82 DAYS ON OKINAWA

82 DAYS ON OKINAWA

ONE AMERICAN'S UNFORGETTABLE
FIRSTHAND ACCOUNT OF THE
PACIFIC WAR'S GREATEST BATTLE

COL. ARTHUR SHAW (RET.)

WITH ROBERT L. WISE

wm

WILLIAM MORROW

An Imprint of HarperCollins*Publishers*

HarperCollins books may be purchased for educational, business, or sales promotional use. For information, please email the Special Markets Department at SPsales@harpercollins.com.

FIRST EDITION

Image facing title page: Landing craft supply U.S. forces on Okinawa, 13 days after the initial invasion. Beyond are U.S. battlewagons, cruisers and destroyers. April 13, 1945. Photo by Everett Historical [Shutterstock, Inc.]

Title page image: Part of F.D.C Personnel holding Japanese flag, Leyte, Philippines, June 1945. Courtesy of the author

Image on page xvi: The Shaw family. Courtesy of the author

Library of Congress Cataloging-in-Publication Data has been applied for.

ISBN 978-0-06-290744-8

20 21 22 23 24   LSC   10 9 8 7 6 5 4 3 2 1

For the brave men and women who laid down their lives in World War II with courage and honor. Their valor still challenges us even to this hour.

Contents

Maps:
Allied Invasions of Iwo Jima and Okinawa . . . . x–xi
Okinawa, April 1–8, 1945 . . . . xii–xiii
Okinawa, April 9–June 30, 1945 . . . . xiv–xv

Authors' Note xvii

PROLOGUE: PRELUDE TO BATTLE 1

1: OKINAWA 9

2: SURPRISES AHEAD 17

3: SETTLING IN 24

4: THE ENEMY EMERGES 29

5: COMING ASHORE 36

6: A PRICE TO BE PAID 44

7: SHARPENING THE FOCUS 50

8: THE SNAKES COME SLITHERING IN 55

9: TRUDGING ON 61

10: THE END OF THE HONEYMOON 66

11: NO REST FOR THE WEARY 71

12: DARK DAYS 77

13: TOMBSTONES EVERYWHERE 82

14: CACTUS HILL COMING UP 88

15: CUTTING THE CACTUS 93

16: TIME OUT 99

17: TRAGEDY ON THE RIDGE 105

18: SLAUGHTER 112

19: THE STRUGGLE TO ESCAPE 118

20: BRAVERY UNEQUALED 124

21: VALOR 130

22: NO LETUP IN SIGHT 135

23: A STORM UNABATED 140

24: DARKNESS DESCENDS 147

25: IN THE DEAD OF NIGHT 152

26: WHILE NO ONE SLEEPS 157

27: WHAT NEXT? 162

STARTING OVER: THE NEXT PHASE

28: THE NEXT STEP 167

29: STRUGGLING ON 172

30: NONSTOP! 177

31: CLEARING THE CRAGS 183

32: GOING ON 187

33: THE ESCARPMENT 193

34: ONE MORE HILL TO CLIMB 199

Contents

35: ONWARD AND UPWARD 204

36: DEADLY DEADEYES 209

37: ENDLESS STRUGGLE 214

38: DIGGING IN 220

39: MAKING DO. 226

40: PLOWING AHEAD 231

41: DISASTER. 237

42: CONICAL HILL. 244

43: NO CHIVALRY LEFT. 250

44: MONSOON SEASON 256

45: THE LOST PLATOON 262

46: AIR STRIKES 272

47: STALEMATE. 278

48: ROLLING ON 285

49: THE BIG APPLE. 290

50: THE HOME STRETCH. 296

51: THE FINAL BATTLE 302

52: THE BOMB. 307

53: THE ROAD HOME. 313

54: MORNING COMES AGAIN. 322

Acknowledgments 333

Index 335

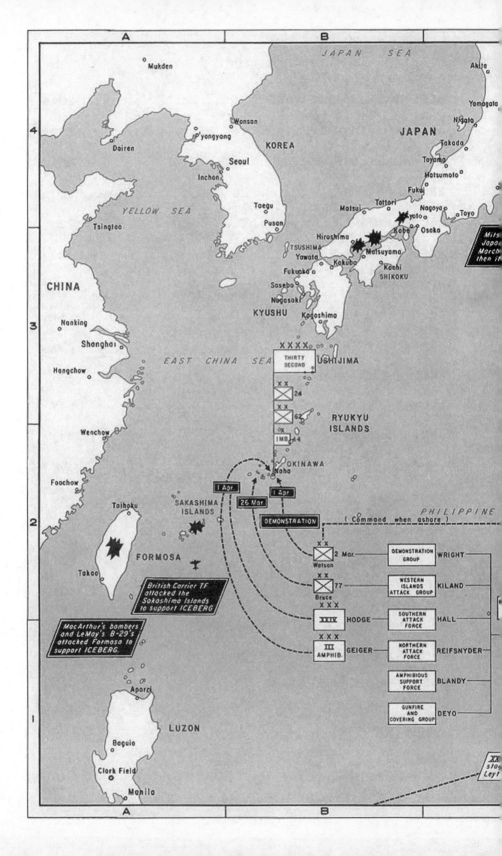

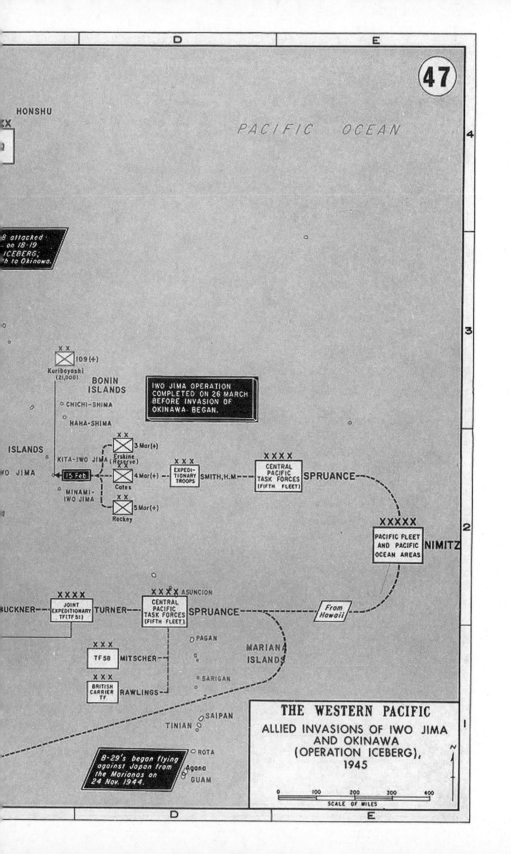

47

HONSHU

PACIFIC OCEAN

B attacked
on 18-19
ICEBERG;
h to Okinawa.

X X 109 (+)
Kuribayashi
(21,000)

BONIN
ISLANDS

○ CHICHI-SHIMA

HAHA-SHIMA

IWO JIMA OPERATION
COMPLETED ON 26 MARCH
BEFORE INVASION OF
OKINAWA BEGAN.

ISLANDS

KITA-IWO JIMA

X X 3 Mar (+)
Erskine
(Reserve)

WO JIMA   15 Feb

X X 4 Mar (+)
Cates

○ MINAMI-
IWO JIMA

X X 5 Mar (+)
Rockey

X X X
EXPEDI-
TIONARY
TROOPS

SMITH, H.M.

X X X X
CENTRAL
PACIFIC
TASK FORCES
(FIFTH FLEET)

SPRUANCE

X X X X X
PACIFIC FLEET
AND PACIFIC
OCEAN AREAS

NIMITZ

BUCKNER

X X X X
JOINT
EXPEDITIONARY
TF (TF 51)

TURNER

X X X X ASUNCION
CENTRAL
PACIFIC
TASK FORCES
(FIFTH FLEET)

SPRUANCE

From
Hawaii

○ PAGAN

X X X
TF 58   MITSCHER

○
○ SARIGAN

MARIANA
ISLANDS

X X X
BRITISH
CARRIER
TF

RAWLINGS

○ SAIPAN
TINIAN ○ ○

THE WESTERN PACIFIC
ALLIED INVASIONS OF IWO JIMA
AND OKINAWA
(OPERATION ICEBERG),
1945

○ ROTA
Agana ○
GUAM

B-29's began flying
against Japan from
the Marianas on
24 Nov. 1944.

0   100   200   300   400
SCALE OF MILES

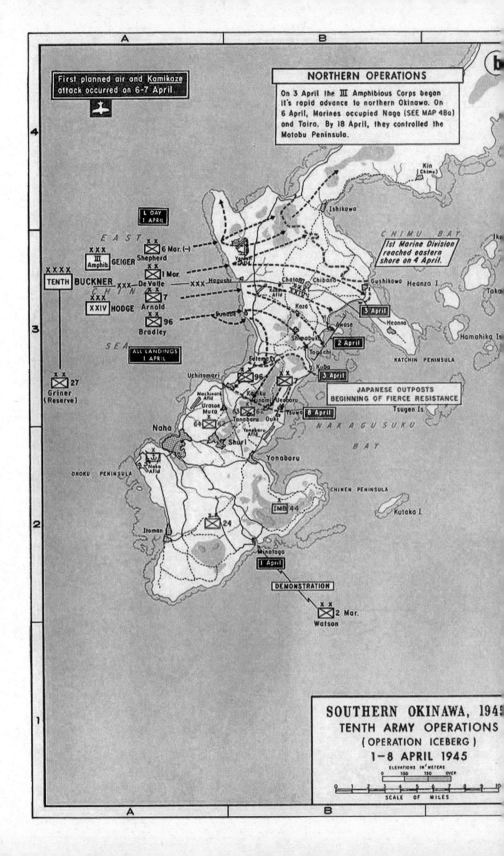

First planned air and Kamikaze attack occurred on 6-7 April.

NORTHERN OPERATIONS

On 3 April the III Amphibious Corps began it's rapid advance to northern Okinawa. On 6 April, Marines occupied Nago (SEE MAP 48a) and Taira. By 18 April, they controlled the Motobu Peninsula.

b

L DAY
1 APRIL

Kin
(Chimu)

Ishikawa

C H I M U   B A Y

E A S T

XXX
III
Amphib GEIGER

XX 6 Mar. (−)
Shepherd

XXXX
TENTH BUCKNER

XX 1 Mar.
xxx—De Valle xxx—Hagushi

C H I N

XXIV HODGE

XX 7
Arnold

XX 96
Bradley

1st Marine Division reached eastern shore on 4 April.

Chotan Chibana

Gushikawa Heanza I.

Ike

Taka

3 April

Heanna

Hamahika Is

S E A

ALL LANDINGS
1 APRIL

Koza

2 April

Awase

Shimabuku

Tengan

Kuba

KATCHIN PENINSULA

XX 27
Griner
(Reserve)

Uchitomari

Machinato Afld
Urasoe
Mura

XX 96

XX

JAPANESE OUTPOSTS
BEGINNING OF FIERCE RESISTANCE

Tsugen Is.

3 April

8 April

N A K A G U S U K U

Naha

Kadena
Afld

XX 64
XX 62

Tanabaru Ouki

Yonabaru Afld

Shuri

Oroku

Naha
Afld

OROKU PENINSULA

Yonabaru

B A Y

CHINEN PENINSULA

Kutaka I.

XX 44

XX 24

Itoman

Minatoga

1 April

DEMONSTRATION

XX 2 Mar.
Watson

SOUTHERN OKINAWA, 1945
TENTH ARMY OPERATIONS
(OPERATION ICEBERG)
1-8 APRIL 1945

ELEVATIONS IN METERS
0   100   150   OVER

SCALE   OF   MILES

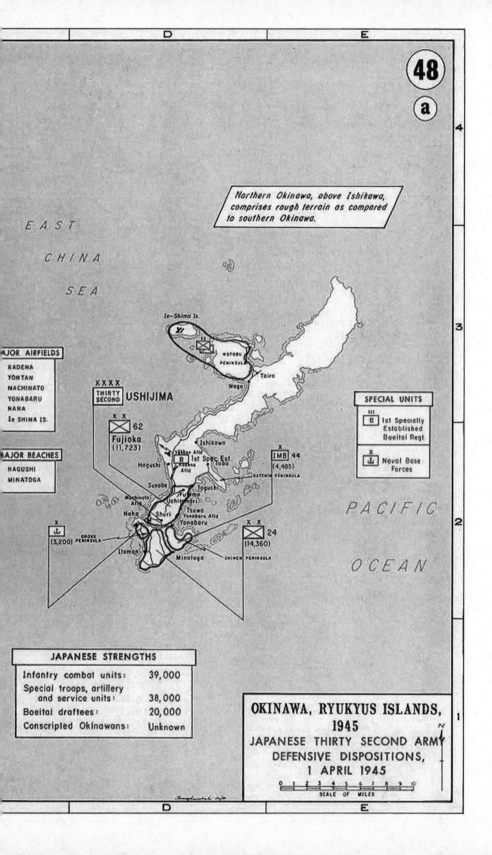

48

a

Northern Okinawa, above Ishikawa, comprises rough terrain as compared to southern Okinawa.

EAST
CHINA
SEA

MAJOR AIRFIELDS

KADENA
YONTAN
MACHINATO
YONABARU
NAHA
Ie SHIMA IS.

MAJOR BEACHES

HAGUSHI
MINATOGA

XXXX
THIRTY SECOND   USHIJIMA

XX
62
Fujioka
(11,723)

Ie-Shima Is.

MOTOBU PENINSULA

Taira

Nago

Ishikawa

Yontan Afld
B 1st Spec Est
Taba
Kadena Afld

Hagushi

KATCHIN PENINSULA

X
IMB 44
(4,485)

Sunobe

Toguchi
Machinato Afld   Futema
Uchitomari
Tsuwa
Yonabaru Afld
Yonabaru

Naha   Shuri

X
(3,200)   ORUKU PENINSULA

Itoman

Minatoga   CHINEN PENINSULA

XX
24
(14,360)

PACIFIC

OCEAN

SPECIAL UNITS

B   1st Specially Established Boeitai Regt.

Naval Base Forces

JAPANESE STRENGTHS

Infantry combat units:	39,000
Special troops, artillery and service units:	38,000
Boeitai draftees:	20,000
Conscripted Okinawans:	Unknown

OKINAWA, RYUKYUS ISLANDS, 1945
JAPANESE THIRTY SECOND ARMY DEFENSIVE DISPOSITIONS, 1 APRIL 1945

0 1 2 3 4 5 6 7 8 9 10
SCALE OF MILES

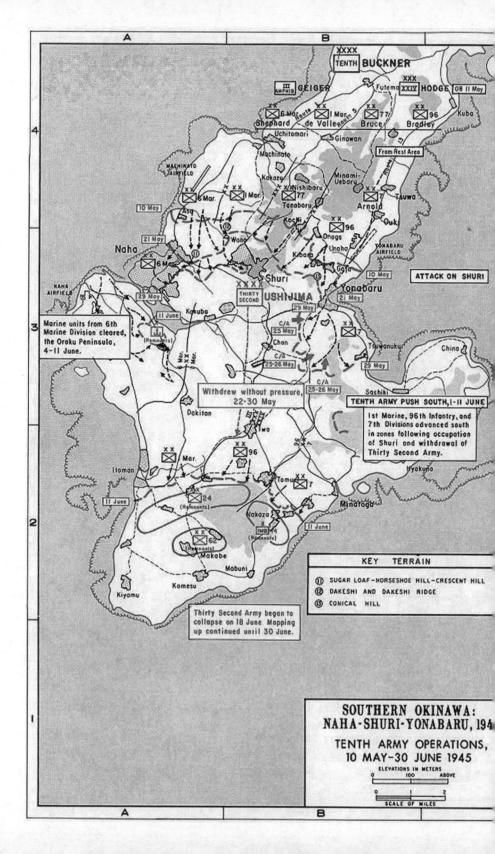

SOUTHERN OKINAWA:
NAHA-SHURI-YONABARU, 194

TENTH ARMY OPERATIONS,
10 MAY-30 JUNE 1945

AMERICAN REINFORCEMENTS

The 27th Infantry Division entered combat on 18 April and was replaced by the 1st Marine Division 29 April. The 77th Infantry Division replaced the 96th Infantry Division on 29 April.

The Japanese main line of resistance generally followed the line of key terrain: 8-9-1-2-4-5-...-7

AMERICAN REINFORCEMENTS

JAPANESE ATTACK, 12-13 APRIL

This attack aimed at splitting XXIV Corps by driving north on an axis Kochi-Ginowan-Kishaba.

JAPANESE ATTACK, 4-5 MAY

This attack was launched with fresh 24th Division troops, but after some local success in the 7th Infantry Division's zone the attack collapsed.

By 6 May, most all of the combat forces of Thirty Second Army had been committed to the line.

KEY TERRAIN

① KAKAZU RIDGE
② NISHIBARU RIDGE
③ TOMBSTONE RIDGE
④ TANABARU ESCARPMENT
⑤ HILL 178
⑥ OUKI HILL
⑦ SKYLINE RIDGE
⑧ ITEM POCKET
⑨ URASOE-MURA ESCARPMENT
⑩ KOCHI RIDGE

TENTH ARMY

With the arrival of III Amphibious Corps, General Buckner assumed direct command of operations against Shuri on 7 May.

SOUTHERN OKINAWA: NAHA-SHURI-YONABARU, 1945

XXIV CORPS OPERATIONS, 9 APRIL-6 MAY 1945

ELEVATIONS IN METERS
0   100   ABOVE

SCALE OF MILES

Authors' Note

When we began this manuscript, Colonel Arthur Shaw had just turned ninety-seven. His memory remained as sharp as ever. With his faithful companion and friend, his boxer dog Dexter, we unfolded the story he had packed away with no intention of ever visiting again. To remember the unspeakable remains an act of courage.

Some of the names of soldiers had slipped away and had to be replaced with pseudonyms. Consequently, some of the characters here will never be found on a roster of the Ninety-Sixth Infantry Division. Other names were changed for the sake of families. While some of the dialogue is imagined, the events occurred as described.

We thank Susan Conway for her assistance in working with the manuscript and her most helpful suggestions. Her family knew well the cost of war.

82 DAYS ON OKINAWA

Prelude to Battle

SEPTEMBER 1944

Somehow or the other, the rumor had leaked out that the entire division was going to Yap.

"Yap?" I said. "Where in God's name is Yap?"

The soldier with the Intelligence unit whispered so softly I almost couldn't understand him. "Major Shaw, Yap is on an island called Leyte about a thousand miles east of the Philippines."

"You're kidding!" I know my voice sounded somewhat indignant.

"I don't know for sure, Major Shaw. Hell, Yap may be an island by itself. Can't tell. Never heard of any of these places."

I looked at him skeptically. "Could we end up on Leyte?"

The lieutenant shrugged. "Who can say? This I know for sure. Keep your helmet fastened tight, soldier, 'cause we're all headed for a big-time showdown."

And you're wondering where Yap is. Well, I never got there. Turned out we ended up on Leyte, which had become the center of the struggle as the war was winding down and the Japanese sun began fading into the darkness of a night of defeat. The island of

Yap was bypassed. We soon found out that Leyte had good beaches for landing, but our vehicles plunged into the ominous swamps that were everywhere just beyond the beaches. The thick, sticky mud could stop a truck in its tracks. A musty, tropical smell hung in the air along with the muggy humidity. Anyone without vaccinations might well have ended up in the hospital with malaria. Tall grass standing six to eight feet high covered the interior of the island. You could get lost in that turf before you even knew what happened to you. Careful attention was essential. Most of the soldiers had never seen anything like this isthmus, but we knew the Japanese were certainly out there somewhere.

After we landed, I didn't think much about Yap or Leyte or anywhere else. I was hunkered down in a foxhole while Japanese Kawasaki Ki-102s and Ki-61 Heins strafed Leyte and made any previous conversations seem like they'd happened decades ago. The command told the boys not to shoot at the Japanese fighter planes when they flew over, but no one in this war was going to pay attention to that nonsense. After all, the Japanese were trying to kill us!

A thunderous explosion sprayed dirt in my face. The smell of gunpowder and smoke filled my nose. One of those Zeros had caught it from our boys. An airplane had crashed close to the beach, causing the ground to shake.

How do you handle a catastrophe like that? Many of us had only been farm boys before the war. A few had been merchants, clerks, or schoolteachers. Our families barely survived the Great Depression. After Pearl Harbor, we had marched off to make the Empire of the Sun pay for their cowardly attack on our unsuspecting ships. Most of us were just kids trying to do our patriotic duty without any idea of how devastating, deadly, and dastardly the war really would turn out to be. But we were finding out fast.

I grabbed my helmet and pushed it down tight. Machine-gun fire had opened up somewhere out there. Maybe it wasn't aimed my way. Maybe it was. I ducked.

"Major!" A voice yelled from out of the dense tropical forest. "Major Shaw! Need a medic. Got a man down."

I started crawling across the open space toward the bushes. Gunfire sent me rolling over on my back. "Medic!" I hollered. "Somebody get me a medic!"

"I'm one!" a soldier hollered back from somewhere in the thick jungle bush.

"Get the hell over there in the trees. North of you. Got a soldier down."

"Yes, sir. I'm on my way."

An explosion made the ground shake again. Scare me? Are you kidding? Frightened me to death! But by the time we landed on Leyte and settled into the bloody conflict, I already expected to be terrified when I went to sleep at night and to wake up mortified in the morning. Just the nature of war.

My outfit, the 361st Field Artillery Battalion, could pump 105-millimeter howitzer shells at high and low angles so fast that the Japanese thought we had automatic weapons. The cannon had a good compromise between range and destructive power. A single caliber simplified logistics. Most of the time we were no more than a thousand yards behind the infantry, firing over them like crazy. The battles raged with a ferocity that could leave you deaf or delirious.

Sometimes we called them Japanese, but mostly we labeled them *imperial forces*, *enemy*, and a couple hundred obscenities. By the time we landed on Leyte, we knew the enemy's tactics well enough. They lived off the land. The war roared on somewhere far on the other side of grotesque and obscene. Most of the enemy troops didn't survive. Their live troops were so scarce that our higher-ups offered a bottle of whiskey for any Japanese soldiers brought in alive. The few that were found usually looked like a truck had run over them several times.

The abrupt roar of a Japanese fighter plane caused me to hit the foxhole again. Rapid machine-gun fire sent everybody plunging back into the ditches. Some of the men stood up and fired rifles as well as machine guns at the airplane circling overhead. Once again, the acid smell of gun smoke filled my nose.

A captain named William Carpenter jumped in my foxhole. "Major Shaw, the report that we got says that the Japanese Navy is going to circle the island with their big guns aimed right at us. If they get through and open up, we could all be hamburger. Get the picture?"

I nodded. "What are we up against?"

The captain's voice lowered. "We think there's at least twenty-five thousand Japanese in the area with a hundred seventy-five fighter planes and thirty bombers. If they get their navy turned around the tip of the island, we're looking at big trouble."

"I got the picture."

"We've got several other batteries firing heavy artillery at them. I understand that Admiral Halsey is deeply concerned." The captain peeked over the top. "I know one of our fighters was shot down. The pilot killed." He shook his head, jumped out, and took off running back into the trees. "Keep firing!"

I took a deep breath. "Okay, men!" I shrieked, "Get back to firing the big guns. Make this battery spit fire!"

Men crawled out from under cover and assumed their positions to fire the 105-millimeter shells at the Japanese. The roar of the cannons again shook the ground.

"Come on, boys!" I shouted when the first wave of firing paused. "Let's blow those enemy guns off the map!"

The artillery started up again with a roar that could leave a man deaf. The war was back on.

When morning broke, Intelligence told us that we had turned the forest in front of us into toothpicks. They weren't sure, but the enemy appeared to be in retreat. The scuttlebutt said they were getting pushed off the island. No one knew for sure.

A colonel came by. "Looks like the Japanese really are running. We are aiming our artillery down the island to focus entirely on their ships. If we can break the back of their navy, this war could be close to finishing. Our boys got to keep hitting them hard."

"We're already at it," I said. "We're firing toward the high cliffs." We swung into action once more. The artillery roared like a volcano exploding.

As the afternoon began to fade, we had a little slack time. We didn't have a sophisticated radio, but we did have a crystal receiver that if we twitched just right could pick up broadcast messages. We almost always tuned in Tokyo Rose whether we wanted to or not. The Japanese woman sounded like your next-door neighbor in Peoria, Illinois, and worked diligently to needle our troops. No one could figure out where she got her information, but she had an uncanny ability to say things like, "Lieutenant George Smith in the 361st Field Artillery unit, are you aware that your wife is about to have a baby with the cook down there at the country club?" We knew she was a piece of the Japanese propaganda efforts, but to hear her calling your name over the radio was unnerving.

We were scratching on the crystal and had picked up a radio broadcast when the battalion medical officer joined us. Sergeant Robert Raleigh had been with our unit for some time. We were talking about whether the enemy really was on the run when we were interrupted.

"Major, could I have a moment of your time?"

I looked up. The sergeant before me appeared to be like any other soldier. "Sure. What can I do for you?"

"I'm Jesus Christ," he said slowly but with certainty. "You don't have to worry. I'm going to take care of you."

He was as serious as a hand grenade. I studied his face. His eyes were blank.

"What about me?" the medical officer asked.

"Well, I don't know," the sergeant said. "I haven't given you any thought, but I'll consider the matter." He turned back to me. "Thank you, Major Shaw. Don't worry." The sergeant walked off. "You'll be fine."

"He's gone psychotic," Raleigh said with a gasp. "The guy's stark raving nuts!"

"I'll report him to the division psychiatrist," I said. "They'll have him shipped out of here immediately. Sometimes that's what happens after a couple of beach landings. Men just fall apart. Their minds explode."

———————————

By morning, it was clear that the imperial forces truly were retreating. The rumor circulating through the division was that their navy really had turned around and beat a hasty retreat back up the way they had come. Of course, everyone wanted to know why the Japanese were running.

The captain who had jumped in my foxhole earlier came trotting by. "Hey!" I hollered. "Captain Carpenter! Please come over here."

Carpenter stopped and looked at me for a second before it clicked who I was. "Oh, yeah. Major Shaw!"

"Captain, can you tell us what the hell is really going on? Is it true the Japanese are on their way out?"

The captain grinned from ear to ear. "You won't believe what developed. Admiral Halsey sent a message north to Guam saying that we needed help and they should send the fleet down. The admiral up there fired back a message, 'I'll be there in a few hours.' They put that exchange out where the Japanese would intercept the communiqué. Scared the pants off the enemy! They started pulling out immediately." The captain broke into laughter. "It was all a sham. It would have taken days to get that fleet down here anyway." He kept laughing. "While the imperial soldiers were retreating, we blew their ships apart. Our fire has crippled their fleet. The Japanese are on their last leg."

"Then we'll be going home?"

"Oh, no," Captain Carpenter said. "We're going to Tokyo! We're going to beat them bastards like a drum just like they did us at Pearl Harbor. The train is pulling out. Our next stop is Okinawa!"

1

Okinawa

You take landings for granted until you've been on a couple of them, and then Christmas is over. The first time around you think hitting the beach is like a football game. Lots of hurrahs and excitement because everyone will be alright when the contest is done. Maybe you write a letter home telling the ones you love that they were in your last thoughts if hitting the beach didn't work out, but you know everything will be fine. You give it to a buddy to mail if you don't make it. However, the second time around everything changes. After you've walked up a beach where a soldier is lying facedown in the sand with the ocean lapping at his feet, reality sets in. A rifle stuck in the beach with a helmet resting on the butt jars you to the core.

The second landing leaves you terrified and keenly aware you may be about to die. This time around you've written many more letters home. You give those letters to a number of buddies because you know a good number of you will end up in the sand. Your stomach aches and you fight nausea.

If you make it to a third landing, you are swallowed by the hard, cold facts. Most of you won't walk past the edge of the water. You've written a bundle of letters and given one to everyone in sight. You know that your chances of survival are slim.

"Major Shaw," Sergeant Arthur Bushboom called out. "Here's some material from Intelligence that will tell you about the island." The soldier shrugged. "Possibly a bunch of junk, but you'll want to read it. You'll need the dictionary of their native language. Might want to read it carefully. The papers give you an update."

"Got anything else worth reading? A nice novel?"

The soldier laughed. "Are you kidding?" He walked on.

I was riding in an APA, a troop attack transport, that left Leyte with the officers while the entire battalion loaded onto an LST (landing ship, tank). You almost couldn't sink one of those LST ships, so I figured my men should be riding in good shape. The salty smell of the ocean drifted across the deck when the waves rocked the ship. My mind was fixed on what might be ahead, but I glanced at the report I was holding.

None of us had heard of Okinawa. The island was no more than some obscure hunk of dirt stuck out in the middle of the Pacific Ocean as far as we were concerned. Intelligence said they had their own language called Ryukyuan, related to Japanese. Most natives under twenty couldn't speak it unless they'd been raised by grandparents in a rural area.

Okinawa looked like a twisted-up snake sixty-seven miles long and from three to ten miles wide. The northern half of the island had rough, mountainous land that was militarily unimportant. We were coming in from the southern end, where most of the island's residents lived. North of us was Kufus, where the Japanese trained kamikaze pilots, and even further north was Yokohama, where their main base was located. I was sure that along the way we'd be hearing from them.

I laid the communiqué down. There couldn't have been a less promising area for a seaborne invasion than Okinawa. Coral reefs would be everywhere in front of the beaches, and the crumbling reefs would present a real danger. On the other side of the island, no beaches bordered the Pacific Ocean, making a landing suicidal. Consequently, we'd be coming in the back door from the East China Sea. Apparently, this area was lightly defended, and resistance should be marginal.

"All personnel be alert," the microphone boomed. "We will be landing tomorrow morning at zero-eight-hundred hours. Be prepared."

I looked at my watch. Time was running out.

———————

Officers were running all over the ship. Hard to believe the day was Easter Sunday, April 1, 1945. A year earlier, the division had been part of a sunrise service. General Kane had given an eloquent address.

The date was the anniversary of the fall of Bataan. General MacArthur had called those blood-soaked ravines of Bataan our Holy Grail. He'd said, "We cannot lay down our arms, we must not hope for peace, we shall not even rest until we have recovered it and restored it to a more worthy hand." Those soldiers who heard him would six months later spearhead MacArthur's return to the Philippines and Bataan. They would hurl themselves against the enemy that had perpetrated the desecration of Bataan.

Now, with landing at Okinawa imminent, everyone needed to make final preparations. The LST boats would eventually be loading an entire battalion of three hundred to eight hundred men. If the tide stayed high, the LST could go all the way up the beach; if not, the men would load in ducks for a beach landing. Ducks were undersized amphibian boats that carried a much smaller number of men. Not much ammunition on the ducks: the ammo would come in later.

My artillery battalion would soon be scrambling down a sixty- to ninety-foot rope webbing to drop into landing boats if the LSTs couldn't hit the shore. Each man would be loaded with everything he needed on his back when he cautiously climbed down from one rope hold to another. While he intended to end up on a landing craft, the boat could jerk five to ten feet up and down in a rough sea, making entry difficult. If he slipped and fell, the soldier would probably drown. The weather had been rough sailing in from Leyte, but on this Easter Sunday, the climate shifted. Couldn't have been a lovelier day. Perfect for our task.

We would be coming in north of the town of Naha. An escarpment of steep, high cliffs stretched from Naha across the island to Yonabaru. The towering bluffs were rumored to essentially cut the island in half. We knew the Japanese were on top of them, but Intelligence said there wasn't much below, where we were coming in.

The waves beating against the APA ship reminded me this would be the last time in a long time that I would be on our territory proper. Once I landed, I would be on Okinawa until it was over one way or the other. At least one enemy airborne division was known to be on Kyushu, and the waters were reported to be infested with suicide craft. What was left of the Imperial Fleet was reported to be up north. In the last few days, I had studied the maps long enough to know that winning Okinawa was the key to final victory. We had to endure.

———————

I surveyed the island in front of us as I lined up to leave the APA ship. Okinawa looked serene from a distance. The ocean gently washing up on the beach with tropical trees swaying in the breeze might have made a great vacation sight if we weren't in a deadly war.

"Hey, Major!" a soldier hollered to me. "Want a free ride in?"

I laughed. "You mean it won't cost me a dime?"

"I'm a tank commander," he said. "Gonna make an exception. Hop in my amphibious craft and you will be the first one ashore."

"Sounds like my kind of deal," I said, and climbed down the rope ladder. "I suppose I can sit anywhere," I joked. "Since there are only two of us, shouldn't be crowded."

"Always wanted to come in first," the tank commander said, "but never had the opportunity. Today, I'm going to fulfill my wish. Hang on."

We shot through the waves like a racing craft. I hunkered down when the spray washed over us. As we got closer, I could see the tide was at least partially coming in if not all the way. Landing would be relatively easy.

Behind me I could see a few of the ducks circling. These smaller boats always made wide circles before they landed. As each boat followed the same pattern, they created substantial waves that made it easier for the ducks to get up the beach. Clearly, they were getting ready to follow us in.

The waves parted, and the wheels touched the ocean floor.

Our craft plowed right up the beach until the tank commander pulled it to a halt. I jumped out.

"Congratulations," he said. "Major Art Shaw, you did it. You're the first man on Okinawa!"

"Well," I said, "Intelligence has likely already been here. I imagine the amphibian boys maybe swam in earlier. Maybe somebody else. I'm among the first."

The soldier laughed. "Yeah, technically maybe some other guys have rolled in. But you are the first 361st Field Artillery Battalion solider to set foot on Okinawa; the first actual fighting man. You still got congratulations coming your way."

———————

We started walking around the beach deciding where our troops and the artillery should be located. Intelligence said there wouldn't be any enemy snipers around this end of the island, so we could be more casual than usual, but we still paid attention to what might be out there.

When nightfall came, we sat around a campfire and talked. The smell of burning wood and the crackle of branches popping reminded me of home. By morning, all the troops would be landing, and the war would be on. The Ninety-Sixth Infantry, called the Deadeyes, would be there along with eight divisions of army and marine infantry. The Seventh, Ninety-Sixth, First Marine, and Sixth Marine divisions would be in the assault.

The men sitting around the embers had differing views of our enemy. On one hand, the Japanese had to be respected. They'd die before they surrendered. Their training taught them that if capture was inevitable, they should commit *hara-kiri* as the honorable way to die. A Japanese soldier would stab himself in the stomach.

As he fell forward, an aide would chop his head off. Gave us something to think about.

On the other hand, they seldom took prisoners. If one of our soldiers held his hands up in surrender, he'd be shot on the spot. An enemy soldier would have a man behind him with a machine gun on his back. The first man would drop while the second sprayed bullets at the people surrendering. To say that scenario didn't sit well was the understatement of the day.

The enemy hid in "spider holes," narrow, small foxholes that were well camouflaged. You could nearly step on them and never see what was right under your feet. Once you walked passed, they'd hop out and kill you. Then they'd jump back in the hole and wait for the next victim. No matter what anyone says, atrocities breed atrocities. At the same time, our boys weren't raised with such desperate approaches. However, we had to take their tactics seriously or we'd end up getting killed.

By morning, the beaches were hopping and popping. Men were running everywhere, and the big machinery started coming ashore. At that point, the difficulties created by the coral slowed us down. The weight of bulldozers and large machinery made the coral crumble, and the vehicles would sink into the ocean. The beach was secure, but the coral wasn't. The ordeal of getting the equipment onto the beach gripped everyone's attention.

When the Deadeyes of the Ninety-Sixth Infantry surged ashore, they were taken with the thick grove of trees that bordered the beaches. I watched a soldier named Fred Long and his buddy walk into the shrubbery. They spotted an extremely large snake in a tree, which they shot. They pulled the huge snake by the tail back to their bivouac area, and some of the guys strung the reptile up on a pole. The snake measured eleven feet in length, but nobody knew what kind of serpent it was. The only thing that fit the description was a king cobra, but they were not indigenous to the Philippines. A soldier suggested that the monster could have come in when it was small with some unsuspecting shipment from elsewhere. Fascinating creature to behold.

Not long after this, Fred Long was walking through the jungle with a young native who showed up from somewhere. The local tapped Fred on the shoulder and motioned for him to be quiet. He slowly slipped Fred's rifle from his shoulder and took aim into a tree. Long immediately thought a sniper had him in his sights, but when the native pulled the trigger, a huge lizard fell from the tree.

Long asked, "What are you going to do with that thing?"

The native said, "Eat it! You eat chicken, we eat lizard."

Well, Dorothy, we certainly weren't in Kansas anymore.

2

Surprises Ahead

You probably wonder why I haven't mentioned my wife. The truth is the pace of the operation and the possibility of getting blown away pushed the most important thoughts right out of my mind. Sure, I thought of Joan, but the roar of kamikaze enemy diving at us kept my mind on the war.

Joan's face floated in and out of my mind, but when we left the USA, we might as well have landed on another planet. San Francisco sank in the sunset and the Philippines came up with the morning sun. The world of my past faded like the evaporating fog. My past blurred into a distant yesterday.

Actually, I was a gunnery instructor at Fort Sill, Lawton, Oklahoma, when I first saw this blonde sitting with a couple of women in Gilbert's Drug Store. They were talking, drinking Cokes, just killing time. I didn't know it, but during the winter Joan Payne Terry was a student at Oklahoma College for Women at Chickasha,

Oklahoma. She caught my eye, so I grabbed a napkin and scribbled, "You're the most bored blonde I ever saw. What's your name? —Artie Shaw (you know, the band director)"

I watched her reading my note. Without missing a beat, she started writing on the same napkin. When the waiter brought it back, I read, "None of your business, signed Dinah Shore." I started laughing. The name of a famous popular singer made an intriguing response. I thought for a moment and decided I'd find out her actual name if it killed me.

After a few inquiries, I discovered her name was Joan Terry and she was going with a captain at Fort Sill. A second lieutenant like me had to do some fast footwork to beat his time. During my search, I discovered that she worked at the Western Electric plant. That was all I needed to know. I walked in out of the clear blue and shocked her down to her toenails!

Through the years, Joan and I laughed about that encounter over and over again. I broke the ice on May 26, 1942. By the following November, we were married. With the war going on, you couldn't wait around. Sure enough, I was soon on my way toward the Pacific.

The training our soldiers received for landing in the Philippines had been realistic enough. We learned to coordinate between tank and infantry attachments as well as to respect what a flame-thrower could do. One good shot from the torch and you'd be roasted toast or a charcoal briquette. We participated in joint exercises with artillery and amphibious tank battalions to put everything in place for when we hit the ground. They even gave me a dictionary of the Ryukyuan language and I practiced pronouncing some of the words and phrases.

Supply problems had developed because General MacArthur had all the necessary items going his way during the pivotal battle in Luzon. However, most of the issues were worked out by the time we started moving into Okinawa.

Our destination turned out to have a surprising difference from the rest of the Philippines. Far from the tropics, Okinawa had rolling, terraced hills. We weren't plowing through vine-covered jungles but walking through attractive farmland. As it turned out, the Japanese had miscalculated where our ships would come in and we had no resistance on the beach landing.

Morning broke. At straight-up 8:00 a.m., the rest of the beach landing began pouring in with deadly earnest intentions. The ducks rolled in filled with the troops, and the heavy equipment began coming ashore. Of course, the problems with the crumbling coral reefs affected the efficiency of hauling in the tanks and big guns. Usually, we had a two-and-a-half-ton truck to pull the artillery into place, but that wasn't enough. We needed to bring in three batteries and a bulldozer to carve out a place for the big guns to be positioned.

I was responsible for situating and firing the heavy artillery pieces that could shoot clear to the other end of the island. These units were placed about three blocks apart. The men began hustling to get us set up.

"Sergeant Williams!" I shouted. "Get the bulldozer over here to flatten these knolls."

"They're coming!" Williams yelled back.

The roar of a bulldozer drowned out the rest of the conversation. I hurried over to the plot where I wanted the first artillery placed. The 105mm guns had to be carefully set in place to achieve the results we were after.

"Let's move it!" I kept yelling at the troops. "We're running out of time. Come on!"

The men said little but pushed to get the area cleared and ready. Out of the corner of my eye I saw a woman appear in the bushes just on the other side of where the bulldozer was pushing dirt. I whirled around, and she was gone. I studied the terrain and couldn't believe I was hallucinating.

"Level it out!" I shouted to the bulldozer driver. "Get the area smooth."

The big caterpillar dozer cracked the small trees to the ground and pushed them out of the way.

The woman popped up again. This time I could see her olive-colored skin. As quickly as she stepped out, she was gone. I jumped over a small bush and headed for where she had been. Nothing! No one! Like a magician's assistant, she had appeared and disappeared almost in a puff of smoke. I walked back to the clearing shaking my head.

The bulldozer quickly leveled the terrain, and the soldiers started to maneuver the 105mm howitzer cannons into place. I stepped back to make sure the ground was level enough. For the first time, I noticed several circular brown spots in the ground. As I walked around, I found more of these faded areas that looked like someone had sprayed grass killer over the ground. Why in the world would anyone be killing the ground covering in this uninhabited strip of land? Made no sense. I waved for one of my men to come over.

I pointed at the ground. "Make any sense to you, soldier?"

Sergeant Kent shook his head. "No, sir. Never seen anything like it." He stooped down and tugged at the dead grass. "Strange," he muttered.

"Will it burn?" I asked.

"Let's see." The soldier pulled out a Zippo lighter and set the dead grass on fire. "Seems to burn," he said and tugged at the grass. "Comes loose too."

"Take your shovel off your backpack and see if you can get the chunks loose."

He started digging around the edge. Abruptly, the entire brown piece broke loose and turned over. "I'll be damned! This is the door to a cave!"

I stared down into the hole. Six people looked up at me with fear in their eyes. The women were shaking. They were huddled together and looked terrified. "God almighty! That's where the woman went. We got a village hiding down there in a cave."

The soldier motioned with his shovel. "Come out! Come out of there," he shouted. They began to move.

Two men, three women, and a boy started to climb out. The men had on short pants and long, short-sleeved shifts. The women's dresses hung down to their ankles with a rope tied at the waist. Long black hair draped over their shoulders and they were bare-footed. The boy wore only short pants with no shirt.

Their eyes said it all. I was sure they expected me to shoot them on the spot. They huddled together like captured prisoners. Obviously, they were only natives trying to escape the war.

"How do we talk to them?" the soldier asked.

"Well . . . I've got a dictionary of their language . . . Maybe . . ." I pulled the small red book out of my back pocket and started thumbing through it. Even saying the words was tough. Finally, I tried, "Friend. Am friend."

Their eyes flashed, and they started bowing.

"You hit the jackpot, Major!"

Slowly, I said, "Here to help you."

The oldest woman held up her skinny arms and cried something or the other. The men continued bowing and almost scraping the ground. The little boy hugged my legs.

"Looks like I've become a hero," I said to the soldier. "Let's open the rest of these hiding places."

The men began chattering. I had no idea what they were saying, but I could guess. We'd seen this before. The Japanese told the locals that the Americans would torture and kill them. The enemy had carefully instructed villagers that we were savage murderers and if they cooperated with us, we would kill them. Discovering this wasn't true must have seemed like a voice from heaven offering solace.

"Get some of the men over here to help you," I instructed the soldier. "We've got to get these villagers out of the caves."

He nodded and trotted back to the soldiers setting up the 105s. We quickly had a crew opening up the ground covers with my sergeant overseeing the task. Villagers huddled together while I tried to tell the first six people we would help them. They seemed to get the idea and started passing the message along. The mood of the locals quickly changed from apprehension to relief.

"Get a truck over here," I told my sergeant. "We need to get them evacuated and out of the line of fire. Once our attack starts in earnest, it'll be dangerous for them to stay around."

"Will do." The sergeant hurried away.

The natives kept huddling around me. Obviously, I was their only source of communication, and for the moment I had their total trust. Of course, conveying that Americans were good guys would take some time. We needed to get them down the road, fed, and sheltered. In time, they would know we were for real.

A large truck with the rear covered by canvas started lumbering toward us. I could see that the locals weren't going to get close to any of the other soldiers, so I kept nodding to them, smiling, and making folded hand gestures that said they were okay.

When we started putting them in the back of the truck, they kept looking at me with fear returning to their eyes, but I kept smiling and saying, "It's okay, it's okay." Over and over I repeated the phrase.

"Take these people over to an area where registration is going on," I told the driver. "Treat 'em nice and don't let anyone frighten them."

He nodded and waved through the rolled-down window. "Yes, sir. We're on our way."

As the truck pulled away, the villagers kept waving to me. Keeping my big smile in place, I kept waving to them until they were out of sight. With luck, we'd made a good start with the locals.

3

Settling In

Once the big guns were in place and the people hiding underground were sent on to registration, I knew the infantry would soon be heading toward the escarpment, the high cliffs where the Japanese were dug in. Intelligence told us that we shouldn't have any confrontations until we got closer to the towering bluffs. I watched my men finish setting up the three 155mm artillery batteries. We weren't fooling around.

I kept walking around and looking down in those holes in the underground caves where the natives had dug in. The Japanese had terrified those poor people into believing we were the dragons from the West who were going to devour them with fire blowing out of our noses. When the roar of our bulldozer started, the noise must have confirmed their every fear. The volcano god had descended on them for lunch.

I watched the men stack the wooden boxes of ammunition. For once, I decided to take a breather and let someone else worry for a while. Sitting down on the trunk of a tree the caterpillar had knocked over, for the first time in days I thought of home. For the moment a million miles away seemed right there under my feet. I started walking down the sidewalk again in Ada, Oklahoma, where I'd always delivered the papers. *The Oklahoma Times* and *The Daily Oklahoman* came down from Oklahoma City and that's how everyone got their news. The Great Depression had turned everything upside down and Oklahoma had fallen out on the floor. Making a nickel was big time. A dime put you over the top. Back in the thirties everyone was poor.

On my paper route, I soon discovered that the people who still had money were the hardest to collect from. That was probably why they still had money: they were so tight. For instance, Howard Smith owned the most prosperous business in town. At some time or the other, everyone needed his hardware store. Smith had the best flow of money around, but you'd think that he was about to fold at any second.

"Mr. Smith," I said politely, "you're a month behind and owe me a quarter."

"Don't have time to talk to you now," Smith grumbled. "Got a customer. Come back later."

"But—"

He turned around and walked off, leaving me furious. Finally, I told him I wasn't delivering any more newspapers until he paid the twenty-five cents he owed me for the month and paid another twenty-five cents in advance for the next month.

"Robbery!" Smith nearly shouted. "Absolute robbery."

I walked off saying nothing. A couple of days went by and he stopped me on the street. "Where's my paper?" Smith growled.

"You ain't got a paper coming until you're paid up," I said with determination in my voice of someone well beyond my age.

"Listen, you little snap. If I don't get a paper, I'm not paying you a quarter."

"Then you ain't getting any newspapers," I said defiantly.

"You drive a hard bargain," Smith conceded, sticking his hand in his pocket. "All right, here's your quarter."

"And I need another quarter for next month," I insisted.

"Highway robbery!" Smith squealed. "A hoodlum holdup!" But he put another quarter in my hand.

"Here's your newspaper, sir." I handed him the news and walked off.

When I glanced over my shoulder, I saw a grin on his face. Later I learned that he thought I was a real businessman.

Old man Smith was indeed a businessman. He sold caskets on the second floor of his hardware store. He was the only person in the town of Ada selling caskets, so business kept booming. (Pardon the expression.) Of course, every kid in town wanted to go up and look in to see what a casket really was like. We'd try to sneak up there and take a peek. What we didn't know was that Smith had installed a pipe that ran from his office through the ceiling into the casket room. When he'd see a kid sneaking up the stairs, he'd wait until the boy tried to look into one of the caskets. Then Smith would say through his secret tube, "What are you doing looking at my rest place?" The kid would go flying down the stairs and run out of the building.

"Major Shaw," the sergeant said.

I jumped and stood up. "Got lost in my thoughts. What can I do for you, Sergeant?"

"Looks like the Deadeye Ninety-Sixth Infantry Division is getting ready to march north. They're preparing to pull out."

I nodded. "Okay. We need to be ready to give them artillery support. Are we so positioned?"

"Just about. Give me another hour or two and we'll be done."

"You got it," I said. "This lull won't last long, and we'll be back in the thick of it."

The sergeant saluted and hurried away, knowing the 361st Artillery Battalion provided support for the 381st as well as the 96th Division.

I sat down again. My mind drifted back to Ada. The newspaper route taught me to respect people like the villagers down in those dark caves that we uncovered. You learned that people like Smith had a place in the town and they were important even if they didn't seem so then. That was true of Aunt Molly. At least that's what we all called her. She lived out on the edge of town, so it took some walking to get to her house with a newspaper.

I didn't know her very well, but she took a newspaper every day. Three days had gone by when I realized her newspapers were stacking up. Something had to be wrong. Of course, no one locked their doors, so anyone could walk in. I decided maybe I should see what had happened to Aunt Molly, so I let myself in.

"Aunt Molly? You in there?"

I heard a groan from a distant room.

"Aunt Molly?" The groan came again.

I peeked around the door. The poor woman looked terrible. I knew she was in a bad way, so I ran for the phone and called Doc Seibert. I was surprised how fast he got there.

The old town doctor took one look and said, "Son, you did the right thing. I'll take care of her from here. I know Molly's got some cows out that probably haven't been milked in three days. I think there's three of 'em. You go out there and take care of them poor cows."

I stared at him. "Sir, I never milked a cow in my life. I wouldn't know what to do."

"Ain't nothing to it. Just start pulling on those tits. Them cows is probably about to bust as it is. Now get out there and take care of 'em and I'll handle business here in the house."

I had no idea what to do, but I was about to learn. When I got out to the barn, the cows were throwing a fit. They were obviously in pain from going three days unmilked. I grabbed a stool and a bucket and went to work. Somehow or the other, I got the task done.

I brought the buckets of warm milk in and set them on the counter in Aunt Molly's kitchen. Dropping into a chair exhausted, I waited to see what would happen. Finally, Doc Seibert came out and started washing his hands in the sink. I just watched.

"Son," the doc said, "you got some grateful cows out there." He laughed. "Yes sirree, grateful indeed." His countenance changed, and he looked serious. "Art, you probably saved Molly's life. She'll be thankful."

"Major Shaw!" a soldier yelled, running up the trail the bulldozer had dug. "Anyone know where Major Shaw is?"

"Over here!" I called. "I'm Major Shaw."

The corporal stopped and caught his breath. "We just got word that there's a resistance movement out there. Villagers who opposed the Japanese. We don't know where they are, but probably the resistance is roaming around. Just wanted you to be aware."

"Thank you, Corporal. We'll pay attention."

4

The Enemy Emerges

Watching the troops quietly come ashore gave us optimism that turned out to be short-lived. The successful landing extended the beachhead for three and a half miles. Fighting the coral and the mud had appeared to be the worst of it, but change was soon in the air. King's battalion working up the island ran into a struggle but ended up killing twenty-one Japanese without one casualty. The Eighty-Eighth Chemical Mortar Battalion laid down fire for over twenty yards ahead of the front lines. These struggles amounted to ominous clouds ready to descend on us.

That afternoon two platoons of B Company ran into a bitter battle with enemy entrenched in tombs and pillboxes. The ferocity of those battles clearly signaled what was ahead. The Japanese were going to hang on to the bitter end. We could expect extreme confrontations.

Our soldiers proved equal to the task and valor was equally evident. Lieutenant John Restuccia led the attack and was wounded three times. The lieutenant didn't slow down or retreat even with serious wounds. In the fight, another soldier was seriously injured. Lieutenant Restuccia crawled out to rescue the wounded man and was finally himself mortally wounded. Lieutenant John Restuccia would be the first in the Okinawa struggle to receive the Distinguished Service Cross.

In the middle of the island, the Second Battalion discovered a significant number of the enemy waiting on the high ground to the north. Tanks, dive bombers, and artillery pounded the enemy and cleared the area for a while. Taking Okinawa was not going to be a picnic.

Sergeant Jim Kent came walking up during a lull in the firing of our 105mm howitzers. "We've found something strange straight just ahead of us. At first, we thought we might find the enemy inside. Really strange. Could you take a look, sir?"

"Sure. How far away are we talking?"

"I'd guess . . . maybe three football-field lengths down the road."

"Shouldn't take long," I said. "I'm leaving Lieutenant Ryder in charge. Okay. Men. Unless orders come down to the contrary, wait till I return before firing again."

The soldiers started sitting down, pulling out cigarettes, and talking. We hurried down the narrow dirt road ahead of us.

"You sure this area is secure?" I ask the sergeant.

"Our scouts went through the whole patch," Kent said. "No problem."

Kent had always been reliable, so I kept walking. The dense brush swished by my legs. The field had a damp smell, but Okinawa was far ahead of those other island jungles with monkeys screaming and vines that could certainly trip you up. We climbed up a short hill and found the site.

"Never seen nothing like it." The sergeant pointed. "When we stumbled onto this area, we knew the worn stones meant it was really old. Maybe historic."

"You mean prehistoric," I said.

"Whatever." The sergeant shrugged. "You need to see inside the cave we found. Come on down."

Huge stones had been positioned to suggest a woman's womb. The entry to some sort of cave looked like it had been dug out centuries ago and then large blocks of shale or igneous pumice, maybe blocks of coral, had been positioned. The front of the area had been shaped to look like a courtyard, leading to the entrance of a cave. The structure appeared to have been dug out of the hill and then cemented or plastered to form a formal doorway. A four-foot square hole was the only way in. Around the sides of the entire structure were stone blocks arranged to frame it. Weeds and grass had grown up over the top and the sides.

Kent cocked his rifle and cautiously crept toward the entrance. "Want to make sure no one's crawled in there since we left." He flattened himself against the side of the worn entrance. "Anybody in there!" he shouted.

A slight echo rolled back. Kent stuck his rifle around the opening and fired one shot. The crack of his gun and the bullet ricocheting off the rock wall roared back at us.

"Guess the hole is empty," the sergeant said, and stooped to crawl in. "Come on in."

I slipped in but immediately jerked back a step. Five bodies lay on the floor with their throats cut.

"They're natives," Kent said. "Not Japanese. Looks like they've only been dead a few days."

I swept the interior with my flashlight. Stone sarcophagi and urns lined the walls of the large cave. The sides looked like they had been scraped with some kind of primitive tools.

"You've found a graveyard," I said. "This is where the locals buried their ancestors. The suicides were probably the result of Japanese propaganda. Maybe these men thought we'd skin 'em alive or some such atrocity. They probably saw our ships coming in and ran up here to die."

The sergeant scratched his head. "This crypt would make for a good bunker. Bet there's more around and you can bet the enemy are in there."

"Yeah, we best pay careful attention when we come on another one."

Kent took a deep breath. "You bet!"

The lack of combat didn't mean the Japanese weren't out there. We knew they were somewhere waiting, picking their own place to fight. Waiting, just waiting. Waiting *for us*.

The 381st Infantry had been slowed by the up and down terrain as well as mines and tank traps. They made steady progress covering two miles and were able to take the town of Shimabaku with only scattered resistance. Unfortunately, the struggle had taken the life of one of the battalion's most valued men. A veteran of twenty-nine years' service, First Sergeant Walter Korejwo of K Company fell. War was strangely just like that. Whether a recruit had just shipped in or a longtime warrior had been around forever—made no difference when the bullets started flying.

At three o'clock, General James Bradley brought his command

ashore. Actually, his troops were operating well ahead of schedule. The Seventh Division and the marines in the north had split the island. General Bradley had made himself well aware of the situation. By the time this fight was over, there would be plenty of scars to go around. The Japanese weren't in the habit of surrendering and they sure wouldn't here. The clock was ticking and there was plenty of action ahead.

As the sun drifted toward the horizon, we figured our perimeters ought to be secure. Intelligence indicated combat fighting would be north of us anyway. We hadn't seen any Japanese in the area, so that was a good sign. The men secured the cannons, and as soon as it was dark, we prepared for the night. We'd be back up and at it by the crack of dawn. A little shut-eye was more than necessary.

The bulldozer left gutters and ditches that made good foxholes. I found a trench with covering that made an excellent pit for a bed . . . considering the alternatives. I crawled down into the entrenchment and stretched out in a semi-sitting position. I knew I'd slept in worse. I closed my eyes and let the day drift away.

I don't know how long I dozed, but I awoke to noise somewhere out there in the trees. I could hear talking. I listened carefully. The chatter got louder, but I had no idea what they were saying.

Japanese! I thought. *They've penetrated our lines and are making a night attack.* I strained to see if I could decipher the sounds as the talking got louder, but I couldn't. *Got to be prepared.* I pulled my .45 pistol out of the holster and cocked the weapon.

The jabbering became more hushed because they were crouching ever closer. I heard footfalls kicking the dirt not five feet away.

I slowly turned and pointed the pistol at the dark opening to my foxhole.

I'd shoot first and ask questions later.

A woman abruptly jumped into my trench!

"Aah!" she screamed and held her arms up in the air. The small woman rattled off something and then said in broken English, "Resistance! Resistance."

I sat up, turned on my flashlight, and pointed my .45 at her. She certainly wasn't a Japanese soldier and her eyes registered sheer terror as she stared at my pistol. The woman's dirty tunic hung to her knees with pants underneath.

"Resistance?" I said.

"Hai! Hai!" she insisted and kept her hands held high.

I took a deep breath. "You nearly got your head blown off."

"Yes!" she broke into English. "Yes! Good!"

"I think we have a communication problem." I lowered my weapon.

The woman stood up and waved to three men, who hurried over.

"I'm Emiko."

The largest man in the group pushed to the fore and in broken English said that his name was Akio and that he was part of the resistance, fighting the Japanese.

"Interesting," I mumbled. "We need to get you to our Intelligence people."

Akio turned to the others and rattled off something. They all kept nodding. Finally, Akio said, *"Arigatou gozaaimasu."* Even more emphatically he said, *"Domo arigatou gozaaimasu."*

The other four kept nodding and repeating the same words. I watched as they scurried over by the cannons and settled down on the ground. Didn't take an expert to tell they weren't the enemy.

I probably should have hustled them off to Intelligence, but those guys would be sleeping, and the matter could wait until morning. Emiko and Akio would still be here for sure and someone in Intelligence could speak their language.

All I wanted was a good night's sleep.

5

Coming Ashore

With the first light of dawn, the roar of engines and the clanging of tank treads plowing through the sand broke the silence. The completion of the invasion had already started in dead earnest. Bellows of black smoke curled up toward the blue sky and the scent of diesel fuel filled the air. We knew we had landed on Japanese soil and the enemy would consider that giant footprint to be the supreme insult.

Our earliest incursions had been in response to Pearl Harbor: we'd liberated the islands the Japanese had taken in their murderous assaults on innocent civilians. We had won conflicts like Midway and were confident we could finish the job in a fairly decent amount of time. At least, we hoped so.

Our men were battle-seasoned with their minds fixed on the task at hand. We clearly understood this was an "us or them" battle to the finish. They wouldn't be taking prisoners and we could depend on their trying to slit our throats at every opportunity.

Climbing such deadly hills with bombs flying down from the top made one realize there could be no fooling around about what we were doing. We had to be ready for any and everything.

Under the command of General Claudius Easley, by two o'clock, with the afternoon sun blazing down, the tanks and artillery were ashore. Resistance turned out to be so limited that the landing felt like a free ride. The 382nd Reserves came rolling in along with the engineers. Two hours later three light battalions were set up in firing position. We had completely outsmarted the Japanese expectation that we would land halfway up the island where they were fortified for bear. Their mistake allowed us to land, set up shop, and prepare to blow their pants off.

When the Ninety-Sixth Infantry hit the shore, they had their running boots on and guns loaded. Those guys didn't stop for nothing. They had come ashore for an invasion and weren't slowing down. They aimed for the village of Shimuku and weren't going to stop until they got there. Unfortunately, that's when good men started getting killed.

The Japanese Imperial Army had infiltrated every corner of Okinawa with propaganda declaring Americans were beasts with voracious appetites to devour the locals. Once we landed, every islander would be our target for brutal attacks, raping girls, killing children, and mutilating the elderly. The enemy left the locals terrified, believing death was better than capture by the American pigs. These poor people were terrified of what we might do to them.

"The Ninety-Sixth shore is moving on," Sergeant Art McQuiston said. "We gonna have to get some artillery in behind them. Wanna follow the big guns up the road, Major?"

I thought for a moment. "Well, with the general and his staff onshore and the beach secured, we probably ought to follow them while our unit sets up shop. Yeah. Sure. Let's go. Start the jeep."

The Ninety-Sixth moved at a good clip through the flat fields. We rode behind at a slower pace with a couple of trucks pulling the howitzers. The day seemed pleasant enough and deceptively nice for an invasion, but I knew it wouldn't be long before we got hit. Sure enough! The cracking of rifles meant that one of our companies had found Japanese land.

"Watch out!" the sergeant said. "Troubles ahead."

I pulled the rifle from my shoulder and leaned it against the windshield. "Keep your eyes open," I told McQuiston. "They're out there in the bushes ahead of us."

"Don't worry," he said. "You can bet that I'm payin' first-rate attention."

The shooting faded, which meant the enemy might have retreated—or of course it could mean nothing at all. Or they were getting ready to come running straight at us and cram it down our throats. Our forward movement came to a halt. An infantryman broke through the trees and came running toward us.

"Hey! We hit the jackpot," the soldier said. "When we were setting up our big guns, we exposed a number of locals hiding underground and then turned up another batch in a local boneyard of some variety."

"Interesting," McQuiston said.

"Yeah," the soldier said. "We got a machine gun set up in case some Japanese are hiding in there among 'em. Don't know what to do next."

I climbed out of the jeep. "Stay low, McQuiston. We don't want our luck to run out."

"You bet!"

We followed the soldier through a clump of trees and came out on top of a sharp ravine. At the bottom against the side of a cliff was the opening to a cave. The dark entrance didn't reveal whether anyone was hiding, but of course they were.

"Just stumbled onto it, Major," the soldier said. "We could hear talking inside, but thought it might be the enemy, so we didn't walk in."

I nodded. "Don't suppose you've got anybody around that can speak to them."

"You've got the dictionary business," McQuiston said.

I looked askance at him. "You're suggesting that I just walk in and start thumbing through the pages to see if I can find something to say?"

"Oh, no. No."

"We got one man who grew up in Hawaii," the soldier offered. "Worked there with the Japanese. He's down there by the lookout. The man's a private. Maybe the two of you could work something out."

I took a deep breath. "Where is he?"

"Follow me." The infantryman started down the side of the ravine and stopped near the bottom. "Hey, Higa! The major here can speak a little of the local dialect. How about you? You know some Japanese, right?"

The soldier stood up. "I can talk a little. Probably the rumble of our ships floating in sent the locals running for shelter. Maybe, if we each got on one side of the entrance, we could shout for them to come out."

"Getting close to the entrance is more than a little dangerous," I said. "We'd be out in the open."

"Expect we'd have to crawl some," Higa said. "But we know

there's nobody on the other side of the ravine. Already checked it out."

"Look at what you got me into," I said to McQuiston. "Any more bright ideas?"

The sergeant looked down and didn't answer.

"Okay, let's go."

We worked our way through some trees and then edged along through the ground cover but found no resistance. When we got near the entrance, I could hear crying and mumbling.

"Americans will not hurt you," Higa shouted in Japanese. "They will not harm women, children. Don't kill yourselves."

I'd been thumbing through my Ryukyuan section of the dictionary and shouted, "Friend! We friend!"

We listened. Seemed like a conference going on in there with women crying and children screaming. I yelled "Friend" a few more times. Finally, some man began shouting questions to Higa. For several minutes, the exchange went back and forth.

"He says they are willing to come out," Higa said. "The Japanese gave them hand grenades to kill themselves, but they're going to put them down. The leader says they got a truckload of people in there."

"Tell 'em to come out single file with their hands up," I said. "We don't want any surprises."

Higa nodded and shouted my message.

After about a minute, a man in a long brown robe tied at the waist with a piece of rope slowly stepped out. He looked around like maybe a tiger was going to leap on him and tear his head off. His crumpled brown hat with a flat top pulled down to his ears made his head look flat. The guy's sandals were as worn as his eye. Terror was written across his forehead.

"Friend," I kept saying in Ryukyuan. "Me friend."

His face brightened. The locals waiting behind him started filing out. The women had poles across their backs with large sacks dangling from the ends. Their stringy black hair had been pulled tight at the back of their heads and tied with coarse string. Every last one looked mortified.

The line appeared endless. These frightened Okinawans kept marching down the ravine back toward the beach where we'd come from. Young girls hugged small children walking next to them and refused to look at us. I was sure the Japanese had frightened them severely enough to last a lifetime.

"My God!" Higa gasped. "I bet there's a thousand of them in there. Can you believe it?"

"This won't be the last time we see such," I said. "I bet there's caves all over this island."

McQuiston waved from above us and yelled, "Lousy place to hide. Once you're in, you're a sittin' duck for anybody aiming at the entrance."

"Afraid so," I said.

———————

After returning, we discovered the First Battalion of the Eighty-Third had landed on the wrong beach. Whoever messed this one up really threw the attack into confusion. The First wouldn't move out until the correct direction to the southeast had been cleared. While the command was straightening the maps out, Company B ran into a hornet's nest of Japanese. Bullets started flying in front of Sergeant Fred Hale's unit. "Hit the ground!" he yelled.

The men dived into the bushes and waited for more fire. They didn't have to wait long. Another round ripped through the trees, just missing our heads. Sergeant Hale rolled over and motioned for the men to spread out.

Some soldier lying near the front pulled out a grenade and slung it. While he missed the enemy, the blast sent another round of machine-gun fire back at Company B and clearly identified where the Japanese were.

Hale took a deep breath and screamed, "Charge those bastards!"

The unit inched forward with guns blazing. Finally realizing they had taken off a bite too big to swallow, the Japanese grabbed their weapons and started to retreat. They didn't get five steps away before rapid fire dropped them.

Company A sent another squad of the elusive enemy on the run. Because they weren't far from the town of Momobaru, they figured these bad boys would try to hide in a pillbox in front of their unit. They were right on target.

"The enemy are holed up in that pillbox over there," the PFC explained. "We been shootin' at 'em but getting nowhere. That cement fortress got no give in it. Gonna try a flamethrower." He pointed to a soldier creeping toward the cement structure.

I watched as the fire eater carefully worked his way through ground cover toward the base of the gun turret. The Japanese kept firing but were too far above him to hit our man. The soldier swung the long black nozzle around and fire blasted out like a volcano erupting. The flames wrapped around the pillbox like a runaway blowtorch and sent the smell of smoke drifting through the trees. The flamethrower kept roasting the doorway, but nothing happened. The Japanese were just too well insulated and far back in the structure.

"Can't get 'em!" the fire eater called out. "Gotta retreat." He started backing away.

"I'll fix those bastards," the sergeant grumbled, and picked up the phone unit hooked to a radio box on the back of one of the soldiers. "Give me a round from one of them big boys! Give 'em hell!"

The Japanese opened up another round that kept everybody close to the ground. They weren't budging an inch.

"You just wait," the sergeant hissed. "You're gonna see some real fireworks in a moment."

Periodically the enemy fired off a round or two, but not much seemed to be going on until somewhere behind us a rumbling noise began increasing in volume. The sound of grinding wheels cutting through trees and debris shook the ground. An M4 Sherman tank rolled up and stopped.

"Get out of the way," Hale warned. "Those steel monsters make quite a racket."

We retreated into a clump of trees and covered our ears. I could see a long steel barrel leveling on the pillbox. The tank fired two quick rounds.

With smoke flying out of the crumbling rubble, the sides of the pillbox slid into a pile of broken concrete. No more gunfire erupted. Their guns were silenced.

The Japanese were finished.

6

A Price to Be Paid

None of us had any idea how terrible the cost would be before we finished taking Okinawa. The casual observer might have concluded that the landing was so easy, war must be a walk in the park. Some park!

As the postwar decades passed, I realized that the average American's view of death was shaped by movies and television shows. In thirty minutes, you'd watch a number of people get killed, break for a couple of commercials, get a beer out of the fridge, change the channels, and watch another detective kill some other guys. Finally, you'd turn the set off and go to bed. All those killings were imaginary, impersonal, abstract; they meant nothing. Just show business.

The situation changes when the dead are your buddies, a brother, a friend whom you'd played poker with and shared stories of what you hoped to do when you got home. The cost of war mounts up and takes a staggering emotional toll on every soldier.

Weeks after we had come ashore on Okinawa and fought a good number of battles, Sergeant McQuiston and I were in my jeep driving in the opposite direction from the front lines and following a set of tracks that our boys had cut through the remnant of what had once been a footpath of some sort. The smell of war hung in the air, but by this time we'd gotten used to it and just kept going. We happened onto an area where bodies of soldiers were kept, awaiting burial. After men fell in battle, they were usually carried to the rear and eventually ended up in black body bags.

Somebody had set up a shelter under tarps tied up on wooden poles. Underneath, corpses were stacked like firewood. The pile must have been three to four feet high. The soldiers' dog tags were fastened on the end of the zippers, the only remaining identification of who they had been.

McQuiston brought the jeep to a halt. The anonymity of the body bags only added to the pathos. Could have been us. We sat there staring at that heap of cadavers. Each one was someone's son, brother, maybe fiancé, and now they were gone. Forever gone. We stared.

No break for a television commercial there.

———————————

Lieutenant Colonel Ed Stare's Third Battalion of the 383rd Infantry made the most spectacular advance of the day pushing south from the landing beaches. Company I marched along the coastline until they stopped for a flag raising. Someone had brought an American flag from the States. The soldiers hoisted the flag to signal American sovereignty; the men cheered as the flag went up. Let the Japanese think on that one for a while!

I wasn't with them at the time, but later the men kept talking about what followed. The experience proved to be so vivid, I couldn't forget it. The soldiers shared the struggle with me in great detail.

The battalion kept moving; they knew a river was ahead. The men were prepared for a difficult time crossing the waterway. Could be a big-time problem as all the enemy had to do was set up machine guns on the other bank and fire at the approaching soldiers. Amazingly enough, they had forgotten to destroy a bridge. Our men rolled across without missing a beat. They hadn't gone far up the road when they finally ran into the opposition. About twenty Japanese had set up a machine-gun nest and were waiting for our boys. Battalion I hit the ground and began returning the fire.

Captain Gordon Wheeler yelled that they'd found the enemy.

The gunfire went back and forth while the battalion tried to position itself. Bullets were flying in rapid fire. Soldiers dropped behind boulders or downed trees.

A soldier called back that there weren't many of them but they were dug in below ground level. We needed to hit 'em from both sides.

The enemy answered with a blast of machine-gun fire.

Wheeler called for the unit to spread out, to split up and work both angles.

The battalion divided on the flanks and started working their way around the opposition. A blast much larger than a simple machine gun ripped through the air. Sounded like they had a 155mm artillery piece over there.

Two American soldiers fell to the ground. A third man screamed and rolled over into a ditch. For thirty minutes intense fire went back and forth. The unit didn't seem to be making any progress. Casualties were quickly mounting.

The voice of Captain Wheeler echoed through the trees that he needed help. He'd caught it in the leg and couldn't walk.

Someone called for a medic.

An anonymous man called from the left to keep the captain on the ground.

Men began pulling in behind where Wheeler lay sprawled.

The medic called for them to drag him out and get him behind shelter. Three men pulled the captain across the grass and finally propped him up behind a large boulder.

Wheeler groaned that he'd gotten smoked in the thigh and the pain was killing him.

The medic gave him a shot of morphine. He worked feverishly over the captain, telling him they'd quickly get him out of there.

The soldiers around Wheeler nodded, but a burst of machine-gun fire sent them diving to the ground again. A sergeant crawled over and informed them that they had killed some of the enemy but the rest, though outnumbered, were still dug in below ground level. The battalion couldn't hit them, and trying would only get them killed. They needed an ace in the hole. Something different.

The radioman crawled over with the phone pack on his back. The sergeant jerked the receiver off and reported the problem. Captain Wheeler had been hit and so had a number of other men. The Japanese weren't budging. They needed a tank or something big of that order. A weapon that packed a punch. The sergeant listened for a moment before hanging up.

In five minutes, a soldier poked through the trees carrying a long black tube at his side. He said Command had sent him and he had to make it fast because "I'm busier than a one-legged tap dancer over there in my unit."

The sergeant asked what he'd brought.

The soldier answered that he'd show them.

The sergeant beckoned him to follow and they inched through bushes until they stopped behind a fallen tree closer to the enemy. The sergeant pointed out a machine gun there on ground level that was their problem.

The soldier nodded and told them, "Don't stand behind me. The bazooka has a considerable back blast."

The soldier lowered himself almost to ground level. Abruptly, the enemy fired a round or two. The sergeant and the bazooka man could hear them jabbering.

After putting his finger to his mouth to signal silence, the soldier rested the long, recoilless antitank launcher on the fork of a scrubby tree. For a second, he carefully aimed low, and then he pulled the trigger. A ball of fire spiraled upward before smoke covered the area around the enemy's foxhole. The Japanese were history.

The sergeant couldn't believe the bazooka had knocked them out with one shot.

The two men started inching backward until they rejoined the rest of the squad.

The Japanese wouldn't be bothering them anymore. The bazooka man saluted and disappeared through the trees and scrub just as he had come in.

By then Captain Wheeler had passed out. Apparently, morphine had done the trick but his leg continued to bleed heavily. The sergeant took a second look.

The sergeant knew that they had to get the captain out of there. A couple of the men carried him out. It was getting late enough in the afternoon that they ought to have been digging in for the night. Fortunately, none of them got hit with that 155mm.

The sergeant who told me this story paused then, caught his breath, and gritted his teeth, cursing the loss of their men. The survivors knew that Wheeler would end up in a body bag with a hundred other guys all laid out under a tarp.

Nobody said anything.

At night we'd sit around and talk, sharing this kind of story. I remember thinking how we were really processing what might happen to us.

7

Sharpening the Focus

By morning our end of the island was quiet with little movement, but we knew that wouldn't last long. The men stirred and broke out their rations. I hated the canned "stuff," but if you're hungry enough, you'll eat anything. My battery had already gotten the big guns in position and looked ready to fire. I'd seen enough action the day before to realize that the Japanese weren't going to lie down and roll. The Japanese meant business—and much of the conflict looked like it would be suicide before it was over. I needed to spend some time at headquarters to learn more.

Sergeant McQuiston came over to my tent. "The men are ready to respond to whatever comes our way. Do you have any idea when we'll start firing?"

"I don't," I said. "We'll have to see how far the other units got last night. I'm sure we're okay for the time being. Assemble the troops."

McQuiston left my tent to begin lining the men up.

I knew the soldiers of the 361st Field Artillery Battalion were efficient and dedicated. Standing at the top was Lieutenant Colonel Avery Masters. The colonel didn't hesitate to promote himself and loved to watch the entire battalion go marching by. If he ever made general, old Avery would be holding a parade at every opportunity.

Our battalions had the most highly skilled personnel in the army. Since World War I, many adjustments and changes had been made, and these innovations were put to good use. The size of the battalion depended on the magnitude of the artillery we fired. The larger the big gun, the more men were required for the operation. For the 105mm M2A1 units, we had three firing batteries with four guns in each one. Each battery had a captain with an executive officer who was usually a major. That was me.

Each battery ran around a hundred men. However, it was rare to have the full count because once combat began, casualties were inevitable. The army had a replacement system, but too many fell, so we always came up short. On the European front, in December's Battle of the Bulge, there was such a manpower crisis in infantry units that many of the nonessential artillery personnel ended up as infantry replacements.

In the other batteries, Captains Lorne Martin and Albert Olson ran a tight ship and I knew that precision would filter down through the units. In our battery, First Lieutenant John Hayes was a standby sort of guy. He didn't say much but was as tough as a brick. The men would line up with him. No question about it.

Then there was "Swinging" Bill Arnold. The corporal had a habit of nibbling on the bottle and an amazing ability to come up with forbidden booze. We never found out where he hid the joy juice, but we knew when he'd been drinking. After a few swallows, you'd think he could have whipped heavyweight champ Joe Louis. However, his high-flying right swings were so obvious that anyone could see one coming and duck. The corporal usually ended up in the dirt. Swinging Bill was flirting with a court-martial, but we let it go because his replacement might be hard to come by. When he sobered up, old Bill seemed actually to be on the timid side. Just took a little Jack Daniel's to fire him up, then he'd be out there in line in the morning straight as a stick.

Corporal Hans Goins had always been a guy who had a habit of irritating people by making constant personal jabs aimed at their weaknesses. He wasn't a big guy but he enjoyed being irritating. Nobody really wanted to smack him in the chops because a brawl would follow. Still, the day was coming when he was going to get hit in the face big-time.

They'd all be standing at attention every morning, waiting to hear what I had to say. My message would be clear, and it didn't change. "Boys, this might be the next-to-last big battle of the war. Dig in!"

This one particular morning I stepped out of my tent and slapped my helmet on my head. Off in the distance I could hear gunfire. The infantry boys were already at it.

"At ease!" I shouted. The unit relaxed.

"Okay, gentlemen. This is the big one. After we finish this encounter, our next stop will be Tokyo. The enemy aren't going to allow this to be an easy road to travel. However, the sooner we wind up the engagement with the enemy, the sooner we will be on our way home. We must hit them hard. You know what your assignments are. Get out there and get the job done."

I saluted, and they returned the high sign. "Dismissed!" I shouted, and they broke up.

Sergeant McQuiston stepped up and saluted. "What's the next step, sir?"

"I'm going to be our reconnaissance officer for the time being," I said. "Need to know what Command is thinking and where all this is going. I'm sure we will be shooting before the day is over. Sergeant, just make sure this battery is ready to fire. I'm going to Command Central right now."

"You got it, sir." The sergeant saluted, turned on his heels, and marched off.

The humidity began picking up and I could tell it was going to be a hot day. The day before the men had stretched camouflage netting over the artillery and poked tree branches in the openings to keep the Zeros from flying over and dropping a few bombs on us. Driving my jeep alone, I wound my way through walking trails that lined the rolling hills. I believed this end of the island was safe enough, so I felt relatively secure, but my .45-caliber pistol and rifle offered a little encouragement.

I soon found the Command Center that had temporarily been set up in one of the caves that dotted the island. When I pulled up, I could see officers coming and going. Obviously, they were already well under way. I saluted the guard at the entrance and went in.

The cave still had the musty smell of dirt. Big lamps had been set up all around the walls. Large-scale maps were spread out. The size of the island allowed us to identify every nook and cranny, every ravine and valley in detail. Some officers were already on the communication phones. Others were moving the lines on the maps. We had made good progress in moving toward the towns of Naha and Yonabaru. Looked like a small airfield at Yonabaru would soon fall. I studied the maps carefully.

"What do you see, Major?" the familiar voice of Lieutenant Colonel Avery Masters echoed in my ears.

"Looks like we're moving, sir," I said.

"Yeah," Masters answered, "but the train's about to stop." He pointed his finger to the map. "We outsmarted the Japanese in our landing on beaches they weren't expecting. That's given us a good hunk of land taken with minimal opposition. We're about to run out of that advantage."

I studied the map. "I see." I rubbed my chin. "Sir, I've taken the unusual position of being the reconnaissance officer for the time being. I want to make sure we are hitting our targets."

"Oh?" Avery frowned. "On the unexpected side, but damn! If it makes your soldiers aim more accurately, I suppose it'll work."

"Yes, sir."

"Look here, Major Shaw." The lieutenant colonel traced a line that ran across the island. "We call that barrier the escarpment, a high bluff and ridge that nearly cuts the island in half. We'll have increasing resistance as we approach this area. Names like Sugar Hill, Flattop, Cactus Ridge, Charlie Hill will become familiar to you. However, nothing will be like what the Japanese will throw at us once we hit the big divide, the escarpment. We'll need all the artillery support we can throw at that ridge. Won't be there soon, but that's where we're going."

"I see," I repeated myself. "Gonna be tough."

"Tough?" Avery snorted. "Major, it's gonna be hell."

8

The Snakes Come Slithering In

Command wanted artillery to "soften up" the enemy, let them know we were coming. A couple of rounds or so ought to wake them up. At least, that's what some of the boys back at headquarters seemed to believe. Personally, I thought they were wrong. We might have caught the Japanese off guard by where we landed, but they'd already figured out where we were and by now had settled in for the real fight. I knew the conflict was going to take a hell of a lot more than a few blasts from one of our 105mm howitzers.

"Ready!" I shouted. "Fire!" The ground shook when howitzers fired.

The men immediately tossed the shell casing aside and slid in another round. I counted to thirty and yelled again. "Fire!"

We kept this routine up for thirty minutes. I had no idea what we hit, but whatever was out there would be confetti by now. The Ninety-Sixth and the Seventh Division had moved to our right on the downhill side of the island. The Deadeyes would have started bearing down on the enemy's main line of resistance.

No one was quite sure where the name Deadeyes came from. The Ninety-Sixth Infantry had been trained under the supervision of General Claudius Easley, who was one of the army's crack marksmen. Actually, marksmanship had always been one of the general's passions. Many a time during training, a PFC would be jarred to look over his shoulder and find General Easley sprawled out in the grass beside him ready to instruct the trainee on the fine art of hitting the target. That old sharpshooting Texan left his mark on all the men. They were expected to have eyes like a mountain lion and trigger fingers as steady as Easley's. Somewhere along the way that translated into Deadeyes.

The Ninety-Sixth had evolved into a triangular division built around three infantry regiments: the 381st, 382nd, and 383rd. What had been a machine-gun battalion in World War I had now become field artillery. We were supporting the forward flow of combat.

"Fire again!" I continued to command.

When the 105mm erupted, the big gun literally jumped off the ground. After a few rounds, the pad was getting hot. Men jerked their shirts off as the big blasts continued. The air was heating up. The pungent smell of smoke filled my nose and I had to step back. If this was what Command wanted, we were certainly providing.

The communication line rang and Corporal "Swinging" Bill Arnold took the call. "It's for you, sir."

"Yeah," I answered.

"Listen. Lieutenant Johnson's First Battalion has pushed two miles in on your left flank. You can stop firing for a while."

"Got it." I hung up the phone.

Lieutenant Colonel Charles Johnson was one of the youngest infantry commanders. He obviously had his men on the move. While he was charging forward, Company K attacked a hill and came under heavy fire. They got hit not only from the front but from both sides. Several of their men fell in the exchange. Speculation had jawboned the idea that the Japanese were now dug in. My earlier suspicions were proving true. The party was over.

The phone rang again. "Yeah," I answered.

"K Company needs assistance. Here's some new coordinates. Shoot in this direction."

As he rattled off the numbers, I wrote them down. "Gotcha. We'll fire over there."

I hung up and began passing out the new numbers. The men responded quickly. Maybe Lieutenant Johnson would get some relief.

That night the situation began to change. Colonel Ed May's Third Battalion ran head-on into the opposition. The company had made good progress through the day and in the late afternoon had settled down for the evening. May ordered the men to dig foxholes and prepare to spend the night on the edge of what had been the front line. I was with them checking out how the howitzers were firing.

The sun began to set, and sentries were placed around the camp. The men talked, smoked, and stretched out to relax from the wear and tear of the day. The situation appeared to be under control. Finally, night settled over the soldiers exhausted from the day, sleeping with their rifles beside them.

Around eleven o'clock, PFC Jesse Rice heard a noise. "Hey, Smith! Did you hear that?"

The other sentry listened. "Get down," he called back. "Might be something coming our way."

I looked out to see what the noise was about.

After ten minutes of waiting, they stood up again. "Don't know," Smith said. "Maybe an animal broke a branch."

"Okay." Rice started walking slowly again.

A Japanese soldier came rushing out of the brush, swinging a saber. Rice caught the first blow with his rifle, but the strike was so forceful it knocked the gun out of his hand. Rice grabbed the Japanese by the collar and swung him to the ground. The two men rolled back and forth, each jockeying for the best position to throttle the other. Finally, Rice got one hand under the man's chin and squeezed his throat with all his strength. The attacker began to choke and swing with both fists, but Rice wouldn't let go. The attacker slowly stopped resisting.

The other sentry didn't have time to yell when the attacker hit him in the throat. Smith fell straight backward, and the Japanese soldier was all over him, stabbing him repeatedly. Blood went flying all over the ground. A third rushed in and jumped on top of one of the sleeping men. When he plunged his sword into the Yank's stomach, the soldier screamed and that brought everyone to their feet. Once the ambush was exposed, the fourth man dropped to his knees and opened a backpack filled with satchel charges.

"Get that son of a bitch!" a sergeant screamed, and tried to get his rifle to fire, but it jammed. "Shoot 'em!" he kept yelling as he tried to get his gun to fire.

The Japanese started to pull out a charge, but one of the men who'd been sleeping with his rifle fired and hit the invader square in the chest. He didn't get the explosive out.

"They're all over the place!" the sergeant shrieked. "Grab your weapons!"

Some idiot in the unit started firing indiscriminately and nearly hit two soldiers. He finally dropped back into his foxhole and stopped.

The Japanese soldier who killed Smith charged the sergeant and swung his saber down on the man's head. By pure reflex, the sergeant pushed his rifle over his head with both hands and the blade crashed into the barrel, splintering the Japanese's weapon. The slam unlocked the rifle, causing it to fire and sending a bullet flying off into nowhere land.

The Japanese soldier's eyes opened wide in consternation. Apparently, he wasn't sure whether he had been shot or not.

"You bastard!" the sergeant screeched, and fired again.

The Japanese fighter had turned to run when the bullet hit him in the back. He tumbled over dead.

By this time, a couple of the enemy had jumped on a jeep parked to the rear. They seemed to be trying to disable the vehicle. Rapid fire from several of the soldiers dropped them in the dirt at the back side of the jeep.

An eerie stillness settled over the camp. For a couple of minutes, no one moved until it was clear the enemy had gone south. Finally, the sergeant stood up. "I think they're gone."

The soldiers slowly emerged from their foxholes.

"Got one casualty over here," Staff Sergeant Horace Jones called out. "He's slumped over in the hole. Don't think a medic will help."

"Medic!" the sergeant shouted anyway. "Where's a medic?"

From the back of the camp, a man answered, "I'm coming."

From across the encampment, men slowly crawled out and assembled around Smith's body as well as the man in the foxhole. Seeing a buddy lying there with a deadly wound stunned the senses and left you numb—if not ready to scream. A sober silence settled over the entire unit.

"Sneaky bunch of snakes," Rice said. "Striking in the dark and as poisonous as rattlers."

Nobody said anything.

9

Trudging On

Funny thing how war affects one's identity. We all started out as average young guys growing up in average American towns doing average things like playing baseball or tormenting the girls before going after them. Many of us grew up milking cows on farms. Just easygoing kids trying to wiggle a dime out of someone so we could see a cowboy movie that included a serial each weekend. Most of us were a little on the mischievous side but meant no harm.

Then Uncle Sam picked us up, shaved our heads, and ran us through thirteen weeks of hell. When we came out of boot camp in uniforms, whatever had been was gone. We were loaded up on ships and sailed off into a world that we virtually didn't even know existed. Guys we'd never seen before became our buddies and brothers. We were supposed to survive on K rations that became as monotonous as eating rubber. About all that was left of us was something called "a soldier." We had become killing machines. Our motto was "Kill them or they will kill you." All those easygoing good times were gone.

Take for example what occurred north of the town of Kami-yama. The Japanense felled trees across the road and laid mines in there, which knocked out two of our tanks from the 763rd Battalion. Colonel Cyril Sterner figured out how to avoid the confrontation by swinging his battalion to the right off the road. The tanks and infantry moved through an open field for over five hundred yards without encountering any opposition. When the enemy appeared, Sterner's men let them have it big-time. By the end of the shootout, 148 Japanese had been killed. While I wasn't there, I quickly heard all about the skirmish.

Around 5:45 p.m., the battalion rolled into the town of Ginowan. As the sun dropped to the horizon, the enemy opened up with a fierce round of fire. In front of the town was a low clay ridge that gave them an opportune position for shooting at us. The Second Battalion didn't retreat but knew they were digging in for the night on dangerous ground. E Company grabbed their shovels and went to work.

Sergeant Charles Reber started shoveling out his foxhole, telling the men to keep their heads down because the Japanese might be aiming at us.

"Don't worry," PFC Bill Synder answered. "I ain't stickin' my head up none."

"You don't understand," PFC James Bolger said. "We're invincible. That's what the army will get you. Absolute virility."

"Ha ha," Reber answered in a flat, emotionless voice.

The dirt kept flying. Sporadically a burst of gunfire cut through the trees. Sometimes the Second Battalion responded; sometimes they didn't. The sun faded, and night was coming on. E Company was ready for dreamland.

Out of nowhere, four Japanese came rushing in, hurling grenades. The explosions sent shrapnel flying in all directions. E Company began firing at the shadows, but Charlie Reber fell over in his foxhole. Grenades kept exploding in a deafening roar. Bolger caught it in the hand and couldn't shoot. Synder kept firing his pistol but wasn't sure he was doing any good.

Three of the attackers fell, but the fourth one came straight for Lee Bland with his bayonet aimed at the sergeant's heart. PFC Joe Mikula knocked the gun down before the enemy could stab Bland. Mikula grabbed the man's arms and pinned them to his side. PFC Kenneth French leaped up and began pounding the Japanese in the face.

"Kill the bastard!" Bland screamed.

"Hit 'em again," Mikula said, while holding the man's arms down.

French didn't say anything but kept pounding him in the face until he brought his rifle butt down on the man's head several times. The Japanese man slumped.

"I think he's dead," Mikula said. "I heard his skull crack after that last blow." He let go and the Japanese soldier crumbled in a heap on the ground, his face turned into a bloody mess.

"Looks like the attack is over," Bland said. "Can't tell you how much I appreciate you boys jumpin' in. That imperial force would have killed us for sure with that bayonet."

French kept rubbing his knuckles. "Musta hit him with all my strength. My hand is killing me . . . pardon the expression."

Bland laughed. "You really whacked him."

"Oh, my God!" Joe Mikula gasped. "I swallowed my false teeth! Can't believe it! I actually swallowed my whole set . . . My teeth are gone."

"What'll you do?" French asked.

Bland laughed again. "Why, it'll take surgery to get those back."

I sat there and chuckled.

That's how your identity gets altered. Never in a thousand years would you expect to get your teeth knocked down to your stomach. After you've been through some of those firefights and killed a few enemies, the encounters change how you see yourself. You know you *can kill* someone. Sometimes a man gets swallowed by guilt. Other times men recognize that now they know what it means, "kill or be killed." Some of the guys just take it in stride.

But no one talks about the killing.

Clearing out that road that Sterner's men had avoided became the job of Lieutenant Howard Tway's Regimental Mine Platoon. While they were deactivating fifty-pound mines, the Japanese kept shooting at them with mortar and machine-gun fire. Tway's men were swatting mosquitoes that could blow their heads off.

The fireworks back and forth lasted through the entire time it took to clear the road. When the debris and mines were cleared and the job done, one man had been killed and five other soldiers wounded. The men called the trail "a thousand yards of hell." Unfortunately, the clearing process was necessary because we needed the road open to bring in rations, ammunition, and water to the men on the front line. Nasty business from top to bottom.

The Japanese kept up their attack and backed off only when pressured to the hilt. Whatever ground they gave us in our landing, they were dead sure trying to take back now. One of their worst strikes came when a sniper killed Captain James Barron, the F Company commander. We knew he had proved himself to be one of the finest officers we had. During the battle of Leyte, Barron had demonstrated exemplary courage. Some Japanese had been sitting out there in the trees and got a lucky shot. Captain Barron was gone.

I watched these events for the clues about where our artillery battery should fire. We needed to be exactly on target. I knew that the 383rd section of the Second Battalion had covered seven hundred yards without opposition. Then the firestorm broke out. The enemy hit them with everything they had. Intense mortar and machine-gun fire rained bullets down on them. All forward motion came to an abrupt halt.

The 383rd had been after a target labeled Cactus Hill. The Third Battalion came in from a different direction and was after the same objective. They too came to a complete halt. The soldiers had worked their way in to the front on the coastal flat. Obviously, they were in an exposed position. The Japanese had certainly paid attention to this fact.

No matter which way our people moved, we had a big problem. The Japanese weren't moving. I knew what was needed. Time to get back to the battery. Our targets weren't a mystery anymore. A little artillery working-over would turn Cactus Hill into Boot Hill.

10

The End of the Honeymoon

The next day broke with a sunny sky and relative quiet. You could hear Corporal "Swinging" Bill Arnold singing all the way back to the beach. That wasn't a good sign as it probably meant he'd already been nipping. If a ruckus started, Arnold would be in real trouble at such an early hour. We hadn't heard anything from Corporal Hans Goins, which was a good sign. A least he wasn't out irritating people yet. Stay tuned.

A check on the data revealed Cactus Hill was farther off than I might have suspected. Once our battery started firing, we soon got word that the advance had slowed and weren't near that target. I wasn't sure what was going on. McQuiston was already on the phone.

"Sergeant McQuiston, any updates on where the front line is going?"

He pressed the phone against his head and listened more closely.

"McQuiston! You picking up anything? Any details?"

The sergeant put the phone down. "Looks like the motorized patrol of the Ninety-Sixth Reconnaissance got hit hard. They were on the move with vehicles sandbagged to protect against road mines. As they approached the village of Uchitomari, they came out on a stretch of open ground. The Japanese were waiting and hit them hard with antitank and sniper fire, even got in a machine-gun barrage. The Reconnaissance guys were up against a well-camouflaged installation. A forty-one-millimeter shell smacked the lead half-track. Captain Kyle Riley and their radio operator were knocked out. Turned out to be one damn big mess."

"Sounds like they got hit from every possible angle," I said.

"Yeah," McQuiston said. "Sergeant John Cain ordered the men to abandon their positions while he covered them with a thirty-seven-millimeter gun. They contacted one of our other batteries to open up a barrage. The whole unit was cut off and pinned down. They were liberated only when some tanks and foot soldiers showed up from the rear."

"How many did they lose?"

The sergeant rubbed his chin. "I believe six men were wounded and two killed. Five vehicles got blown away, but I'm sure they saved the infantry heavy losses."

"I guess we softened up Cactus Hill for nothing."

"No, Major. They are still after the same objective. Trouble is we got hit sooner than expected. We got some new sites to worry about. Hills like Clay, Coral, and Quarry. There's even one in there named Mishabaru Hill."

Sounded unexpected to me. I wasn't sure where we should be aiming now. I remembered seeing those sites on some of the maps back at headquarters.

"I need more information," I said. "I'm going to take a hike and see what turns up. You keep the unit running and stay in phone contact."

"Yes, sir." The sergeant saluted.

I took a road that wound up to the front. Lieutenant Colonel Ed Stare's Third Battalion had pressed forward behind the Recon boys even though they were under constant harassment. By the time I got to the front, I could see that K Company was taking heavy fire from Cactus Ridge, so we really weren't out of the game we had been fighting. The enemy continued to hit hard.

"Get down," a soldier yelled at me. "They ain't gonna stop firing."

A mortar blasted the area. For a few minutes, I lay there and waited for the next blast. It didn't take long.

"How bad is it?" I asked one of the majors lying just ahead of me.

"They've really kicked up a storm," he said. "Those sonofabitches are hitting us with everything they got. Problem is that the Cactus Ridge area is lined with caves and pillboxes. Hard for us to get at 'em."

"Got ya," I said.

"We're getting it from the rear as well," the major explained. "There's a rock formation down there by the shore where they can hit us. Command dubbed it the Pirates' Den. They're using us for target practice."

"I think I can get our artillery to fire their way. You got the coordinates?"

"You bet." The major pulled out a map and made notations. "Will that work?"

"You got a radioman?"

"Over there." He pointed to his left. "He'll fix you up."

I crawled part of the way and ran the rest. Sergeant McQuiston got my information and started making adjustments.

Meanwhile the C Company of the 763rd Battalion began taking heavy hits from 76mm shells. I worked my way down to where they'd stopped. As I watched, three tanks broke into flame. Suddenly, a soldier leaped into action and started pulling men out of the tanks and away from what would soon be an explosion.

The Japanese kept shooting at him with every sniper they had. At the risk of his own life, the soldier started saving men. One of the C Company men crawled up beside me.

"Who is that guy down there risking his life?" I asked.

The soldier blinked several times. "Looks like . . . like . . . a sergeant. I believe that's Sergeant Orvil French."

"That man should be awarded for his bravery," I said. "He's really risking his life."

"You bet!" the soldier said, and hurried away.

Much later in the conflict, I learned that French did receive the Silver Star for his efforts.

I crawled down closer to the action to see if we could bring artillery fire to bear on their situation. Just as I reached the edge of their command post, a shell exploded, and men scattered everywhere. As the smoke cleared, we struggled to get up from the ground.

The regimental commander, Colonel May, staggered to his feet with blood running down the side of his face. I guessed a piece of shrapnel must have caught him.

"Damn it to hell," the colonel moaned, and grabbed his head. "Don't stop for me. Keep firing!"

A medic ran up with a large bandage. Colonel May paused long enough for the dressing to be tied to the back of his head and then charged ahead even though he walked with a limp and must have had a headache the size of Chicago.

"Keep firing!" May kept shouting. "Keep firing back!"

I realized that I had walked into a highly difficult position and wasn't sure how to get out. Turned out that Colonel Stare had a similar problem. A firestorm had broken loose forty ways to Sunday and the Japanese weren't letting up.

Colonel Stare called in that he was seriously worried that his battalion had become isolated and wasn't sure how to proceed. They had him covered on all sides.

His voice roared out of the phone, "We are in danger of being wiped out if they counterattack." The line went dead.

I looked around. Eleven men had been killed and fifty-four wounded. Stare was right.

We were in deep shit.

No Rest for the Weary

When darkness fell, I knew this was the only opportunity I would have to get back to my battery without getting blown to smithereens. Trudging toward the rear at night wasn't the best idea in the world, so I stayed with a unit of soldiers, hoping our boys wouldn't think I was a Japanese infiltrating. By the time I got back, Sergeant McQuiston and most of the men were dug in for the night.

After I passed the sentinels, I walked into the encampment. Swinging Bill Arnold lay there snoring like a bull charging a matador. His sound sleep probably had more to do with Jack Daniel's than anything else. Because we'd start early in the morning, no one was wasting any time getting enough shut-eye. Didn't take a rocket scientist to see the wisdom in that decision. I bedded down quickly.

The next morning, the phone call from Command informed me that a withdrawal had been made to the town of Mashiki and Colonel Stare's unit had escaped any serious problems from a counterattack. The Ninety-Sixth Division had clearly reached the first line of the Japanese defense. The holdup for forward advancement was the need to clear out Clay Ridge and Tombstone Ridge. Those obstacles had to be taken for our soldiers to keep moving forward.

Tombstone got the name from three prominent look-alike tombs on the western slope. The ridge ran about eight hundred yards north and south. Just reaching Clay Ridge would probably take several days. Before our infantry could get there, we had to take two small hills, Coral and Porter. I knew the 382nd Infantry would be faced with a tough job and I had to get our artillery unit ready.

With so many caves and tombs dotting the area, we had to carefully sort out where those shelters were located because the enemy would be shooting from those covers. We'd be ready to grind it out.

———————

Two hours later the Command Center called again.

"Major Shaw?" the voice barked over the phone.

"Yes, sir," I said. "The 361st Artillery stands ready to fire."

"Good. You've already been around those damn caves the Japanese use for firing at us like we're ducks in a shooting gallery. We need you to help inspect that scene for information on what we should do next. The boss wants you to get over there and take a good look. Get near Nishabaru Ridge. Keep your eyes open for all action related to the Cactus Hill area. We'll communicate with your battery by phone when and where we need them to fire."

"As you say, sir." I hung up the phone.

"What's happening?" McQuiston asked.

"They want me to take a hike up to the front. You keep the fires burning here. If you get a call for artillery support, you know what to do."

McQuiston saluted and I took off.

Colonel Sterner had moved his command post and mortar section closer to the front, but they'd barely gotten set up when the Japanese started hitting them exactly where they were positioned. Because the Japanese had excellent field visibility from their hill locations, they could follow our every movement and so immediately knew where Sterner moved. Once the colonel settled in, all the Japanese had to do was start shooting.

With mortars flying, the colonel realized they'd have to retreat. By the time they'd rounded up their gear, fifty shells had landed in their vicinity. The infantry took off running back to their previous position at Ginowan. Two were killed.

When I passed one of the caves that had been evacuated, I saw a woman and her two children huddled under a bush. Fearing the Japanese might have wired them in some way to make them a booby trap, I could only watch from a distance. I could tell the baby was nursing at the mother's breast, so I had to assume they were all alive. I watched for a moment. The women's eyes were closed, and she didn't move. The other child stayed huddled behind her and stared at me. I'd report the situation and move on.

Nothing I could do, so I kept moving.

Sterner's battalion weren't about to give up ground to the Japanese, and the battle didn't cool off. G Company kept pushing until they had taken the western end of Clay Ridge. Anyone watching the encounter could see the tremendous effort they made.

While this action unfolded, the Imperial Army unleashed a terrifying new weapon. Three mammoth projectiles came screaming down into the Second Battalion's line. The explosion sent dirt and rocks flying in every direction like a volcano erupting. Anyone near the explosions could feel their ears wilt. The ground shook under my feet. Finally, I made my way into their camp.

Three men were standing around one of the huge craters. Down inside the hole, another soldier appeared to be examining what was left of the tail fins that brought the flying pain-making pineapple cruising in on top of our men. I joined the soldiers.

"What do you think?" I asked.

"Unbelievable! That doomsday machine made every other missile in the world look puny," the sergeant said. "Bigger than anything I've ever heard of."

"Must have been at least a three-hundred-twenty-millimeter mortar. The damn thing shore was a flying boxcar. Scared the pants off me."

The men broke out cigarettes and kept talking.

"That hole is thirty to forty feet across," the third man said. "Big as a swimming pool."

"They're trying to scare us to death," I said.

"Well, if so, they've won that round," the sergeant said.

Another explosion to our right shook the ground.

"Hate to say it," I said, "but I don't think I want to stay around you boys. You seem to be drawin' the really big mosquitoes these days."

"Do tell," one of the soldiers said, and extended his hand to help the soldier in the crater back up to ground level.

"I'd say the Japanese blew a swimming pool in our backyard, but there's a disadvantage to this flying monster," the sergeant said. "All the fragmentation gets absorbed in the sides of the crater. Didn't splatter on any of us. Whatever they're after, the enemy better hit it head-on or all they get out of the blast is a big hole."

"Good point," I said.

"Hell," one soldier said, "I still don't want to be around when another flying boxcar drops in."

"For sure," the sergeant said, and the men walked away.

I went back to my task of taking a hard look at the caves and pillboxes that dotted the area. In a short time, I found nothing exceptional about them except that they were well located for maximum visibility as we approached. I sat down and rang up Command.

"Hey, I've been looking at the fortifications you asked me to inspect. I have an initial report."

"Give it to me."

"Nothing special going on. Just well-positioned units that are blowing the hell out of our men. The Second Battalion is taking savage resistance from Tombstone Ridge. They're not letting up on hitting us."

"Keep your hat on," Command said. "Colonel Johnson called in an airstrike on Tombstone because the enemy are moving tanks toward us. They ought to be hitting about now. Watch out." He hung up.

I crouched down behind a small rise and peered over the top. Within a couple of minutes, a formation of airplanes appeared on the horizon. The roar of the engines carried a disquieting, chilling threat. The airplanes began to turn out of their formation and dive straight at Tombstone. Bombs and explosions went off like the Fourth of July.

From my position, I could see the enemy had now figured out they'd best retreat before they got obliterated. The screaming dives must have panicked them as much as the flying boxcar bombs scared us. Their tanks came to an abrupt halt.

Didn't take long for Colonel Johnson's men to bring in two platoons of American tanks that started planting mines as a defense against any further advance of Japanese armor. For the moment, the enemy assault was stopped. I crawled away and went back to my task of sniffing out the pillboxes and burial caves.

Before I started back, I made one last check on the bunkers in the area to make sure nothing had changed. I thought to myself that anyone with any doubts about the status of the war ought to check this place out. They'd know for sure that the Japanese weren't slowing down or quitting, even though we kept steadily pushing them back. Sniper fire remained heavy.

Virtually crawling, I maneuvered out the way I came in. As I got closer, I realized that the woman I'd seen earlier was still sitting there like an oblivious statue just as she had been. A second look revealed what I missed at first glance. The mother was already dead. I just didn't see the wound. I couldn't miss that the children were now dead.

I clamped my eyes shut, stumbled away, and kept walking.

Those drawn faces wouldn't leave my mind.

12

Dark Days

Calling the ridge "Tombstone" turned out to be way too appropriate.

The Japanese weren't letting go. We began firing our howitzers almost continuously. Seemed like our constant rounds made no difference. The enemy had dug in for the duration and returned our blasts as fast as we fired them. Throughout the morning, our 361st Artillery unit blasted away constantly.

The humidity picked up and the heat from the big guns sent the thermometer rising. Many of the men took their shirts off, but no one slowed down. Handling the shells and the shell cases proved to be an arduous task, but no one backed away. Each man knew that the entire Tombstone Ridge area had to be hammered in order to protect the units trying to move forward. Our frontline soldiers were still getting killed.

Around noon, we got a call from the Command Center. The Second Battalion had made some progress pushing forward but ended up pinned down by the incessant fire from the other side. Company B had moved in and taken a small knob northeast of Tombstone. Command wanted us to stop firing until the situation had been clarified.

I shouted to the men, "Cease firing until further notice."

The men stepped back and appreciated a break. As usual, they broke up into little groups, reflecting friendships, buddies, or whatever. McQuiston's inner circle usually included Hans Goins as well as Swinging Bill plus a couple of other guys like George Morris and Lee Lewis. They busted out a pack of cigarettes and lit up. I stood on the edge and watched.

"Noticed that your hands were shaking today," Hans said to Morris.

George flinched at first and then took a breath. "Well, ain't you observant, since a slight tremble always comes with fatigue. You wouldn't know about that since you never worked that hard."

Hans grinned. Just one of his usual jabs for laughs.

McQuiston leaned back against an empty wooden box that had once held artillery shells. "I wonder what'll come next after we finally push the Japanese off this island. Major, you know?"

I rubbed my chin thoughtfully. "I understand that our next stop will probably be Tokyo. From what we are seeing here, doesn't look like they are going to surrender until we've nearly wiped them out. Afraid that's not good news."

Swinging Bill looked thoughtful for a change. "How bad's that gonna be, Major?"

"They say women and children will meet us on the beach with bamboo spears sharpened to a point. We might be shootin' at them. Not a pretty picture no matter how you color it."

"Why, hell! Old Jimmy Doolittle and his Raiders bombed them

and made it clear we were coming. You'd think they got the picture."

"I knew one of those pilots," Hans said. "A guy named Jack Sims. One heck of a pilot. Good man. After they smoked the enemy, Sims crash-landed in China and finally got out through the back door. Quite a story. Just think of how many guys never made it home."

Soberness settled over the men and for a while no one spoke. Finally, Morris said, "I guess them Japanese just don't think like us."

Swinging Bill nodded. "Afraid so. I wonder if they ever think about home, a girlfriend, and dreams. What do you think?"

"They're just different," Lee Lewis said. "The imperial system trains them to die, to die fighting. I heard they call it the honorable way to go. They appear to be more focused on death and honor. I guess going down for the homeland is considered glory for them."

The men smoked for a while. Hans looked up at me. "You think about home, Major?"

"I got a wife," I said. "She's waiting for me. I know that for certain. But we all know how war swallows your best thoughts. We're on the other side of the world. Light-years away from home. Sometimes, it's hard to stay focused."

"I had a girlfriend at home." George's words sounded loaded with poignancy. "Haven't heard from her in a while. Her letters began to sound distant. I'm not sure she's still there. I got a feeling she doesn't want to tell me good-bye while I'm out here maybe dying, but that's where her head is. Don't know about her heart."

"Ooh," Sergeant McQuiston said softly. "That's a tough one."

"I imagine this'll sound silly, but I've got a horse at home out on our farm," Bill Arnold said. "I loved to ride old Thunder. Grew up riding in the saddle. I just want to go back and ride my horse one more time."

"I want to go fishin' again," Lee said, and took a big drag off his cigarette and sent a ring of smoke rolling overhead. "I'd just like to be sitting on a bank under a big willow tree and feel a jerk on my line. Why, I'd yank my pole and start reelin' in one of those big fat bass. Now, that'd be something!"

Once again, the men settled into silence and quietly smoked.

"Do you think we'll ever get back to normal, Major?"

I took a deep breath. "What is normal? I don't know anymore. I once knew what normal was in Ada, Oklahoma. Could see the streets and walk down them—at least in my imagination—but I don't know anymore. Maybe, by the time we get back, that past will all be gone. Normal will have become something else, something different. I fear that what was once normal for us will have disappeared."

A hush settled again. Each one of us knew that life was going to be different in ways that we might not be prepared for. Out here on this godforsaken island nothing was like what we once remembered. Sometimes it was hard to even recollect what had been what.

McQuiston suddenly said, "You know . . . war has *changed us.* That's one reason why everything will be different. *We're* not the same. We ain't ever gonna be normal again."

Swinging Bill Arnold abruptly got up and walked away. He didn't want any more of this kind of talk.

I didn't either. The faces of dead children and men in black body bags already haunted me. Pushing those dastardly images aside remained a struggle that I had a hard time managing. I didn't know whether Joan could understand any of this. For sure,

I wouldn't be telling her. We'd all come over here like American farm boys going out to milk the cows. The army whipped us into line and turned us into killing machines in only thirteen weeks. Now we were all human torpedoes, butcher boys, gunmen. Killing had eaten a hole in every last one of us.

Of course, there was no other choice. They'd get us if we didn't get them first. Understandable? Not really. Just the way it was.

When Command finally called, we trudged back to the big guns and started firing again. Must have gone on for at least three hours. Tragically, the afternoon turned out to be one intense struggle.

Company B had tried to come up on the northeast side of Tombstone but got hit by intense mortar fire. Two platoons led by lieutenants Robert Jackson and John Fox had been forced to retreat. They jumped into an antitank refuge to escape the intense barrage. Anticipating a retreat, the Japanese had set up a machine gunner at the far end of the trench. As soon as the platoons hit the ditch, he opened up like a runaway maniac. The report said that at least two men were killed and eighteen others wounded. Both Jackson and Fox got hit hard.

C Company rushed up to stop the annihilation but got pinned down as well. Captain Robert Best moved in with a medical station, trying to evacuate the wounded from B Company. Tech Sergeant Frank Hartzer moved out alone and started spraying the ground with his flamethrower. The bloody chaos revealed the heroic efforts of every man. The struggle continued without relief. The evacuation did not end until six thirty that evening.

McQuiston had been right. We'd never be normal again.

13

Tombstones Everywhere

The Japanese opened up with everything they had. Command was reporting they were particularly firing at Clay Ridge. An 81mm mortar hit a hole filled with soldiers and killed every one of them. Eventually, they even blasted the Command post and destroyed a jeep and a trailer and blew up the ammo dump. What we had earlier thought might be Christmas turned into Halloween. The Japanese were stopping for nothing and laying a meat-ax job on us.

We found it particularly difficult to deal with their infiltrations. The Japanese weren't deterred from slipping through the front line and hitting our camps in the dark. These attackers seemed to be everywhere at once. In one night, sixteen infiltrators got whacked.

Tombstone Ridge remained our prime objective. Our battery was firing with as much accuracy as we could muster, but we had limited information. Of course, we were concerned not to rain fire down on our own men. The issue had gotten tricky. For several days Lieutenant Colonel J. R. Lewis attacked one of the foothills that B Company had been hitting from the west. No matter which way Lewis turned, the Japanese brought mortar fire down on the company. The battle lines were so close that we couldn't call in airplanes without a high probability of hitting our guys. The issue had become deadly.

"I need to do some reconnaissance," I told McQuiston. "I'm not sure what coordinates we ought to be using. I'm gonna try to get up there where I can observe the exact nature of the action."

The sergeant saluted, and I took off through the trees. Gentle rolling hills dotted the landscape. Most of the island was flat with fields planted with rice and similar crops. Plenty of bushes around, so one had to pay attention. No telling where one of the infiltrators might turn up. They had obviously penetrated our front lines and could pop up from out of nowhere. I kept walking.

By the time I got to the front, I learned that I and K Companies had been hit with everything but the refrigerator door. The men were hunkered down while the Japanese continued to blast them endlessly. Even when they reached the edge of a rise, our boys remained prime targets.

Four soldiers came hustling through the bush carrying a man on a makeshift cot.

"What happened?" I asked the first man.

"They got Captain Garland Campbell," he said. "He's been the captain in command of I Company. Machine-gun fire brought him down. One hell of a good man."

I saluted.

They hurried past.

Lieutenant Jack Carr of I Company ran into the same barrage.

Carr and several men were working their way through bush covering when they stumbled onto a rise with an entry in the center. Small scrubs had grown up around the entrance opening, which had been created from centuries of rain and floods.

"Be careful," Carr cautioned. "Looks like there could be a stash over there. Makes a perfect hiding place. That cave would be a good den if the enemy are already in there."

The men watched. Finally, one of the soldiers slowly approached the cave with his bayonet fixed in front of him while PFCs Earl Chambers and George Glover covered the soldier. With an ear-splitting scream, three Japanese charged out of the cave. Two were slinging hand grenades and the third dropped to his knees to set up his machine gun.

Our men started firing like crazy. Glover hit the first Japanese soldier loaded down with grenades. The man literally exploded when the other grenades went off as well. Shrapnel blew everywhere as well as body parts. Chambers shot the next attacker, but Lieutenant Carr was wounded in the blast.

The third Japanese had been knocked over by the blast and his machine gun didn't look good. He leaped to his feet and charged Carr. One of the soldiers fired and hit the Japanese in the shoulder. Even though wounded, Carr grabbed the attacker and hurled him to the ground. Carr pulled his trench knife and plunged it in the infiltrator's chest.

For a few moments, the soldiers stood there, waiting to see if anyone else might charge out of the cave. Silence finally convinced them that the assault was over.

"You took a nasty wound," Chambers said.

Carr sagged slightly. "Afraid they got me on this one."

"Yeah, but you shore put that attacker out of service," Glover added. "Man, what an attack."

"You're gonna need help getting to the back where you can get medical attention," Chambers said.

Carr shook his head. "Damn it! I only got a scratch. Keep movin' forward!"

"Sir," the PFC said, "that's a nasty, deep wound on your leg. You gotta have attention to that area."

"Didn't you hear me?" Carr shouted. "I said . . . I said . . ." He crumbled to the ground.

"Carry him to the back," Chambers said. "Couple of you guys take him out of here away from the line of fire. Put a tourniquet on that leg first. He's really bleeding."

The men immediately went to Carr's aid.

———————————

By the time I got back to my artillery battery, I knew that more had to be done and I was sure Command must understand how the conflict was fast becoming critical. We quickly were descending into a "do or die" predicament.

The sergeant met me coming into our camp. "How we doing?"

"Looks like artillery's needed bad," I said. "Just not sure where we should aim. I need to talk to the big boys and see what they are putting together."

McQuiston pushed his helmet back and rubbed his forehead. "Sounds bad."

"Yeah. Good men are getting cut down right and left, but they're giving the Japanese everything they got. This fight isn't gonna stop for a coffee break."

The radiophone rang. Sergeant McQuiston answered, identified our outfit, and handed the phone to me.

"Get down here," the voice said. "We're getting ready for heavy
planning. Don't fool around."

"Yes, sir," I said, and hung up. "I'll drive my jeep down to Command Central. Gotta get there as quickly as possible. Sounds like
something big is coming up."

McQuiston saluted and I headed for the jeep.

I knew that as long as I didn't run into a sniper, I could get there
in record time, but the infiltrators had put fear in all of us. I did
drive a little faster than usual.

I pulled up beside a number of other jeeps and entered the
large tent. Lieutenant Colonel Avery Masters nodded to me and
gave a snappy salute. Colonel Ed May, the commanding officer of
the 383rd Infantry Regiment, stood up at the front next to a large
map of the island.

"Attention!"

Major General James Bradley abruptly walked in from a side
entrance and everyone snapped to.

Bradley nodded. "At ease." His voice sounded sharp, slightly on
edge, signaling he was clearly all business. "Gentlemen, we are
now at a critical point." He turned and pointed to the map. "Right
now, they are kicking the shit out of us. This must be corrected.
You can see the Kakazu village and where the Nishabaru Ridge
runs on the other side of Highway Five. Right now, the Japanese
are killing us in this battle for Cactus Ridge. We must develop a
coordinated response. Any questions?"

Masters held up his hand. "Is our artillery doing the job?"

"Yes," General Bradley said, "but we must sharpen your strikes.
We have to hit them more squarely where they are lodged. As

of this hour, I am proposing a three-regiment assault against the Tombstone-Nishabaru-Kakazu corridor. We *must* make a breakthrough and push the enemy back. At 6:00 a.m. tomorrow, we will unleash our assault. I want the artillery to pound these bastards into the dirt. Understood?"

I saluted. Avery Masters did the same.

"In the next few minutes, we will plan how this assault will unfold," Bradley continued. "We got a free pass when we landed, but that ticket's been canceled now. If the Japanese come to believe they can push us back and make us retreat, we're going to be here until Christmas. This is the moment when their assault stops. Agreed?"

A murmur of affirmation went around the tent. The general was exactly right. Their counterattack had to be repelled.

14

Cactus Hill Coming Up

When the sun rose, the 361st Artillery unit stood ready. At straight-up six o'clock, I gave the order and the men began firing. Even under heavy military boots, your toes could feel the ground shake. My unit pounded the target area, and I knew other howitzers were firing from different angles. I thought the Japanese were going to be in for a long, long day.

No one had to tell me that the assault on Cactus Hill would prove costly for us as well. By now, we were aware that the Japanese had every play in the book down pat. While no one liked it, you just had to respect their self-sacrifice. Infiltrating at night and rushing headfirst at our soldiers certainly had to be acknowledged as an act of courage. We didn't like them any better, but we did recognize their dedication.

While we were firing, Major Prosser Clark's men began to move toward Cactus Hill. Their earlier attacks had proved futile and cost us good men. This morning Clark's F Company started around the hill to flank the target from the west.

Clark knew the enemy would pepper us with everything they got in the shaker and that would be a hell of a bad one.

The men kept crawling forward. Abruptly, the roar of airplanes signaled that dive-bombers were about to strike.

Clark yelled that the airplanes were our boys.

Soldiers rolled under logs or jumped under the edge of boulders sticking out of the ground. The dive-bombers began to hit hard and fast. We could feel the impact clear back to our howitzers. The Japanese had to be running for cover. For thirty-five minutes, the strikes continued. Black rings of smoke erupted straight up into the sky, followed by bellows and puffs of gray and sometimes white flames. Smoke slowly covered the countryside. The battle line turned into a forest fire squeezed into a killing field. Unfortunately, when the American planes left, the Japanese continued firing with the same intensity they had before.

Clark bellowed that they were still at it. He called for the men to charge forward.

F Company started inching their way up the hill again.

As the morning progressed, fighting only intensified. Each side of the front line returned the exchange with the same ferocity. Nevertheless, Clark wouldn't back off and kept pressing the men forward.

The men could see a pillbox ahead. The enemy had a damn good perch to shoot at us with accuracy. We couldn't see them, but they were able to spot us. Our soldiers knew they couldn't get out in the open.

Clark called for them to take the west side, recognizing that we had to get on their back side.

The men spread out. One guy worked his way around to the back of the cement bunker and started climbing. The enemy machine gunners kept blazing away without any idea that a soldier was above them. The infantryman worked his way to the front edge. He pulled the pin on a hand grenade, waited a second, and then hurled the pint-sized bomb over the side into the gunners' nest. Before the Japanese could move, the building shook with the explosion.

The soldier rose to his knees and signaled with his thumb sticking straight up. One less problem on the trail!

Not far ahead, the squad ran into another concrete barrier. The bunker encased another machine-gun nest, firing away like it was shooting July Fourth fireworks. PFC Lloyd Smith crept up the side and began shooting. The gun battle didn't last long. The enemy couldn't get their machine gun turned around before Smith killed three of them. A fourth soldier came out the side opening and started throwing grenades at him. The surprise package exploded, showering the area with shrapnel, but nothing hit Smith. Recovering, he shot the Japanese guy, who fell backward.

Someone shouted like a proud hunter that he got four and knocked off their grenade man.

When he bent down to look at one of the bodies, he shuddered. The dead person was a woman! The squad walked by and took a look. Sure enough. No question. "He" was a woman. They looked the other way and kept moving.

Not far ahead another bunker appeared. The Japanese had covered the island with these cement fortresses. The moment F Company came out of the bushes, the bad boys started hemstitching like they'd never run out of bullets. Clark's men hit the ground and rolled for cover.

They knew they couldn't move without getting killed: they were pinned down.

The Japanese blasted away for another twenty minutes, which seemed like twenty hours to F Company. Nobody moved. Finally, the *ack-ack* stopped. Near the front, the soldiers could hear the Japanese chattering. The sudden quiet suggested they might have concluded they'd killed the Americans.

During the lull, Sergeant Bernard Baar leaped up and charged the bunker, catching the Japanese by surprise. One of them grabbed a pistol and fired, hitting Baar. Baar barely slowed his dash and killed both Japanese.

The sergeant finally slumped to the ground in front of the pill-box. The rest of the unit gathered around him. The sergeant knew he'd gotten hit in his side but didn't think it was that bad or had struck anything vital. The men wanted to move him, but he resisted. Someone called for a medic even though Baar insisted he was okay.

Major Clark ordered him out of the line of fire. He knew Bernie was tough, but he didn't take chances with a gunshot wound.

Baar protested.

Clark firmly demanded they haul him away.

The unit kept working through the trees and shooting at anything that moved. F Company hadn't gone far when knee-mortar fire opened up.

In exasperation, Clark cursed and demanded that the men "push the enemy back to Tokyo!" They rushed forward.

The enemy's grease guns didn't slow down any, but their constant fire made it possible to identify where they were staked out. Clark's snipers took careful aim through the bushes. After several tries, the machine-gun nest went silent, but the mortars kept coming.

PFC Ralph Phillips started crawling forward with his BAR. The gas-operated M1918 BAR (Browning automatic rifle) was a magazine-fed, air-cooled automatic rifle. The BAR gave all the power of a machine gun to one soldier, and Phillips knew how to use it. He suddenly jumped up and charged forward, firing like a fullback going for a touchdown! Japanese fell right and left.

Clark's men finally made it to the top of the hill. The dive-bombers, artillery, and F Company had finally broken the back of the intense and ferocious arsenal that the Japanese had unloaded. The rumor was that many Japanese committed suicide rather than stand up against the onrushing Americans.

———————————

When the report of success came in to my 361st Artillery unit, we stopped firing.

"Our cannons got blazing hot, Major," Swinging Bill said to me. "Almost melted the barrels."

I nodded. "Yeah, that's a heap of shells we fired."

McQuiston came trotting over. "Headquarters just phoned and said to continue holding our fire. They need more information about exactly where our troops are located. Sounds like we're really moving."

"Ought to make General Bradley happy," I said. "Take a break!" I called out to the entire unit.

The unit sat down, and the men began to smoke. They talked, joked, just chewed the fat.

But I knew we were far from through.

15

Cutting the Cactus

During the night, we received instruction about our coordinates for the following morning, but I kept hearing a racket. My unit was already on edge. Too many enemy infiltrations were coming from too many angles. The idea that a Japanese might drop in your foxhole with a *gendaitō* sword aimed at your skull didn't exactly give soldiers the best dreams. Of course, we had sentries posted, but the Japanese developed a clever way of cutting throats before an alarm could be sounded.

Somewhere out there in the dark, I could hear what sounded like a man crying. I cautiously cocked my pistol and crept forward. The closer I got to the edge of the encampment, the louder the sound became. I realized the noise was coming from a foxhole.

Swinging Bill Arnold lay down there huddled up in a ball weeping.

"What's going on?" I asked. Never had I seen a soldier cry like a baby.

Swinging Bill didn't move.

"Bill? What's happened?"

He peered up at me with bloodshot eyes. Obviously, he'd found a bottle somewhere. He said nothing.

He barely whispered, "I'm scared."

I watched him for a moment, trying to decide whether to call a guard and ship him off to the brig or be a good guy and listen to a drunk tell me a story. His watery red eyes seemed to signal throbbing anxiety.

"What are you afraid of?" It was a silly question because there were about a thousand and one things to be anxious about out here where strong men died about one a minute.

Bill kept shaking his head. "Been this way for years," he said. "Was so before I got out here in this godforsaken wilderness. Only thing that helps is a little booze. Tonight, that ain't even workin'."

"Where'd it start?"

He covered his head. "My ma . . . my ma . . . was lighting a stove. She'd been using kerosene or gasoline, something like that. Guess when she struck a match . . . the whole business exploded." His whimpering got louder. "I saw her run out the back door trying to stop the flames . . . They covered her . . . her hair smokin'." Bill stopped for several moments. "I saw her burn up," he barely whispered.

I took a deep breath. I couldn't imagine a worse story.

"That's what comes rushin' up inside me at night," Bill said. "Terrifies me."

For the first time, his habitual drinking made sense. What could I say?

Quiet fell between us. "She's gone," I finally ventured. "We're in Okinawa. Your mother will never come over here. She's gone. You can go to sleep."

He looked up at me and blinked several times. Finally, Bill said, "I guess that's right. Sure. It is." He pulled his helmet over his face and became quiet. "Sure."

Ten minutes later, Swinging Bill hadn't made a sound. I went back to my foxhole.

For the first time, I had an idea about what made him a drunk. I'd let it go.

The 361st started firing early. I figured we were the first go at softening up the enemy's hold on the Cactus Hill area. Swinging Bill turned up at his position beside one of the cannons like nothing had happened the night before. He looked surprisingly good, although his eyes were still red. He said nothing; I said nothing.

Command called in. "There's an open stretch between Cactus Ridge and Hill," the voice said. "E Company got slowed to a stop at the edge of this exposed area. Looks pretty rough. Write these coordinates down. Want you to fire beyond the enemy. Be careful you don't get too close to E Company. They're only a few yards away from the enemy."

I scribbled as quickly as I could. The line went dead.

I called to Sergeant McQuiston. "Here's where we should be shooting." I handed him the paper. "I need to do some reconnaissance to make sure we don't hit too close to E Company. Sounds like they're in trouble."

McQuiston nodded. "Be careful."

I grabbed my rifle and took off with binoculars bouncing at

my side. When I reached a ridge near the front line, I could see G Company had also ended up in a fix. Following their own tanks, they'd gotten halfway across the open field when a holy mess exploded. The tanks got hit. One of those Big Boys had gone over a mine that disabled it. Another tank looked like it had just been left when the crew ran for cover. Probably 47mm fire had rained down on them: that would have been destruction on wheels. You didn't need hearing aids to understand that rifle fire and mortars were flying in from every direction. Men were hitting the dirt and looking for shelter anywhere they could find it.

The bombardment didn't stop. Through the afternoon, the reign of terror continued relentlessly. I didn't know how our soldiers endured. From my observation perch, I could see the Japanese were bringing in trucks and their own tanks. A counterattack had to be imminent. I felt certain Command had already been informed of the situation. I only wished that I'd had some way to describe to them what I was seeing. Surely, both G and E had signaled the danger.

A roar came from behind me. I looked up and recognized a host of our airplanes descending on the Japanese. Before it was over, I counted sixteen Curtiss SB2C Helldiver airplanes blowing a hole as big as Chicago in their counterattack. The next roar nearly knocked me off my perch. The blast had to have come from three of our navy destroyers parked off the coast. So much for whatever it was that the Japanese had in mind.

I crawled back through the trees.

The next day, April 6, the report came in that the frontal attack on Cactus Hill had proved to be costly for us. Command concluded we needed to attempt a different approach. Consequently, Major Clark sent F Company out on an alternative attack coming in from the west. Eventually, the company took Cactus Hill, but the Japanese weren't finished.

Our doughboys spent the night on the hill, but at ten the next morning a crazy Japanese soldier came tearing through the perimeter surrounding their camp. Screaming like a wounded tiger, he started shooting in all directions. Soldiers leaped into foxholes or any other place where they could hide. The wacko kept firing while our men threw hand grenades at him. After a dozen grenades, the nutcase finally fell backward.

The issue was not settled yet. A 150mm artillery shell hit the company's location. During the confusion and death, E Company discovered a number of enemy were gathering on the eastern end of the hill. They concluded that a counterattack must be assembling to come roaring at us. I watched to see what would follow.

Sergeant Virgil Purtlebaugh watched for a while and then turned back to the men around him. "I think we ought to banzai them before they have a chance to get their act together."

The men mumbled their approval.

"Okay!" the sergeant said. "Let's blast those sonofabitches all the way back to the nearest cemetery."

Leading the charge, Virgil came out shooting like John Wayne in a cowboy movie. The Japanese began to fall left and right.

Sergeant Joe O'Donnell called for mortar fire twenty-five yards ahead of our men, aiming at where the Japanese were congregated.

"Heads up!" O'Donnell shouted. "Here they come!"

Explosions erupted all along the engagement line. The Japanese scattered like frightened rabbits. O'Donnell counted the enemy falling. Looked like one mortar had taken out at least a dozen of them.

When the skirmish was over, Purtlebaugh had personally killed eighteen bad guys. The final count revealed fifty-eight Japanese down. Needless to say, their counterattack was history. Cactus Hill had fallen.

When McQuiston got the last call from Command telling us to hold up firing, he shared the story of what had happened with our men. Most just nodded a silent acceptance. A couple of guys clapped. Swinging Bill said nothing.

16

Time Out

Funny how time can drag along in a war and then take off like a rocket. We arrived on Easter Sunday, April 1, 1945, and now it was April 7. Just a week had passed and yet it seemed like a year—and then again, like yesterday. The passing of hours and then days gets scrambled. When the fighting is intense, you lose all sense of duration. There's morning; there's night. In between, you are working so hard, everything blurs together. And then the fighting stops, and the minutes seem to tick by like a snail crossing the street. And then, bingo! Here we go again.

We were in a lull, still shut down from yesterday's heavy shelling and expecting today's changes in planning from headquarters. The men sat around the cannons talking, waiting, seeing what would come next.

I leaned against the howitzer, which had completely cooled off, and listened. An executive officer needed to know what the men were thinking and their temperament when they were under constant attack. Sergeant McQuiston appeared to preside over the give-and-take that went on among the men. Hans Goins pulled out a pack of Camels and passed the cigarettes around. George Morris took one, as did Swinging Bill Arnold. Lee Lewis leaned back against the big, wide tire on the cannon. A breeze drifted in. We relaxed.

"How long do you think we're gonna be here?" Lewis asked.

"Why? You got a big business deal cookin' somewhere?" Goins chided.

McQuiston looked up at me. "Tell us, Major. How you calculating the outcome?"

"Couldn't say," I said slowly. "The Japanese been puttin' up a hell of a defense."

"Shore have," Morris chimed in. "They ain't messin' around none." He blew smoke overhead.

"No," McQuiston said. "I believe this struggle is harder than Leyte. We're just getting started and we already lost a good number of men."

No one said anything for a while. Finally, Arnold asked, "Any you guys think about home?" His eyes weren't red, and he sounded sober.

The silence lingered. Finally, Morris said, "Sure. Think about it all the time."

"I don't," Hans Goins said. "Gets to be too much."

"That's a rare confession out of you." McQuiston sounded scornful. "You're always stickin' somebody."

Hans rubbed his chin. "Hell, that don't mean that I don't care none."

"Caring will get to you," Swinging Bill said. "If you get thoughtful, it can come back and bite you." He took a long, hard puff on his cigarette.

"Yeah," McQuiston said. "I had a girl back in Richmond. She was something special. Her name was Sally. First time I went out with her, we went to a movie. Came home afterwards and she stopped me at the door. I never been kissed like that in my life! I mean she curled my socks. I tell ya, she was no little girl. She was a big-time woman."

"So, you turned into Mr. Hot Pants," Hans said.

"Shore nuff," McQuiston said. "I had a fire in my belly for her. I mean big-time foolin' around. And then I joined the army. Sally told me she didn't want none of that. She figured I'd go off and find another girl."

Hans jabbed him. "Was she ever right!"

McQuiston eyed him caustically. "No, ain't been like that at all. One thing's for sure, ain't no enticing women running around out here in the bushes. The only ones I've seen either looked malnourished and needed a hamburger or had a knife behind their backs ready to stab me."

"Ain't that the truth," George Morris added. "No other locale is as accommodating for someone to take a slice out of you or blow a hole through your head."

"Come on, Major Shaw," Goins said. "Tell us about yourself."

"Not much to tell," I said.

"We're you a hot dog in high school?" Goins persisted.

"You might be surprised," I said. "Would you have figured me for the class valedictorian?"

"Probably," Hans said. "You got the smarts in this outfit. That's what put you in the driver's seat."

I laughed. "Let's face the facts. When you curl up in that foxhole at night and close your eyes, everything changes. Some of you start praying, 'O God, save my worthless ass.' Like McQuiston, a few of you think of that girl back home. But my hunch is that most of you are so tired that when you close your eyes, you're gone in thirty seconds. When you wake up and the big guns are going off somewhere on this island, you're too busy trying to survive to think about home thousands of miles away. Out here we're all just trying to keep from getting our heads blown off. Time don't matter much."

Swinging Bill looked intensely at me. His mouth opened like he was going to admit a painful truth and then he looked away. Arnold and I had a secret and he wasn't going to spill it.

The phone rang, and Sergeant McQuiston picked it up. The war was back on.

——————

While my soldiers were chewing the fat, the First Battalion set out to take an unimpressive ridge Command called Kakazu. The area appeared to be an easy target and the Battalion moved easily and quickly. Another unit took the high ground above a draw just north of Kakazu. Looked like another walk in the park, until . . .

Around three o'clock, with the afternoon sun beating down, the enemy made their counterattack. In the exchange, twenty-five of the bad guys and one of their officers were killed. The fighting was fierce. Over our phone, I kept getting reports of what was unfolding.

A private named Delmar Parrish kept firing so rapidly that he ended up burning his hands from an overheated rifle, but Parrish killed sixteen enemy fighters with his BAR automatic rifle. Japanese had dug in on the high ground and started pouring fire down on them. The exchange proved merciless. By nightfall, we had lost six men as well as six officers. Fifty-one enlisted men were wounded.

Kakazu turned into another slaughter alley. The Japanese were coming on big-time. The Second Battalion got caught in the same entanglement. Enemy artillery kept pounding them with everything they had. Our soldiers struggled to avoid fire from above, but shelter proved scarce. The Japanese hit our leadership hard. Major Clark and Captain Vanderlinden, who led H Company, were wounded. Half an hour later, Captain Leo Smith got smoked. Command fell to Major Austin Thorsen.

With all of this mayhem exploding, the Japanese threw in their "boxcar" mortar that could blow a hole the size of a swimming pool. The enemy wouldn't give an inch. Smoke, fireworks, bullets, and flying muck showered the entire unit. We listened to the continual reports of the confrontation between our soldiers and the enemy. The day lengthened, no letup in sight.

The next morning, the Third Battalion of the 381st Infantry was relieved by the 383rd in the town of Mashiki. With two tanks and two assault guns rolling beside them, the replacement troops stormed the Pirates' Den. Earlier, they had taken heavy casualties because of the boulders jutting up from the stony ground, but this time the unit was on the march.

The 383rd began a push forward and then turned and swept away from the coast. The fighting remained intense, but the Americans maintained their forward motion. Finally, they merged into the First Battalion on the high ground north of Kakazu Gorge. The lines were drawn.

Lieutenant Colonel Ed Stare told his soldiers they had some unfinished business to take care of and he intended to keep pushing until every one of those bastards was fertilizing grass. They were not going to get smacked like they did when they got hooked into a disastrous little sally a few days earlier. Stare's intent was to put the enemy down.

The men nodded their affirmation, picked up their weapons, and the battle was on. For the next two days, the assault continued under the most difficult circumstances. The Japanese weren't going to be pushed back easily, but neither were Stare's men. The encounter turned into a day-and-night brawl. Finally, on April 9, the battle was over and the 383rd had prevailed. Every man who survived knew he'd never forget the struggle.

The 383rd too had learned that a clock means nothing when you keep hard-charging into a seemingly endless knock-down-and-drag-out. Yeah, there'd been morning and night, but it was all a blur.

17

Tragedy on the Ridge

I was not surprised when I got the call to come to the Command Center for a briefing. The tumultuous battle fought by the 383rd signaled worse would be ahead. Command Center called the commanding and executive officers in for a briefing on what was ahead. I knew the issues would be tough and demanded significant discussion of what we were about to face. Once again, I drove myself down to headquarters. McQuiston would be needed if the cannons were abruptly called into action and he knew what to do. By now, the general had moved into a large cave that accommodated the gathering of the larger staff.

I parked my jeep and walked in expecting to recognize most of the participants. I already knew many of the men, like 321st Field Artillery Battalion commanding officer Lieutenant Colonel Robert Glenn and executive officer Major David Fierke. The 362nd Field Artillery Battalion commander Lieutenant Colonel Jaroslave Hiavac had been around quite a while, as had Major

Don Alexander. Of course, my commanding officer Lieutenant Colonel Avery Masters had been a close associate. Infantry regiment commanders and officers were also milling around, talking to each other, waiting for the general to show. All good men.

I saluted Avery Masters and he returned the gesture. "What do you think?" I asked. "Got a big one coming up today?"

Colonel Masters nodded. "Afraid so. This Kakazu Ridge business is a real bitch. There's a gorge involved and that's always bad news."

Major General James Bradley walked straight to the front, and everyone snapped to attention. He saluted the group and told the officers to be at ease.

"You have made significant effort in confronting the Tombstone-Nishabaru-Kakazu corridor," Bradley began. "You know that the 383rd prevailed in taking the Pirates' Den and surrounding area. Please convey our profound gratitude to your men for their heroic efforts. These responses now bring us face to face with the Kakazu Ridge and an almost impossible task."

The general turned and looked behind him at the blank backdrop. "You'll notice that we do not have any maps to show you. Most unfortunately, we have not been able to obtain accurate maps and photos of the ridge. Gentlemen, we are going in blind."

I sensed that an atmosphere of nervousness abruptly settled over the room. No one wanted to be part of an attack that lacked any sense of certainty about where we were going. Not a good deal!

"I have asked assistant division commander Brigadier General Robert Gard to detail what we are facing," General Bradley said.

General Gard stepped to the front as two officers pinned up a makeshift map of the Kakazu Ridge. Picking up a pointer, Gard traced a line across the island. "We have a ridge that runs almost the width of Okinawa and is about one thousand yards long. The ridge is separated from Nishabaru Ridge only by a cut and on the west end slopes down to the ocean. You might think that the Kakazu Ridge doesn't look all that formidable. Think again. The deep gorge which now separates the ridge from our forces is worse than anything we've seen thus far. The reverse side is infested with everything from pillboxes to mortars with tunnels and caves. The Japanese are determined to hold the gorge at all costs. Get the picture?"

General Gard looked around the room like a hawk scouting for its next prey. I could tell he was trying to make sure we understood that we were staring at an impossibility that we still had to surmount.

The leaders of the First and Second battalions began asking for clarification. I already knew that trying to climb a steep canyon with armaments and gunnery every five feet would probably prove to be murder.

I raised my hand. "Will reconnaissance be necessary?"

"Absolutely!" General Gard snapped. "This assault is going to require the best that we have to give. Since we lack accurate or virtually any maps of the gorge, we're going to need all the input we can give."

I shifted my weight. In the last few days, I'd taught myself a considerable amount about how to observe and report the unfolding battle scene. Sounded like what I'd picked up would be important in the morning.

The detailed discussion continued for another thirty minutes, and then we were dismissed. The big show would start at five in the morning and we'd be ready well before then.

I started back, thinking about what I had heard. Obviously, we had to cross the Kakazu Ridge to keep moving forward. Probably the Japanese had figured that one out several hundred years ago. They would be armed with everything from grease guns to Big Berthas. Our boys facing those machine-gun nests, I thought, better have their life insurance paid up.

I had the men up at around 4:00 a.m. and in position by 5:00 a.m. We wouldn't be needed for a while, but I wanted to be ready. McQuiston had already taken his place by the telephone and the camp had become totally active.

"I think I ought to observe Kakazu Gorge," I told the sergeant. "The fighting will probably be so close that the coordinates for cannon fire have to be right on the money. The front lines will be too congested for any errors."

McQuiston nodded. "Yeah, I think we're lookin' at a hot one today."

I looked at my watch. "A Company's probably just stepped off about now. They'll be on their way. I need to watch how the Japanese respond."

McQuiston saluted. "Keep your head down!"

"You bet." I took off.

Because the sun hadn't come up, the sky remained dark gray. Broken tree trunks littered the terrain. Torn palm tree branches had been scattered everywhere. Mortar fire had severely blemished the terrain where fighting had occurred. Tropical plants had been trampled into the dirt, and bushes had been stripped of small branches and turned into toothpicks. Here and there, I could see small foxholes where men had once slept. The trail looked like a giant had walked through swinging a club at everything in sight.

Not too far down the road, I came to a hill with good observation of the gorge. The deep drop-off of Kakazu and steep climb up the other side made an ascent extremely difficult with armaments everywhere firing like crazy. Just as I crouched down, I heard steps behind me. An infiltrator might have gotten through the front line in the dark. More by reflex than thought, I whipped my rifle around and clicked off the safety. Flattening myself on the ground, I aimed at the bushes behind me.

The cracking of brush branches got louder. A shape creeping out of the ground cover broke through. An American soldier stepped out. When he saw me, the soldier nearly jumped out of his pants. His eyes widened with fear. "Don't shoot!"

"What are you doing?" I barked.

"I'm doing reconnaissance for the 361st Engineer Battalion," he said nervously. "Captain Albert Kaye . . . Kaye's the name."

I lowered my rifle. "Wandering around in the bushes can get you killed."

"Don't do this often," Kaye said.

"Next time, I'd slip in more like Tonto does on *The Lone Ranger*. Walking around uncovered usually proves to be more than a little dangerous."

"Yes, sir," Kaye said, and sat down.

I adjusted the binoculars I'd brought with me. "Get ready. The show's about to start."

For several minutes we sat in the dark waiting to see what would happen next. Eventually, I noticed a group of soldiers starting up the side of the gorge.

"That's probably A Company," I said. "They are supposed to kick off the assault. C Company's in there with them. Don't seem to be running into much resistance. Looks like they are creeping up the hill."

Suddenly a machine gun started blasting and I could see men hitting the ground. Immediately other artillery opened up. The whole side of the gorge burst into explosive firing. The soldiers started scrambling forward, but the two companies were getting separated.

"That's heavy fire," I said. "Looks like they are going to get pinned down between the gorge and the ridge.

The Japanese came rushing down from the top straight at both companies. I adjusted the binoculars to get as clear a view as possible.

"Good Lord! They are fighting in hand-to-hand combat," I said.

Some men were wrestling on the ground while others swung bayonets back and forth. Riflemen kept firing at the Japanese, but that didn't stop them from rushing forward. Our boys and the enemy both appeared to be standing their ground.

"What do you think?" Kaye asked.

"Looks like a lot of men are going to get killed on both sides. The Japanese are making a do-or-die defense, and our two companies are pinned down by rapid fire. Bad situation. I don't see anything of B Company."

"I've got an EE-8 field telephone. A walkie-talkie," Kaye said. "Let me see what Command can tell me."

"That's a surprise. Sure. Call 'em."

Kaye began ringing. After a few moments, someone answered. "I'm up here watching the attack on the gorge. Can you tell me what's happening?"

For a few minutes Kaye listened and asked a couple of questions. Finally, he hung up.

"The A Company commander Captain Jack Royster just called in," Kaye said. "Either he withdraws or fears being wiped out. Sounds critical."

"Not good."

"They're trying to move B Company up as relief, but so far they are completely pinned down and can't do anything. They tried to get across some open ground north of the gorge, but that's where they got hit. Nobody's going anywhere. What do ya think?" Kaye asked.

"Looks like a disaster."

18

Slaughter

By 8:30 p.m., A Company's situation had become desperate. At the same time, C Company was getting hammered with a strong counterattack on the exposed left flank. Men were hiding, firing, ducking, running for cover while the enemy poured it on, when a mortar blast hurled Captain Royster backward. From my position I could see what was happening and hear the men talking. I listened intently.

"They got him!" one of his men shouted. "Medic!"

Royster rolled over and shook his head. "Where . . . where . . . am I?" He could barely push himself up on his hands. "Oh, my head . . ." His voice trailed away.

The medic dropped down by Royster's side. "You caught a fragment of a mortar. Got it in the head. We'll get you out of here."

"No! No." The captain waved him away. "Just put a bandage across my forehead."

"But you're bleeding like crazy," the medic argued. "I don't believe you can see anything."

"Don't argue," Royster demanded. "Damn it! Get me bandaged so I can get back on my feet."

"But sir—"

"Son of a bitch!" he screamed. "Now! Hurry up!"

The medic began rolling a wide bandage around Royster's forehead and across the back of his head. He tried to tape it tightly enough to stay in place.

"Out of my way," Captain Royster demanded, and got to his feet. "We've got to hold our ground." He paused for a moment and turned to the medic. "Thanks. That helped." He staggered forward, having a hard time seeing with the blood running into his eyes. "Come on, men! Don't let those bastards stop you. Keep firing!"

Royster struggled over to the phone. "Get me Command," he barked.

The sergeant handed him the receiver. "Listen," Royster shouted. "We've got to have a smoke cover in order to withdraw. They're killing us." He listened for a moment. "Do what you can." He hung up.

"What's the score?" the sergeant asked.

"Company B of the Eighty-Eighth Chemical Mortar Battalion has been firing smoke, but the wind's not blowin' it our way. They're going to keep trying."

A mortar exploded, sending shock waves across both men. The captain grabbed the bandage across his forehead to keep it in place. The two men tumbled backward. Royster wiped away the blood that had trickled down into his eyes.

"God almighty!" Royster mumbled. "We got to get out of here."

The company kept firing, but the shelling didn't let up. Around ten o'clock either the wind shifted or the smoke became thick enough that the unit could retreat. Captain Royster waved to the men.

"Okay! We're backing out. Keep your heads down."

Lieutenant Dave Belman and the C Company men followed, but the withdrawal proved as desperate as staying put.

"Get the wounded out first," someone yelled.

The soldiers moved as quickly as possible, but as soon as they reached the open ground where the unit had been pinned down, they found the same desperate situation. The Japanese kept their mortars trained on the ravine. They knew they had the upper hand for the moment.

By 10:30 p.m. some of the reserved members of A and C Companies finally reached the gorge. Captain John Van Vulpen, commander of B Company, came in with forward elements to reinforce the attack. Quickly surveying the numbers of the survivors and the overwhelming nature of the conflict, he at once called headquarters.

"Sir, the enemy is all over us. We're struggling to survive."

A mortar exploded, scattering shrapnel around the area.

Van Vulpen picked up the phone. "Hear that? Tells you where we are." He listened for a minute. "That's what you want? Oh, man! Okay. We'll try."

He slowly put the phone down and looked at the soldiers waiting for the order.

"Our orders are to attack!" The captain stopped and made a quick head count. Only forty-six soldiers had survived. "This is a tough one, but we're the Deadeyes. We don't stop. Grab your gear and prepare to move to the south bank. We're moving out."

I knew they had to move quickly to survive. I could see how

desperate their position was becoming. I followed their movement closely and listened like a wolf tracking a wounded deer.

A sober look spread over each man's face as if to say silently that they'd probably not come back alive. Another mortar exploded, but they picked up their rifles and prepared to struggle forward. They could quickly see an open field ahead. If they were to continue their assault, they had to get across. The unit had barely gotten into the open area when a barrage of machine-gun fire hit them. The men leaped to the ground, but a mortar explosion slung some of their bodies through the air and scattered others.

"Captain!" one of the soldiers yelled. "They're eatin' us alive."

Van Vulpen looked out from his ground cover and started counting. Seven men had been lost in an instant. Rolling in the tall grass, the captain cussed at the situation and realized they'd all be dead if they kept advancing.

"Make litters from your ponchos," Van Vulpen yelled. "We've got to drag the wounded and the dying out of here. Hurry!"

A sergeant crawled up next to him. "By damn, they'll kill every last one of us if we keep movin' forward."

The captain nodded. "Yeah. Looks like it."

"Ain't there some better way to keep out of the line of that mortar and artillery fire?"

The captain stuck his head up and looked around. "Should be the case, Sarg." Van Vulpen began inching backward. "Retreat, men!"

The doughboys made a hasty withdrawal. The captain kept rubbing his head and thinking. Finally, he called to the sergeant.

"Sommers, we need a litter squad of about six men for the wounded if we are to accomplish a withdrawal. I'm going to call for smoke to cover us. Give me the walkie-talkie."

"When we got hit out there in the open, we lost the phone," the sergeant said. "We got no way to call."

"Shit!" the captain exploded. "We got to have help!" He looked around. "Lieutenant Ford! Come here."

The lieutenant crawled over.

"Take command," the captain said. "Sommers and I got to leave here in order to get fire support and arrange for moving the wounded. We'll be back."

Ford saluted and inched his way back to his position.

Van Vulpen and Sommers began maneuvering back to the battalion command post. Machine-gun fire kept erupting all around them.

"Watch out!" Sergeant Sommers screamed, and started firing his rifle as rapidly as the weapon would shoot. "There's one of the enemy over there!" Two Japanese fell to the ground.

The captain leaped against the base of a large palm tree. "God almighty! I didn't see them."

Machine-gun fire beat out a symphony of terror. Both soldiers grabbed their heads and rolled up in a ball. Then Van Vulpen straightened and hurled a grenade. Silence followed the explosion. They started to stand and run when artillery blasted directly behind them. Once again they fell to the ground.

Back up, both men rushed forward through several clusters of bushes. Gun fire followed them. When the sergeant saw a trench in front of them, he dived in with the captain directly behind him.

"A-a-h!" Sommers screamed and pointed. "Snake! God help us! One big sonofabitch."

What looked like at least a six-foot python slithered toward them from the other end of the trench. Van Vulpen fired ten times, blowing the snake's head to pieces. Both men lay there breathing hard with hands shaking. The sergeant's teeth chattered a frightened staccato.

"God help us," Sergeant Sommers moaned. "I've always been terrified of snakes. Scared silly!"

"We got to get out of here," the captain said. "Come on."

As the men got further away from the front line, direct fire decreased, but never-ending explosions constantly rocked them, sending an unending roar through their heads and sometimes blurring their vision. Both men kept running and falling. They stumbled over pointed rocks and broken sticks that punctured their legs and scraped their arms, as sharp pangs of pain shot through their bodies. The roar of artillery echoed in their ears and left them dizzy.

The sun had begun to sink when they staggered into the command post. Both men approached the commanding and executive officers mumbling, trying to say something that no one could quite understand.

"Need help." Captain Van Vulpen's words were slurred. "Now." The word was almost unintelligible. "Need help . . . bad."

"Where?" an officer asked.

"Out there." Sergeant Sommers pointed and then sank to the ground.

"These men are in no condition to lead a rescue party at the moment," the executive officer said. "They're in bad shape."

Captain Van Vulpen held his head in his heads and kept mumbling to himself.

I had seen bravery before, but nothing like what I witnessed and heard that day. These were soldiers who stood together to the death. The Japanese may have thought they themselves were tough, but they didn't hold a candle to these men.

19

The Struggle to Escape

I had seen enough through my binoculars to realize the Japanese had strategically figured out how to hold the Kakazu Gorge long before we arrived. Their position gave them the edge even without using their tunnels and the caves in the side of the steep cliffs. Even if our soldiers got far enough up the side, they'd still have to deal with those hidden tunnels probably filled with mine fields. I realized that the soldiers who had attacked the Japanese positions might not be able to get out from under the murderous return fire. Everything about the situation looked desperate. I watched a sergeant lead twelve men carrying litters back into the gully. I could hear the soldiers shouting back and forth.

"Stay close together," Lieutenant Leo Ford shouted. "Stay down."

A burst of machine-gun fire answered him. The volunteers who took on the mission kept hustling forward, but artillery fire remained so constant that the sound was nearly deafening.

The unit tried to find cover, but the heavy bullets of the machine guns ripped through everything in sight. Soldiers began to fall.

"Got to have more smoke cover," Sergeant McElheran said.

"We lost the radio," PFC Charles Bassett answered. "I'll crawl back and see if I can find it."

"Hurry!" Lieutenant Ford urged.

Bassett wiggled his way back and forth under the ground cover. Finally, he shouted that he found the walkie-talkie and quickly returned while mortar fire kept pounding them.

Lieutenant Ford worked his way under an outcropping of rock. "Good job, Charlie," he said. "Give me the receiver." They rang headquarters.

"Command!" the lieutenant shouted in the receiver. "Command!" For a moment, he listened. "We've got to have smoke cover. We're out here on the side of the gorge trying to rescue the fallen. Give us smoke cover."

Ford listened for a moment. "You stupid sonofabitch! I don't care who you are. We're out here getting killed. Now order the damn ground cover or you can come out here and carry out all the bodies by yourself!"

Whoever was on the other end of the phone obviously didn't like Ford's attitude. "I'm telling you the enemy are slaughtering us," Ford shouted. "Listen, you ass! Get us ground cover or we're all dead!" The lieutenant slammed the phone down.

"What's the deal?" Bassett asked.

"That worthless piece of shit doesn't know if they got any ground cover left!" the lieutenant howled. "He thinks they may be running out of the supply. We probably will have to pull out without that assistance. Is he nuts or what?"

Bassett shook his head. "No matter what, we got to get out of here."

"What time is it?"

Charlie looked at his watch. "It's about three thirty."

"Okay. Let's get the living together and work our way laterally toward the north slope. I know the men are badly shaken, but we can't lose our heads. Got to play it cool."

Charlie nodded. "Let's get on with it."

With every movement to the side, a burst of gunfire forced the men to the ground. Even the wounded had no alternative but to crawl. Slowly, they inched their way sideward. The litters proved to be more of a burden than an asset, as everyone needed to stay near the ground. Some of the wounded had to be dragged over a nonexistent trail they made up as they struggled along. Finally, most of their supply of ammunition ran out.

By four o'clock they reached a point opposite the north slope of Kakazu west. Abruptly, airplanes began diving out of the sky. The ground shook.

"Is that an F4U Corsair?" a solider asked.

"Looks like a Helldiver," one of the men said.

"Maybe an Invader," someone added.

"They're gonna slam the Japanese," Charlie Bassett said. "Watch out! They're not that far from us."

The men watched airplanes dive straight toward the cliffs, attacking the gorge with rockets and artillery. Rocks hurled through the air. Explosions sent boulders flying down the hillside. Debris struck the soldiers with stinging insult.

"Get in one of the caves!" Sergeant Bill McElheran screamed. "Stay out of the way of the rubble."

Charlie and the remnant jumped into a small cave in front of them. Some of the men leaped headfirst into the rock shelter. The air attack continued relentlessly. For the first time, the soldiers were more afraid of our airplane attacks than of the Japanese. The terrifying explosions continued to rock the mountain. Ford knew they had to get out of there.

Bassett shouted for them not to leave the caves no matter what. The brass could shoot him, but to walk out there would have been nothing but sheer suicide.

Even in the dim light of the cave, he could see their eyes. The bravado had been drained out of them. Obviously, the men had crossed an invisible line that kept them thinking they might be invincible. Now they considered themselves expendable. Fear can do that to a man in the middle of battle.

Lieutenant Ford said as authoritatively as he could that they should give the situation a little time. The sun was going down, after all.

Ford realized that the only way to get the men out had to be to stretch the truth. He waited forty-five minutes, but nothing quieted down. Then he lied, telling the men that the smoke would cover them. He sent them out in groups of twos and threes. The wounded needed all the help they could give them.

Of course, there was no smoke.

With my binoculars, I watched the men emerge in small groups. Soldiers started making a break for it, but the Japanese kept firing. The wounded struggled to stay on their feet and some of the men had to crawl. One man came out from behind a rock and started shooting at the enemy coming in the opposite direction. Men were dragging along behind him, but he kept shooting at the enemy. He ran about forty yards toward the enemy and threw several grenades, silencing one of the machine guns trained on the escaping men.

Only later did I learn PFC Edward Moskala's name. His gallantry proved to be unequaled. As the company withdrew, Moskala stayed behind and kept shooting. His buddies estimated that during the next three hours, the PFC must have killed at least twenty-five to thirty Japanese. Moskala had almost reached the bottom of the ravine when he realized that one of the men had been left behind. He turned around and went back, picked him up, and saved his life.

Without any letup in the artillery, the men slowly got out from under the murderous fire, but Moskala stayed and volunteered to protect their rear. His accuracy took out more of the enemy, but other wounded men needed help. Moskala couldn't leave them on the battlefield, so he single-handedly carried them out. Finally, as he returned for another man, the Japanese shot him and Moskala fell mortally wounded.

When the struggle was over, the army recognized his service that fateful day. They described his actions as "unfaltering courage and complete devotion to his company's mission and his comrades' well-being." He became the first Medal of Honor recipient in the 383rd Infantry.

Through the bravery of men like PFC Ed Moskala, the soldiers were finally able to evacuate and find their way out of the brutal, bloody struggle. A few worked their way out and to the unit's base of operation by dusk. The sun had already set when the majority straggled in. A number of the men didn't get back until the next day.

Some were crawling, a few barely walking. A couple of soldiers were dragging a makeshift litter pulling men too wounded to walk. Two of the wounded crawled in on their bellies. The struggle to escape had proved to be almost more than anyone could endure.

20

Bravery Unequaled

The battle to take Kakazu Gorge continued into the night and the next day. The stories of struggle and survival circulated among the men, and by the next day we'd heard them from many different sources. When I reported to Command headquarters, I listened to the fight to take the gorge from a different angle. Company L of the 383rd Infantry had had their own experience, for which they ultimately received battle honors.

On April 9, the company received an assignment to assault a T-shaped spur on the Kakazu Ridge in the town of Kakazu. Of course, we knew the area was heavily fortified. However, capturing and holding this area would give headquarters complete observation and firing position over the entire Japanese-held area behind Kakazu. Obviously, taking the spur would be of supreme importance.

Company L quietly and carefully started up the hill. Captain Fred Caldwell stopped the men near the top.

The captain told the unit to fix their bayonets. They had the jump on the Japanese so far and were close enough that when the enemy discovered they were there, it would be *mano a mano*. The captain told the unit heads up and good luck.

The men quietly began fixing their bayonets to the tip of their rifles.

Caldwell whispered to not make a sound in order to maintain their advantage. He led the men forward.

L Company had nearly made it to the top when a heavily fortified Japanese unit realized the Yanks were on top of them. They turned to face the attackers.

Caldwell screamed to hit them.

L Company leaped into the midst of the enemy. The Japanese tried to engage the unit, but the Americans fought like crazy men. Some fired their rifles at close range. Soldiers ended up on top of some of the Japanese, plunging their bayonets into the enemies' chests. The dead piled up.

The captain kept yelling, "Don't stop! They're on the run."

L Company fought with an almost tireless vigor. On all sides, men were fighting in hand-to-hand combat. The bloody struggle didn't let up.

Slashing and slinging continued for what seemed like hours but was actually more like minutes. The Japanese ended up being wiped out, while L Company occupied their former position. The enemy retreated.

While the Japanese were going under, G Company charged up the left side of the hill and I Company came from the right. Withering machine-gun fire opened up on both companies.

G Company's commanding officer ordered his men to stay low. They had to kill the enemy first, then advance. The men exchanged bullet for bullet, but the Japanese had dug in like they planned to be there until Christmas.

One of the men called out that they couldn't make any progress and were getting killed.

A soldier in the middle shouted that they were in trouble.

The commanding officer grabbed the phone and yelled over the gunfire that they were stuck and simply couldn't move. He realized their lack of forward progress jeopardized L Company, but he didn't know what to do other than retreat. The enemy were about to counterattack for sure.

The voice on the other end shouted back.

The officer listened for a moment, sighed, and hung up. Then he told the survivors to get ready for an attack.

Over on L Company's side, the Japanese had begun to retaliate. Heavy artillery started blasting.

Captain Fred Caldwell started counting heads. Clearly, their losses had been heavy and were about to mount. Without the soldiers who had fallen, they were in a tough spot. Caldwell called out from behind a boulder and told the men to hang on.

Some of the men grimaced while others bowed their heads. Every one of them knew their chances of survival were zero. No one answered with a grumbling word. They simply hunkered down.

The Japanese returned with a vengeance, but L Company fought like hungry tigers. Again and again, the enemy charged. Again and again, L Company held their ground. Through the remainder of the afternoon, the Japanese kept littering the ground with dead Americans.

Around 6:30 p.m., Sergeant Earl Blevins crawled over to Captain Caldwell and told him they were almost out of ammunition. If they ran out, they were dead for sure.

Caldwell nodded. They had no alternative but to get out of there. He wondered how many had been killed.

Sergeant Blevins had been counting and guessed we had killed about 160 of the enemy. He saw the bodies of a colonel and a major. L Company had knocked out a 320mm mortar when they took the hill. That wasn't exactly a bad day's work.

The captain wanted to know how many their unit had lost so far.

Blevins took off his helmet for a moment and wiped his forehead. Immediately, he put the helmet back on. Ten of their boys were killed and thirty wounded. He couldn't account for five missing out there somewhere.

Caldwell took a deep breath, shook his head, and swore. Without artillery, they had to get down the hill.

Captain Caldwell sounded the retreat. He sounded for the men to cover their asses and start going backward.

The men silently began backing down the hill.

Even with the withdrawal, L Company had breached the enemy's defenses, which allowed the entire command to advance. The bravery and fortitude of all these men could not be overstated.

The next day proved to be equally exasperating.

During the fray, the Third Battalion had been scheduled to launch an attack at 5:00 a.m. but got delayed. Company I ended up getting caught in an open field after the sun had come up. Because they were now observable, the Japanese rained hellfire down on them. The Third ended up being unable to move in any direction. Company L got across the open ground and back up the slopes of the gorge before the Japanese realized they were there. Once the enemy recognized what was coming, they targeted the same open field. The exact area the company had just crossed was now blanketed with every type of mortar and artillery the Japanese had. Company L recognized that I Company had been cut off and that they were isolated.

Lieutenant Willard Mitchell, who had taken command of Company L, wasted no time in taking control of the situation. A southern guy, Mitchell had played football and basketball at Mississippi State College, ending up with the name "Hoss." When Hoss realized they couldn't retreat, he saw no way out except to charge ahead.

With a loud, booming voice, he demanded the men move out. Hoss yelled that they could get to the top of the hill.

The men began firing left and right and didn't stop until they reached the ridge. The hilltop stretched from one side to the other with a shallow saddle between. Hoss and his men kept firing until they had conquered the hill. Unfortunately, the entire area was filled with Japanese who weren't backing off.

Hand grenades flew right and left. Mortars exploded. Flying dirt dropped on the soldiers. Both sides fired back with only a few yards between them. Finally, Hoss's crew observed the Japanese wheeling a tracked launcher out of a cave. The enemy fired a round and then pulled the launcher back into the cave.

Hoss knew they had to knock out that launcher. He asked six volunteers to go down there and finish business.

For a moment no one moved. Slowly, one by one, six hands went up.

The men began crawling at a snail's space toward the cave.

Machine-gun fire never let up. Ducking, rolling, inching along, the soldiers moved ever closer to the cave.

One of the men cried and rolled over screaming that he got hit in the leg.

No one pushed on until a tourniquet had been applied. They again crawled closer to the cave. Two more men doubled and gasped. Rifle fire had hit them.

The remaining three crept next to the entrance. The creaking sound of wheels rolling signaled that the launcher would be coming out momentarily. The three soldiers hurled satchel charges into the entrance. An explosion rocked the cave. Smoke billowed out. The wheels quit rolling.

By the time the men returned, only one was not wounded.

Hoss and Company L hunkered down. More would soon be coming their way.

21

Valor

Even though Lieutenant Bill Mitchell and L Company had taken the hill, the Japanese suspected the unit was small in number and knew they significantly outnumbered the Americans. The stage stood ready for terror to unfold. Around noon, the enemy barreled into L Company with guns blazing.

Hoss Mitchell shouted to hang tight because they could beat the enemy at their own game.

Mortars blasted, and grenades exploded, but the soldiers didn't retreat.

Mitchell encouraged the men to stay with it.

Japanese broke through the bushes only a few yards from the soldiers, but no one retreated. A few of the men rushed forward with bayonets, stabbing the enemy. Japanese were falling on every side.

Hoss kept swinging his rifle right and left, constantly firing. Once Japanese bodies had piled up on the ground, their unseen

leaders apparently called off the attack and the survivors retreated.

Hoss knew they would be back and told the men to stay down.
He figured they were not going to give up when they knew they
outnumbered us.

Company L repositioned itself. Men dug makeshift foxholes.
Others settled in behind boulders with their rifles carefully resting in cracks in the rock. In about thirty minutes the sound of
rustling bushes and breaking branches signaled that the Japanese
were coming again. Without making a sound, Hoss waved his
hand in the air to call for readiness.

The Japanese screamed *"Bonsai!"* and roared out of the ground
cover. Machine-gun fire exploded, but Hoss's men stayed flat on
the ground. When the artillery cover stopped, the Japanese came
rushing in again. L Company didn't flinch and kept firing. Once
the Japanese broke through the thicket, they were virtually out in
the open and made easy targets. The soldiers knocked them out
as quickly as they appeared. In short order, the Japanese's second
attack failed.

Sergeant Blevins asked how long the enemy could endure, since
the Yanks had already knocked out two of their counterattacks.

A guy named Annis answered that they'd fight as long as they
had to.

Blevins shrugged and yelled that it felt like there was a million
more enemy behind them.

Annis yelled back, "We'll kill them as well."

Hoss raised his hand and said they were coming again.

The screaming horde descended once more. They seemed to
be getting closer.

Hoss ordered bayonets fixed.

A Japanese soldier came charging out of the bush with a grenade raised in his hand, but a rifle shot dropped him immediately. The grenade never exploded. Behind him another enemy squad came rushing in. Extremely accurate fire from the Deadeyes kept the Japanese from getting through the perimeter of the company.

———————————

Over on the other end of the hill, when the leader of the First Platoon got knocked out of action, Sergeant John Bradley stepped in to lead the squad forward. From out of nowhere, a slug caught him in the shoulder, sending him spinning backward.

Bradley hit the ground, rolled sideways, and grabbed his shoulder. He knew they had hit him.

A PFC yelled to the sergeant that they should retreat.

Bradley yelled that they had to stop the enemy even if they were all over them.

When the PFC argued that he had a bad wound, the sergeant told him to forget it and get busy rallying the men around him.

The soldier called the platoon together.

Bradley told them they had no choice but to fight their way out of there. It had become a real shoot-out.

One of the men noticed blood running down Bradley's shirt. Bradley ignored him and insisted they had to stop the enemy before they kill them.

Within minutes, the Japanese came rolling in again. The exchange proved vicious. Not only for the enemy, but for the squad as well. Nevertheless, Sergeant Bradley led the charge, wounded shoulder and all.

A PFC shouted and fired his rifle several times. A Japanese fell only feet away from the sergeant's back.

The battle continued through the afternoon, but eventually even Sergeant Bradley knew they had to withdraw.

Bradley commanded that they carry the wounded out first.

The medic told the sergeant to lie down: with one nasty hole in the shoulder, he was one of the wounded. His entire shirt was bloody.

Bradley growled hell no and insisted they get the more badly wounded men out on litters first.

The medic shrugged, and the wounded were evacuated. Even though he slumped, Bradley watched them leave.

The medic warned him that he had lost a lot of blood.

Bradley leaned on a tree branch and asked if they were all out. Once assured he suggested they back out gradually.

When a PFC asked how many he had killed, Bradley shrugged and guessed it must have been around twenty-six. He said he thought it was not a bad exchange for a little bullet hole, and laughed, then grimaced.

The men inched their way back down the hill. That night Sergeant John Bradley died.

In the area held by Company L, the sound of a scream echoed periodically from some man. Hoss knew his men were getting hit, but they had no choice but to keep firing. He had watched PFC Joseph Solch demonstrate extraordinary bravery. Solch had been one of the six men who volunteered to take out the spigot-mortar position hidden in a cave. When the other five men were wounded, the PFC stood over the fallen and began to protect them with his automatic rifle. Round after round had been fired into the attackers. While Solch fired, the wounded began crawling back to safety. Finally, only one man, helplessly wounded, remained. Picking him up on his back, Sloch crawled a hundred yards while machine-gun fire erupted around him. Struggling with his grueling burden, Solch made it back to camp and saved the soldier's life.

Later when a surprise attack left the soldiers momentarily startled and staring, Solch leaped to his feet and emptied three BAR clips, killing fifteen of the attackers. Not one of the Japanese got through. Solch had stopped them all.

Hoss had seen demonstrations of bravery and courage everywhere he looked. The Japanese had to be astonished at the fortitude of the American troops. Eventually, the last Japanese fell to the ground and the enemy withdrew. The fourth counterattack ended in the same way. The soldiers had proven themselves to be mighty men of war indeed!

By four o'clock, the pause in the fighting silenced the company's rifles. Hoss began to count heads. A majority of the men had been wounded with everything from minor cuts to serious holes in their legs or arms. Of the eighty-nine men, only three were untouched. Thirty-seven would not be able to walk. Seventeen were dead.

Hoss crept closer to the bodies of the Japanese. Staying under cover, he started counting the number that he could see. At least 165 Japanese had been killed. Kakazu had become a blood-soaked hill.

22

No Letup in Sight

Memories of watching the infantry units assault Kakazu west would never leave my mind. I had seen the bravest and the best stand against murderous assaults of incredible proportions. The price for endurance had been paid by men of extraordinary courage. After talking with some of the survivors, I filled in more details.

While I headed back to my artillery unit, I thought on a few of the courageous deeds that had unfolded on Kakazu Ridge. Sergeant James Pritchard had refused to order his gunner into a vulnerable position and took the exact location himself. Pritchard sat alone, emptying six boxes of ammunition. When they finally got him, heaven knows how many of the enemy Pritchard took out of this world with him.

Lieutenant Willard Mitchell's performance certainly took the cake. When one of his men had been wounded and remained pinned down under machine-gun fire, Hoss went to the rescue.

He dashed through incessant fire and grabbed the injured man, returning with the guy over his shoulder. Hoss got him and the entire unit out and back to safety. Such astonishing valor continued all day. By the time it was over, the top-drawer brass knew what had occurred. Lieutenant Willard Mitchell and PFC Joseph Solch were presented the Distinguished Service Cross. Sergeant John Bradley received the same posthumously. The other soldiers who survived the day were given either a Silver or Bronze Star.

By the time I got back to my 361st Artillery unit, the sun had nearly set. Sergeant McQuiston already had the figures.

"Looks like the 383rd Infantry had three hundred twenty-six casualities. Company L now has only thirty-eight men left. The First Battalion lost fifty percent of their men. April ninth will be a day to be long remembered."

I sat down and took my helmet off. "Bravest men I ever met. Terrible, terrible losses."

"One hell of a battle," McQuiston said.

Some of the men gathered round. Swinging Bill Arnold sat down next to Captain Hans Goins. George Morris sauntered up. Lee Lewis leaned against the barrel of the howitzer.

"Are we gonna retreat?" Morris asked.

"Hell no!" I said. "We can't let the deaths of all those good soldiers go unchallenged. We'll be back at it in the morning."

"That pile of bodies must be starting to stack up as high as a chimney," Goins quipped.

I looked at him and glared. "You trying to be funny?"

"Oh no, sir." Goins shook his head emphatically. He knew he'd crossed a line with me.

"You boys ought to take a little walk down there where the wounded are," I said. "A quick glance will put today into perspective for you. April ninth will indeed be a day that sticks in your thoughts."

Lee Lewis shook his head. "So many, many men killed." His voice trailed away. "I . . . I . . . just don't know."

"Don't think about it," Sergeant McQuiston said. "Gets to be too much."

"How'd we ever get in such mayhem?" Lewis asked.

"Makes you wonder if there is a God," Goins said in an uncharacteristically sober voice.

"Ain't no God," Swinging Bill growled. "Look around at the legs blown off and the heads splattered like busted watermelons. See any sign of a God in that mess?"

Goins sighed. "Hard to think about the religious stuff when bullets are flying."

"Not for me," McQuiston said. "I pray like crazy."

"How can you pray when there's so much pain everywhere around you?" Morris asked.

"That's the point," McQuiston maintained. "Pain ain't bad. The hurtin' tells you where to pay attention. Without pain, you wouldn't know you'd been whacked."

"I'd be delighted not to know," Swinging Bill said, and spit. "I can figure out when I been zinged without the pain attached."

"Good for you," Goins shot back. "But the rest of us need the hurts to know where to throw the antiseptic."

"Okay," Swinging Bill admitted. "But McQuiston, what'd your pain ever get you? Huh? Prayin' done you any good?"

"I'm still here," McQuiston fired back.

Swinging Bill snorted sarcastically.

"Do you really think there is a God?" Lewis looked at each man as if seeking a response from each one. Everyone nodded but Bill.

"What makes you such a cynic?" McQuiston pressed.

"Things happen in this world 'cause people are mean, nasty, real sonofabitches," Bill answered. "If God made 'em like that, then God is one sonofabitch."

"Oooh!" Goins howled. "I thought I was cynical. But old Bill here wins hands down."

"Listen, you loudmouth gutter snakes! You don't know shit. I've seen people burned to—" Bill stopped and bit his lip. "Well, I've seen grotesque faces that won't leave your mind. Now, if your God made all this happen, that's your problem. I keep my head on straight because I know there isn't a God!" His voice had gotten louder and louder. "There ain't no God! That's not cynicism. That's life. Understand?"

Arnold stopped and looked up at me. Our eyes met and we both understood what he was talking about. He sure as hell didn't want me to spill the beans.

The sergeant sensed the conversation might be getting out of hand. I suppose he wanted a referee. McQuiston looked over at me.

"Major Shaw? What do you believe in?"

"Staying alive," I answered McQuiston. "I don't have time to think about God, Jesus, religion, or nothing. I keep my head down and hope to God we all get out of here alive."

The discussion stopped. I couldn't tell what they were thinking, but looking in empty eyes and watching men die fills one's mind with a grotesque landscape that appears to stretch on without end. The truth was that they *did think* about God. None of these men had been in the predicament of Hoss Mitchell and his men, but they'd still seen enough death that they didn't want any more. When the bullets started flying, they prayed for divine cover.

Swinging Bill brought his ghosts with him. Only he and I knew the truth. Most of the men had just been everyday guys living out the American dream. All they wanted was to get back home and keep on chasing the stars. The trouble was that those little hills like Kakazu and Cactus Ridge filled their heads with nightmares that would go on for decades.

I finally walked away from the group and lit a cigarette. There wasn't much wind at the moment. Even though the big guns had temporarily gone silent, my ears still roared from the day's bombardments. I took a deep breath and wondered myself. God, where are you?

23

A Storm Unabated

With the rising of the sun, the roar of war sounded again. April 10 would be another difficult day. All through the day, the reports continued to filter in. The 382nd Infantry began coordinated attacks against Nishabaru Hill and Tombstone Ridge. The two units should extend fighting on Kakazu Ridge that was to the left of the Nishabaru area. Their attention was focused on making a breakthrough between the hill and the ridge. Like everything else in this war, the assault proved vicious and deadly.

I stood in the command headquarters and listened to the reports coming in as well as conversations between the men. E Company of the Second Battalion got across the eastern extension of Kakazu Gorge and pushed their way about 250 yards to the base of the ridge extending out of Nishabaru Hill. At that point, they started getting hit with intense artillery and took an extremely high number of casualties. Losses made it impossible for the two companies to hook up. In the struggle, Colonel Cyril Sterner got nicked by a mortar fragment but refused to stop or be taken out. The war was back on full tilt for sure.

Out of nowhere, two of the Japanese flying boxcar bombs came hurling down on top of the battalion command post. Dirt and rocks flew in every direction while the roar of the explosion left men nearly deaf. The force of the blast picked up men and slung them in every direction. I hit the ground.

"What's happened?" a soldier lying on the ground muttered.

"Gone?" another man's voice sounded far away. "They're all gone?"

Both men sat up and stared. An entire mortar platoon had vanished in the explosion. The command post, obliterated.

"Medics," a soldier mumbled. "Help!"

"Looks like it's bad." He stood up and shook the dirt off his clothing. Several rocks fell out of the fold in his pants. "Those three-twenty mortars sure dig a crater. God help us."

The men began reassembling themselves. The soldiers found it hard to believe that an entire platoon had been wiped out by two large missiles. They had.

———————

On the other end, the First Battalion began their turn. I watched men start working their way up Tombstone once more. By ten o'clock, B and C Companies had made excellent progress. Working their way west, they came through the town of Kaniku, meeting virtually no resistance. B and C quickly got atop the northern ridge. I could hear them shouting back and forth.

Anyone watching the battle knew that a quick advance with no problems wasn't just good luck. The Japanese had something up their sleeves and before long the bubble would burst. An hour later, the expected came roaring in. Like a horde of wasps, the Japanese swarmed C Company.

The company commander, Lieutenant Robert Bolan, quickly recognized what was coming. I could hear him shout across the valley, "Heads up! A carload of the enemy are dropping in for a visit!"

Enemy artillery streamed into their position. Those god-awful 320mm mortars fell indiscriminately all over the hill. Hunks of turf sailed through the air like pigeons flying. The entire ridge had turned into the target.

"Here they come!" Bolan began firing his rifle.

Men around Bolan started shooting in all directions, but nothing could stop the Japanese rushing toward C Company in almost suicidal formation.

After several minutes, the commander could see that the enemy were only yards away from his men. No more than twenty yards separated the two sides.

"Shoot the flamethrowers!" Bolan demanded. "Hit them in the face!"

Men with tanks strapped on their backs assumed a position on the front line. The propane-operated devices come out roaring like an angry dragon. The pressure of the gas, activated through piezo ignition, produced its own velocity. The flames bellowed in the wind. Operators with the propane tanks on their backs surged forward, which meant they had to stand up in a vulnerable position.

"Attaboy!" Lieutenant Bolan kept shouting. "We're roasting those mothers!"

But the Japanese didn't slow down. After several runs at C

Company, they brought their own flamethrowers. Fire exploded in waves on all sides.

"The bad boys ain't gonna stop!" Bolan kept shouting. "Keep shooting."

The commander stood to change his position. The crack of a rifle sent him spinning backward. For a few moments, he didn't move.

"They got the lieutenant," a soldier called out. "Medic!"

One of the medical staff rushed to Bolan's side. "Sir, they shot you in the shoulder. Need to get you out of here."

"Hell, no," Bolan growled. "I'm not leaving in the midst of a confrontation."

The medic felt around his shoulder and neck area.

"Aaaaah!" Bolan gasped.

"Your collarbone is broken," the medic said. "You're gonna have a hard time moving that side of your body."

"Just sit me upright," Bolan said. "Give me my forty-five pistol. I'm not going anywhere. That's a command."

The medic shrugged. "Well, you're the boss." He took the Browning High Fire out of Bolan's holster and handed it to him.

Bolan started firing and the medic crawled away. I watched in amazement at such courage.

———————

B Company began to experience the same ferocity. The difference was that the Japanese had holed up in small caves all over the area, giving them cover as well as the favorable position. The company had just set up the light machine guns when the enemy came pouring in with rifles blazing.

One of the gunners cranked his machine gun up and almost started to fire. A bullet caught him straight in the forehead, sending him flying backward. The Japanese landed on top of the man's buddy. Before he could get his pistol out, the enemy stabbed him in the chest.

The Japanese were everywhere at once. Rifle fire smacked into the machine gunners. Two of the units began to fire, dropping the enemy almost as fast as they broke through the perimeter of the camp. Finally, the far-left gunner got hit in the chest and his machine gun went silent. The lone gunner remaining kept firing and the enemy retreated.

He called out to see if everyone was okay.

No one answered.

The lone gunner called again. He slowly got to his knees and crawled to the other men. Of the eight in the section, he was the only one who survived. He struggled, crawling from man to man. All were dead.

———————

With the frightening struggle of B and C Companies to survive, A Company was ordered off the northern knob of the ridge and sent to bring relief. They were halfway up the hill when extreme mortar fire stopped them. Once again, the sky split open and another 320mm flying boxcar slammed into A Company. A basement load of dirt covered the men.

A soldier called out to the commander.

Someone answered that he'd disappeared. The men yelled for him.

A soldier pointed to a pile of dirt. The damn thing was moving! The men rushed to the heap and began pulling out rocks and slinging dirt. After a few shovelfuls, a hand appeared. The fingers wiggled.

The men frantically pushed and pulled right and left, slowly wiggling their commander loose from the avalanche. Two men grabbed each arm and pulled with all their might. Slowly his body emerged from the dirt.

Lieutenant Doyle coughed and sputtered. He rolled over on his knees and tried to catch his breath. He couldn't find his helmet in the pile of dirt.

They knew the Japanese would be pouring in again and had to get ready.

The explosions only increased, and the Japanese kept charging. The soldiers of Company A kept firing at the enemy, who were popping up like popcorn. The Japanese were everywhere at once, and the company's ammunition kept getting lower and lower.

At two fifteen Colonel Johnson reported their completely untenable situation to headquarters.

Johnson listened for a few moments and then hung up. He told the men that they had thirty minutes to look for missing men and was particularly concerned about the machine-gun section. They had to get out of there.

The men nodded and immediately began preparations for leaving. In thirty minutes, their own artillery would turn the hill into a fire pit. The search for the machine gunners proved futile. They had all been killed.

The trail back proved arduous, with the enemy on their tail at every turn. Mortar fire and machine-gun fire never stopped. Rain started coming down, signaling the monsoon season was not far away. Company A kept returning the fire while they cautiously inched backward. When nightfall had come, the soldiers dug in to muddy, wet foxholes and prepared to defend themselves in the dark.

The men didn't seem particularly disturbed by their retreat. Constant pandemonium and the uproar of war had settled into their psyches, leaving them numb. Mostly, they were simply too tired to give a damn.

24

Darkness Descends

Remembering what happened in war is hard. Not because you don't remember, but because you can't forget. Nobody wants to talk about what they saw. Remembering brings back images that no human being ought to see *ever*. The carnage erupts in your dreams or pops up before your eyes in the middle of lunch. You try to suppress the faces of dead men, lying there on the ground for two or three days, but they won't leave no matter how long you attempt to push them out of your memories. As the decades pass, one learns not to go there. Just leave it be, but somewhere down at the bottom of your mind, the scene lingers like a movie being played over and over, day after day.

April 10 had been one of those days that hangs around forever. I watched some of what occurred; others told me their stories. Many of the encounters were reported to Command Central while I was there. The events remain graphic in all of our minds.

That same day at nine in the morning, the Third Battalion tried again to take the knolls on the northeast side of Tombstone Ridge. The results were the same. Monsoon season had begun to kick in. Rain had begun to turn the dirt into mud, roads into rivers, and that made it difficult for the tanks to move. Heavy armory couldn't offer any significant help. As usual, the Japanese were hitting us with everything they had. Rain made visibility poor, which worked to their advantage. Because we couldn't see where they were hiding, the downpour protected them.

By two thirty, officers could see that the advance was stymied. Fighting went back and forth with no one going anywhere. The colonel decided to pull his men back to their previous position. The big boys at Command Central needed a new strategy and it would take some time to formulate the next step. Meanwhile the Third Battalion had no other option but to sit still and take any pounding that came in. The enemy held the commanding position and all the sacrifices we made did nothing to change that advantageous posture.

The next morning, the battalion command post got smacked with everything but the kitchen door. Heavy artillery scattered the men, and the assault did not stop.

The men attempted to hide in secure positions, but the task wasn't easy. Two mortars exploded near the camp, splattering shrapnel across the area. Another artillery blast immediately followed.

One more explosion shook the ground, followed by continuous machine-gun fire. The soldiers began returning the fire, their machine guns blasting away, but it was clear we were at a disadvantage. The enemy clearly had us dead away.

Sergeant Dick Hunter, realizing the Japanese were about to counterattack, shouted for the men to get ready. Moments later, the Japanese came pouring in. The soldiers kept shooting, but the ferocity of the attack continued to drop good men.

An explosion interrupted their conversations. Hunks of sod hurled past while the soldiers ducked, crouching down in the foxhole.

Immediately after the mortar hit, another wave of Japanese rushed out of the bushes. The men fired continuously until the enemy retreated.

Machine guns began rapid-firing again. Both men dropped back into their foxholes. Once more, the Japanese rushed forward, and the soldiers fired as rapidly as they could. The enemy fell around them, but American soldiers were also hitting the ground.

Many of the soldiers that day thought, *I'm going to die out here on this godforsaken island.*

By nightfall, the First Battalion took a head count to see where they were. The colonel knew they had come ashore with 770 men. Half of them were dead.

———————

On the north side of the slope, the First Battalion had been preparing their own attack. Company A started the drive at seven o'clock with the sun barely up. They quickly got almost within yards of the crest when all hell broke loose again. The enemy began hammering the top of the hill, an easy target. A Company suddenly found themselves in a tough position to maintain. The enemy kept hurling every possible kind of artillery at them.

The soldiers wondered out loud how long they could hang on.

Sergeant Alfred Robertson answered almost automatically that they would stay there as long as necessary.

With Sioux Indian blood, Al was called "Chief." He took it

good-naturedly and answered to the title without giving it any thought.

PFC Tom White asked Chief if he was gonna do something about this little skirmish.

Chief told the boys to pay attention: he'd show them the Indian way of doing business. He adjusted a bayonet on his rifle.

To the shock of the men, Chief leaped out of the foxhole and charged the enemy. His BAR rifle spit rapid fire and Japanese fell. Chief hit the ground, rolled over, and hurled a grenade. As soon as it exploded, he leaped up and rushed the nearest Japanese, catching him in the stomach with his bayonet. The Japanese screamed and Chief hit him again before dropping back into a makeshift foxhole.

One of the enemy stood up and screamed, *"Takakai! Faito!"* The soldier started to run forward.

Chief calmly shot him in the head.

Another Japanese bellowed, *"Kosen!"*

Chief dropped him without even blinking. The Indian rolled over and slung another grenade. After the explosion, another Japanese machine-gun nest went silent. But Al didn't stop shooting the charging enemy. One of the Japanese broke free and ran straight at him. Chief didn't move. When the enemy swung his knife, the Indian leaned back, letting the knife sail past. In an instant, Al rammed his trench knife into the man's throat. Then Chief stopped because none were left.

The Chief had single-handedly killed twenty-eight Japanese.

Mortar fire fell like the rain. No matter where the 383rd turned, the Japanese were on top of them. Each advance was pushed back by crucifying fire. Even through the Second Battalion got up the hill, they finally had to retreat. By the end of the day, virtually everyone in the army knew the truth: they had to rethink how to proceed.

April 11 ended in rain and mud. Every company was faced with a grim struggle. The slime and the mire seemed to be laughing at us.

25

In the Dead of Night

Our 105mm howitzer long-range cannons stood in place ready to fire whenever the instructions came. The men knew that Command was thinking about how we'd proceed, and our unit wasn't exactly itching to be firing the big guns. Sergeant McQuiston kept pacing back and forth, waiting, just waiting, waiting, waiting.

"Slow it down, Sergeant," I said. "A little rest won't hurt you any."

McQuiston grinned. "We get so used to constant fighting that it's hard to do nothing. The unexpected always gets to me."

"Really?" Swinging Bill Arnold said. "Really? Who are you kidding? I can sit here doin' nothing all day long." He lay down and stretched out on the grass.

"I bet you're good at doing nothing," McQuiston quipped.

PFC Lee Lewis sat down on top of an empty ammunition box. "You think them Japanese might be planning to come flying across Tombstone Ridge and pour down Nishabaru Hill thinkin' they'd drive us out of here? Plunk us back in the ocean?"

McQuiston snorted. "Let 'em try. We'll cut 'em up like low-grade sausage and have 'em for supper."

"Whooeee!" Swinging Bill said. "Are you ever the optimist!"

George Morris sauntered over. "Sounds like you boys got the war all figured out. My hunch is that none of you know shit."

McQuiston started laughing. "I think old George is right on the mark. No telling what's ahead. As the saying goes, 'Ours is to do or die.' However, I wasn't planning on the dying part happening anytime soon."

Swinging Bill kept staring at the sky. "None of us has any control over destiny. Like them clouds rollin' in and then rollin' out, the winds will blow in our fate whatever that may be."

"O-o-u," PFC Lee said. "Swinging Bill has turned philosopher on us. "Come on, Major Shaw. Tell us what you see written on the horizon."

"I'd say you're damn lucky you're not out there in one of those units making a run at the Japanese. Sure, we might get hit by one of General Tojo's flying boxcars and blown to smithereens, but it's not likely. If you stay put and keep your nose clean, you ought to be able to survive what's coming."

"Interesting," McQuiston said. "Let's hope you're right."

PFC Lewis rubbed his chin. "Yeah, I'm sure every one of those men who fell yesterday really didn't think it was comin' for them. Course, they didn't suffer none."

"Suffer none!" PFC Morris exploded. "What in the hell has that got to do with anything?"

"A lot," Lewis insisted. "If it's you getting a hole poked in your chest, I'm sure you'll be hollerin' about it then."

McQuiston laughed. "You boys worry and jawbone about the most ridiculous junk I ever heard. Let's face it. We're sitting out here in limbo, waiting for fate to come walking through our camp. All any of us is gonna get is what hits us most unexpectedly. That's just the way life is. You never know because what usually happens comes sailing in out of the blue anyway." He pointed up at me. "Major, were you expecting your wife to get pregnant?"

I snickered. "Why, you didn't think that was an accident, did you?"

The men started laughing. Abruptly, the walkie-talkie phone rang. Sergeant McQuiston answered.

"What?" The sergeant's voice rose an octave. "You got to be kidding!"

For a moment each man fell silent.

"Sounds like we're gettin' ready to fire up," Morris said.

"When?" McQuiston asked in a softer voice. "I see, I see," he said slowly.

I walked over to take the phone if necessary. Sounded like an attack was imminent.

"Tell everyone?" the sergeant asked. "Okay." He hung up the phone slowly. "Can't believe it."

"What?" I said. "Don't just stand there. Tell us what's happened."

McQuiston took a deep breath. "The president of the United States died. President Roosevelt's gone."

The men stared.

"Can't believe it," PFC Lewis muttered.

"I'll be damned," Swinging Bill said. "Talk about the unexpected."

"What's going on?" I asked.

"Command is sending out the word to all units. The president is dead."

"President of America?" Lewis asked.

"The United States!" McQuiston nearly shouted. "President Franklin D. Roosevelt died of a stroke in Warm Springs, Georgia."

"God help us!" Morris exclaimed.

"Don't get your underwear in a knot," Swinging Bill said. "What's all that got to do with us out here in the Pacific?" He shrugged. "The country will go on. Always does. Whoever is vice president will take over."

"You guys don't seem particularly bent out of shape," I said.

"The truth is we are fighting a war thousands of miles away from the good ol' USA," Arnold said. "All that's on our minds is not getting killed. I'm afraid the president of the United States is light-years away from any of my concerns."

Men began walking over from the other howitzers. "What's this about the president?" Lieutenant Marvin Hoffman asked. "Didn't quite get the story straight."

"Yeah," Sergeant Tom Brown said. "Give us the scoop."

Captain Robert Olson and Lieutenant John Hayes joined in.

"You're sure you got the message right?" Brown asked.

"Came from Command," McQuiston said. "Apparently, the president had a stroke. Must have occurred last night."

Hoffman rubbed his chin. "Guess Harry Truman is the president now."

"Who in the hell is Harry Truman?" Hayes asked. "Never heard of the old fart."

"Come on." Morris sounded irritable. "Show some respect."

"I sure as hell ain't gonna kiss his butt," Hayes said.

"I've never voted in my life," Swinging Bill said. "I don't know Truman from a toad. We're out here fighting for the country and trying to stay alive. That's a bigger deal to me than what's going on with the politicians."

"Roosevelt was the leader of our country," I said. "We might quibble over politics, but he did bring America through a terrible depression. Roosevelt put men back to work and oversaw this war. We need to honor his memory and offer due respect."

"You're right, Major," Lieutenant Hoffman agreed. "I don't know anything about Truman except he was a senator. Must be a good guy of some sort to lead the country. I'll salute him."

The men mumbled their agreement and dispersed.

I walked to the perimeter of our camp. I knew nothing about Truman and not a great deal about Roosevelt. Still, he had been our supreme leader. Now this new guy named Harry Truman had moved into the White House. We were all so fixed on the war and surviving that we paid little attention to the comings and goings of political debate back home. We'd keep on living out that mentality till the war was over.

Still, the news was a shock . . . indeed, the most unexpected!

26

While No One Sleeps

Discussing the president's death and who Harry Truman might turn out to be continued into the evening. Most of the men hadn't been interested in politics, so the conversations didn't amount to much. Back home, none of us got national news anyway except through the newspapers and a few static-filled radio broadcasts. Of course, that meant details were sparse and information often delayed. We came from mostly small towns where life went on its own way regardless of what the bigmouths did in Washington. When the bottom fell out of the economy, the WPA and other public assistance programs kept people alive and in some sort of job. Although the Republicans were always chewing on his case, Roosevelt got the credit for pulling America up from off the bottom. Some of the soldiers liked those facts; some didn't.

Before the war, a group called the America Firsters strongly opposed getting involved in Hitler's war in Europe. Even a national hero like Charles Lindbergh joined in the America First group, opposing getting into one of those age-old far-off conflicts between European nations. That opposition disappeared like morning mist when the Japanese bombed Pearl Harbor. By the end of 1942, America was a different country than it had been.

"When do you think we'll hear something from Command?" Sergeant McQuiston asked me.

"Ought to come fairly quick," I said. "Since we came to a halt in that last drive, the Japanese probably think they've stopped us. We've got to come back with some response before long." I looked at the darkening sky. "Personally, I'm ready to sleep whether the big boys call or not."

"Yeah," McQuiston said. "Getting awful quiet out there."

"Um-huh. Don't like that lack of shooting or rumbling. Not a good sign."

"You think something's up?" McQuiston pushed.

"Probably," I said. "But maybe this would be a good time to stretch out and go to bye-bye sleepland."

"Guess so." McQuiston walked over to his foxhole.

I sat there smoking a cigarette and listening to the quiet settle in. Darkness had just turned a shade deeper when the roar of an explosion shook the ground. A mortar went sailing overhead and exploded behind me. Before I could move, the rattle of machine guns out there in the distance ended the quiet of night.

The war was back on with a vengeance.

"Everybody up and on the cannons!" I yelled. "Keep your rifles handy."

The blasts only increased. No one had reported such activity coming, and I knew the entire infantry probably were struggling with the same surprise that we were. We loaded the howitzers and stood ready to execute. The cracking of gunfire sounded like the enemy were closing in on all of us. No question about it. The Japanese had mounted an offensive.

Swinging Bill ran up to me. "Sounds like they're about a thousand yards in front of us. Right?"

"Don't know," I said. "Just pay big-time attention. Understood?"

The walkie-talkie rang, and I picked it up. "Yeah?"

"Looks like the Japanese have mounted a major counteroffensive. We're getting hit across the entire front line simultaneously. This one is really big. Don't fire until we have better coordinates. Just stand by."

"You bet." I hung up and turned to McQuiston. "Tell the men to lower their sights and be ready to shoot at a moment's notice. We're in for a major assault tonight."

The sergeant took off, running from cannon to cannon.

"Hell of a time to start an offensive," I muttered to myself. "Gonna be a long night."

The Japanese intended to push us off the island, and so the doughboys on the front line got it in the teeth. Apparently, the enemy thought the lull in fighting signaled weakness on our part. Probably, they interpreted our pullback as a retreat and believed we were highly vulnerable. Whatever. The brunt of their attack hit Colonel Halloran's troop in the chops. No question that the Japanese had planned this attack carefully. They came rushing in like walking machine guns and probably would have broken through if it were not for men like Sergeant Beauford T. Anderson.

I don't know where he got the name, but everyone just called old Beauford "Snuffy." Of all places, Snuffy came down from Soldiers Grove, Wisconsin, and was he ever ready to fight. He was one enterprising son of a gun!

Some of the men in A Company had crawled into a cave. Snuffy's mortar squad was good at what they did, but like the rest of us, they had bedded down for the night just before the Japanese hit. When the screaming meemies started racing toward them, Sergeant Snuffy hung tight, not being sure what to do next.

Mortars exploded all around them, and it quickly became clear the squad couldn't get out alive even if they wanted to run. Something radical had to be done.

Snuffy didn't want everybody exposed to deadly fire. He knew they would have to take it one person at a time. If one man went down, the next man must take his place.

One of the men piped up, "You just want us to wait while somebody goes out there and gets killed?"

The sergeant stared at him with harsh, threatening eyes.

The soldier didn't say any more.

Snuffy said that he was going out there first and alone. All he wanted them to do was keep their rifles ready.

Snuffy began crawling toward the ledge in front of the cave. Staying on his belly, he pulled a hand grenade from his pocket, pulled the pin, and threw it straight at two Japanese about to run toward the cave.

The explosion sent both of the enemy flying backward. Snuffy picked up his rifle and began firing in all directions. Enemy started falling on all sides. The enemy kept firing back, but Snuffy returned his response with greater accuracy. In between rifle shots and throwing grenades, Snuffy held them from breaking through. He kept shooting; Japanese kept falling.

A mortar flew over his head and bounced off the rock wall but didn't explode. Snuffy grabbed the explosive and hurled it into the night. A blast signaled the dud had finally worked, but in the enemy's nest.

The sergeant had a new idea. He called for the men to bring a box of mortar shells to the edge of the cave.

The men instantly hauled the shells forward. Snuffy began grabbing the explosives and pulling them out of the casing. He pulled the safety pins, activated the mortars by hitting them against the rock, and hurled them. Off in the distance, the discharge shook the ground.

Snuffy grabbed the shells as quickly as the men put them in his hands, and he slung them into the darkness. Discharge after discharge boomed through the night. Somehow, the Japanese never shot him even though he was in plain sight heaving the bombs.

Finally, the Japanese backed off and quiet fell over the hillside.

The men crept back into the cave. The next morning, the terrain didn't reflect any new movement. The men crawled out and started checking what was in front of them. They found twenty-five dead Japanese, seven abandoned knee mortars, and four machine guns lying on the ground.

Someone heard Snuffy say, "Not a bad night's work."

27

What Next?

Sergeant Snuffy Anderson's bravery didn't go unnoticed. After the war was over, the sergeant and several other men were invited to the White House. On Memorial Day, 1946, President Harry S. Truman pinned the Medal of Honor on Sergeant Beauford Anderson in recognition of his bravery and the lives he saved. Anderson was the second Deadeye to receive the country's highest recognition.

But he wasn't the only hero. Heroes were all over the place. Over in F Company, a Japanese officer came through the bushes mistakenly approaching someone he thought was one of his own men. Apparently trying to get the soldier's attention, he whistled. PFC Tony O'Neil instantly knew what was about to happen and fired almost without looking. The officer and ten men fell dead. E Company's Lieutenant Maurice Douthit had been nearly overwhelmed in the enemy's offense but kept fighting. He heard a shot behind him but couldn't turn around. Looking over his shoulder, he saw one of his men about to be stabbed by a Japanese. Without turning, Douthit shot over his shoulder and killed the attacker. When the day was over, those companies had killed over 196 Japanese.

Hard to believe how many people were being killed hour after hour. They lost their boys; we lost ours. By the end of the day on April 13, we figured that the 381st, the 382nd, and the 383rd had 1,401 wounded and a total of 2,004 put out of action forever. Some of the units had to pull back with half their men gone.

I went down to Command to attempt to understand what was going on. Generals James Bradley and Claudius Easley had already gone to the front and were talking. Finally, the meeting officially began.

"Gentlemen, I believe the Japanese thought they'd push us off the island with their night offense," General Bradley explained. "We've lost way too many men, but we held our position. In the exchange, their bodies littered the fields like fallen leaves. It certainly turned into a bitter night. Even though many of your units bore the brunt of the assault, the Japanese now have a big rethink coming. The Japanese have lost 4,663 men and have no other soldiers to replace them. Attrition alone is cutting them down."

The general kept explaining as he pointed to a large map behind him. "I know that some of you believe we ought to wait for another division to come ashore. I understand, but the stakes are too high to wait. Our chances of success are too good for us to wait. If the Ninety-Sixth and the Seventh can achieve a breakthrough, the war will be shortened and, in the end, lives saved. We need to keep hitting them as hard as we can."

I kept listening, but my mind wandered back to those frontline soldiers and their commanders. Units like the 383rd Infantry that had landed on Easter Sunday and were now radically depleted wouldn't get the bigger picture General Bradley described. The ideas certainly sounded good, but those men had paid a terrible price for what had become a seemingly unattainable objective.

After the meeting, I walked outside and thought about our next move. The first phase of the battle for Okinawa had been completed. We attacked; they retreated. Finally, they attacked big-time; we held. Still, both sides had lost far, far too many men. If the figures kept mounting, eventually the Japanese were going to be finished for a lack of soldiers if for no other reason.

We had come ashore on April 1, and now thirteen days later we had endured what seemed like months of combat. In only a couple of weeks, we had lived through a lifetime of struggle. Thousands had died, and we were still at it. Staggering thought.

Our men had endured horrible conditions, and more were ahead. God help us.

STARTING OVER

THE NEXT PHASE

28

The Next Step

Despair.

Sooner or later, soldiers experience discouragement.

How do you deal with seeing your buddies get bullet holes in the middle of their chests? What do you do with recurring images of dead men lying in a ditch with empty eyes? Sure, it's easy to hate the enemy, but what do you do when you see them sprawled over the ground and find pictures in their pockets? Photographs of them standing next to a Japanese woman, all smiles. She's a pretty thing, just like your girlfriend back home. You can't escape the fact that even with different facial figures and skin tone, they are human beings. *Just like you.*

Despair sinks in if you let yourself think about what's going on. Particularly when the fighting becomes increasingly brutal and your side is getting pushed back. Men in the units get quiet. Sometimes they quit talking to one another. Everyone's trying to make adjustments but aren't sure where it's all going. Gritting your teeth will hold it all back for only so long, and then—

Despair doesn't mean you're afraid, though sometimes you are. You don't want to go AWOL, though sometimes you think about it. The sinking feeling signals that you don't have it all figured out. Maybe Command isn't telling you the whole story. Possibly nobody knows the truth about what's coming down next.

I knew the men on the front line wouldn't understand the "big picture" that the generals were talking about. The top brass already knew the Japanese were licked even if the enemy didn't accept that conclusion yet. The thoughts of the guys in the foxholes were mainly on surviving. Another night assault like what they had barely survived might take out every one of them. Such a situation settles in on you and produces its own emotion.

Despair.

———————

By the morning of April 19, the pieces in the puzzle had been rearranged. During the day and at night, we kept firing at the enemy mainly to keep them off balance. Small patrols kept checking on what the enemy appeared to be doing while we built up our stockpile of ammo. We certainly didn't want them mounting another offensive. However, we were fundamentally marking time while the details were worked out for our response. As the sun came up that morning, we were prepared for the greatest land attack in the history of Pacific warfare.

Out in the ocean, Admiral Turner's fleet stood ready to hammer the enemy with the huge guns on those battleships. Both navy and marine dive-bombers had been loaded with bombs and prepared to strike like lightning bolts. Six battalions of the Ninety-

Sixth were ready to roll. The 198th Battalion's 155mm howitzers stood ready along with the First Battalion of the Eleventh Marine Artillery unit. The big guns were aimed at the face of the enemy. This was a do-or-die campaign to the bitter end. We didn't expect to die.

Command had given me the assignment for the 361st Artillery unit. At six in the morning, we were to begin firing. The sun had barely peeked over the horizon when I gave the signal. Our howitzers bounced off the ground as they rapidly fired shell after shell. The enemy certainly had a wakeup call coming down their chimney. Like monstrous sledgehammers smashing boulders, our bombardment slammed down on them.

Smoke began curling up and then spread across the sky. The entire enemy line became engulfed in a smoky cover as our explosives relentlessly fell. I grabbed my binoculars and raced to get a good reconnaissance view of what was happening. By the time I looked down on the front line, I could see nothing but the enemy shrouded in hazy fog. Dive-bombers kept up their attacks, making the ground shake. I couldn't see how any of the enemy had survived.

The Ninety-Sixth Deadeyes found their place along two lines, ready for the follow-up to the bombing. The Seventh Division stood to the north of Tombstone Ridge and the town of Kaniku. The Twenty-Seventh Division waited on the north side of Kakazu Ridge. Along with other units, each group had their own specific objective. A series of pinnacles we called the Crags gave the enemy excellent cover, and we knew they'd be firing at us from that significant position. The 382nd would have to deal with that problem.

Everyone knew the plan of attack. Our artillery would pound

the Japanese for forty minutes, and then the infantry would move out. Forty minutes later, artillery was to shift to the right and pound that corridor. When we stopped, another battalion would jump off and begin opening up the area for still another battalion to hook up. By this time the Japanese were getting lambasted with everything we had.

I figured the advance should prove easy. We must have flattened the enemy's front line and could walk over them, making excellent progress. Wrong. As the smoke began to lift, machine-gun fire opened up everywhere. Mortars started flying. It turned out that the Japanese had holed up in huge holes and pillboxes. They had survived the barrage and were back in action.

The Japanese were still there and waiting for us.

―――――――――――

The First Battalion of the 382nd Infantry had fought their way up Tombstone Ridge three times. I imagined they'd got to know the area like their backyard. Now the task fell to them again. Once more they started up that treacherous terrain. For the first hour all went well, but from eight on, progress became difficult and costly.

Company A charged up the sheer, rocky cliffs, searching for footholds and watching for cover. The men crept up behind Lieutenant Roger Smith, grabbing at any handhold they could find. Smith kept shouting for them to stay down and keep low.

A machine gunner opened up somewhere above them. The men hit the ground. Smith started shooting back.

Then he stood up and swung his arms to encourage the men forward. A blast of machine-gun fire exploded. The lieutenant flew backward with his arms still extended.

A soldier yelled that Smith was hit and needed a medic.

The paramedic scrambled over the rocky terrain and bent over Smith's body. He listened for a minute before shaking his head and saying he's gone. They called for a litter to carry him back.

The soldiers kept pushing. By three o'clock, the company had worked their way up to the northeastern tip of the slope. The unit kept pressing the enemy and slowly inching to the top. By nightfall, they had taken half the ridge.

Darkness settled in and the infantry began to calculate what had happened. The bodies of 240 Japanese lay sprawled across the slopes. We had knocked out eighteen machine guns and mortars with only six of our soldiers killed. Tragically that loss included Lieutenant Smith and Captain George Gerrans, who had been the commander of Company B. I figured Roger Smith had a posthumous award coming. He did: the Distinguished Service Cross.

Even with these losses, our men had made genuine progress. F and G Companies occupied important high ground. The 381st ran into savage opposition, but the Second Battalion pushed forward. By the time the sun went down, F and G Companies had settled into advantageous positions. No matter where the different units turned, they had encountered deadly opposition.

The Japanese had the advantage of observation that the soldiers didn't. Wherever the doughboys moved, the enemy could hit them hard. We had blasted them big-time, but they still maintained an advantage although their losses were staggering. Maybe this time, I thought, they might be the ones struggling with despair.

29

Struggling On

After a while, you can't miss how men deal with their fear of death. Personally, I shut my emotions off and cram the gruesome specter to the bottom. I got a job to do and that's what I concentrate on. I can't afford to let dread run through my head. The men around me had different approaches. Sergeant McQuiston hopped around like a toad. He'd pace back and forth from cannon to cannon as if inspecting, when all he was doing was marking time. Hans Goins made wisecracks. When he was really nervous, Hans offended everybody in the unit with his deprecating humor before he got through. I suppose that was his way of turning his anxiety outward and onto others—by being a jackass. Whatever.

On the other hand, Corporal Bill Arnold kept getting quieter and quieter. If you looked closely, you could almost see him shrinking inside himself. Of course, I had unexpectedly dropped in on him earlier in the fighting and knew about the horrendous images floating around in his head. When Swinging Bill got completely silent, I knew the fire must really be roaring in his head. Pour a little booze on the bonfire and the man could possibly become dangerous or at least a wild man.

I suppose nobody talks about it, I told myself, 'cause we're all out here to win the war and we just suck it up and go. Ain't easy, though.

Once our second major assault began, every man knew the Japanese had the capacity to drop one of their flying boxcars on us, and that added to our concern. No matter how we did our thing, the issues were tough.

———————

The sun came up on the second day of response, sending the First and Third Platoons pushing off to conquer the top of the ridge. As soon as they started down the back side, all hell broke loose. From their superior observation positions, the Japanese easily followed our movements and could see the soldiers coming down the far side of the hill. Machine-gun fire never stopped. Grenades flew through the air like softballs. Mortars rained down on all sides. The men were bombarded into the dirt.

The night before, Captain Harold Butler had been in charge of Company K when they got hit. While Butler was briefing the men on what to expect, he was killed. Lieutenant Stan Smith took his place and was quickly wounded. Lieutenant Albert Strand filled in the loss. The battle never let up. Like a returning bad dream, Kakazu exploded with intense fire.

No matter how heavy the artillery fire, the men in I Company worked their way to the top, but three men were killed almost simultaneously when they tried to come down the back side. The company commander Captain Sam Hughes got hit. The enemy didn't let up a fraction.

Finally, the company had to withdraw or get wiped out. Using Sherman tanks for protection, they began evacuating the wounded. With tanks providing ground cover, the retreat began. From out of the bushes, a swarm of Japanese rushed one of the Shermans. Our men kept firing, but the Japanese were all over the tank, hitting it with satchel charges. Satchel charges stick to any surface and when manually detonated cause massive explosive damage to anything nearby. Satchel charges can be thrown from a distance and set off through the use of a detonator. Charging like a pack of rabid wild monkeys, the Japanese lost men but completely destroyed the tank. With only four tanks left, the unit tried to work their way through the gap between Kakazu and Nishabaru Ridge.

The First Battalion pushed forward, losing men left and right. They finally got positioned and hunkered down on a hill. C Company had been cut off and couldn't hook up with them until the next day.

As night fell, Major Sanford Fencil gathered the men for a briefing.

The major admitted they were in a tough place. The imperial forces were all around them and they had to be extremely careful. The major warned, "They wouldn't hesitate to hit us in the dark if they can get away with it. Got to stay prepared and at the top of our game."

One of the men held up his hand and asked if the major thought C Company could advance toward them tomorrow.

Fencil nodded and said that's the instructions he had received and he would take them at their word. They had to have a coordination to have a solid front. Nishabaru Ridge remained in enemy hands. Kakazu was behind enemy lines and spitting death with constant artillery fire.

One of the soldiers commented that the enemy were really hitting them hard.

The major agreed but tomorrow would be another day and their turn.

Somebody laughed and said, "You bet!"

The shrill whistle of a falling missile stopped the conversation. Men dived for cover. The ground shook when the bombs smashed into their midst. Dirt and rock flew across the camp. Debris fell on men barely in their foxholes. No one moved. The soldiers waited for the possible sound of Japanese rushing in, but none came.

Somebody ask where Major Fencil was.

A soldier shouted for the major.

Silence.

One of the men inched toward the crater left by the artillery hit. The men stood dumbfounded, staring at their dead leader.

War correspondents had descended on us and were covering this day's action more than they had any of our actions in the past. When the Ninety-Sixth jumped off, at least twenty newspaper people were watching with binoculars. Their stories of watching our men struggle from pillbox to pillbox while advancing only a few yards made good newspaper material and painful memories for us.

Everyone knew the Japanese were fighting with everything they had and hurling their troops into the fray regardless of how many men they lost. Even the reporters could recognize that the

Japanese were fighting from concrete bunkers and pillboxes that were well hidden and strategically placed.

We were probably fighting against the sturdiest Japanese defenses that we had faced in the entire war. On the other side of the front line, the Japanese had built a network of tunnels that gave them shelter and made us an easy target. Their defenses extended back for four or five miles and we were only able to take that ground yards at a time.

No one needed to tell us that no breakthrough was imminent. We were stuck.

———————

The Ninety-Sixth lost more men on April 19 than any other single day. The entire 381st had one particularly brutal struggle. Casualties were high everywhere.

The sun was almost down when Sergeant McQuiston came up to me.

"Major, we've been firing those howitzers all day. They're so hot the barrels are about to melt."

I nodded. "Yeah, I know."

"Think tomorrow's gonna be the same?"

"The Japanese aren't passing out train tickets back to Tokyo," I said. "I expect we'll do it all over again."

"Sure takes a toll on the men."

I shook my head. "We got no choice. We'll fire up again tomorrow."

McQuiston looked at me with those empty eyes that he always got when anguish settled in. We could all smell it. The scent of death was in the air.

30

Nonstop!

The 382nd struggled through a long, dangerous night. Somewhere around midnight, a voice called out to one of the guards, saying they had a message for the company commander.

The guard demanded identity.

The man said he was with the Nineteenth and needed to talk with the commander about hooking up.

The guard asked when.

The voice said tomorrow and that they were pressed for time.

The guard insisted they come out with hands up.

Three men stepped out of the bush. In the black of night, all the guard could see was them standing there with their hands behind their heads.

The guard told them to follow him.

They fell in behind him. The soldier obligingly led them to the commander's tent.

The men were still shrouded by the black of night.

The soldier stuck his head in the door and said three men from the Nineteenth were there.

The colonel stood up and said that didn't make any sense. He started to step forward.

The flap on the tent jerked open and three Japanese stood in the light. The first one swung a pistol and fired. The colonel and the guard dropped to their knees and shot repeatedly. The three infiltrators lay dead on the ground.

The colonel roared his indignation.

The guard mumbled that they spoke perfect English.

The colonel screamed that the guard was an idiot that had nearly got everyone killed. He told him to get his worthless ass back out there on patrol.

The soldier rushed from the tent. Others dragged the three bodies away.

That's the kind of night we had. Have to hand it to the Japanese. They certainly tried a clever move. If their first man hadn't been such a lousy shot, no telling what would have come next.

Early in the morning on April 20, a group of Japanese came crawling up on C Company of the First Battalion. When they opened fire, three soldiers leaped to the defense of the unit. Sergeants Bill Ballard and James Cochran and PFC John MacKennis Jr. instantly moved to the perimeter of their camp to keep the attackers at bay. With the fury of a tornado, the exchange ripped through the dark.

Ballard motioned for a man behind him to get closer. The soldier crawled forward.

An explosion sent shock waves through the bushes.

Sergeant Ballard realized he didn't have many grenades. He asked the men to form a human chain and keep passing them up to him.

The sergeant hurled another grenade in front of him. For a minute, the explosion stopped the gunfire. Sergeant Cochran and PFC John MacKennis scooted away from Ballard and began throwing grenades. In turn, the Japanese threw their own grenades. Because the three American soldiers kept blasting them, the Japanese didn't get any closer.

Ballard shouted to keep them coming. The enemy was taking it in the face.

The explosions went back and forth for what seemed forever. Eventually, the enemy's grenades stopped coming. The machine guns slowed and quit.

Cochran yelled that he thought they'd run out of ammunition.

Ballard shouted to fix bayonets and get ready.

The three frontline soldiers charged into the bushes. They hadn't gone fifty yards when they caught ten enemy trying to get a jammed machine gun to fire. The soldiers cut them down instantly. The next squad was caught up against a rock wall with no way out. When Cochran and company broke through, the Japanese started throwing rocks. Obviously, that wasn't the best strategy.

Sergeant Ballard asked, "Can you believe it? Throwing rocks?"

The men shook their heads.

Maybe the craziest and certainly the most bitter fighting occurred on a tree-covered knoll just east of the southern tip of Tombstone. Lieutenant Robert Glassman led L Company up a hill Command called Hill Seven. The fighting proved to be exceptionally tough, but the men plowed ahead.

Glassman had begun briefing his men on how they might keep control of the area, when the crack of a rifle sent Robert Glassman reeling backward. Soldiers fired in every possible direction, but the lieutenant had been seriously wounded.

The medical personnel hovered around the silent leader. The sergeant concluded that he wouldn't regain consciousness. Who would take command?

Lieutenant James Young said he would. He reminded them about what Bob had said. That's what they were gonna do. Stay close and shoot like hell.

The men spread out on the top of the hill, but the machine-gun fire proved murderous. Mortar flew across the terrain. Soldiers were falling everywhere.

Young told the sergeant they had to retreat. He was to tell the men to cover each other.

With every backward step the soldiers took, the Japanese seemed to increase their fire. L Company kept shooting but were clearly outnumbered.

Machine-gun fire blasted away in a symphony of destruction and death. The Japanese, who seemed to have choreographed their assault as one long crescendo of terror, began emerging on the perimeter of the unit with bayonets drawn.

Young groaned that the Japanese were running through the fire of their own machine guns. The enemy were in a suicide attack posture. This had to be a to-the-death deal.

L Company kept firing at every Japanese that broke through. Bodies began piling up, but they didn't stop coming.

Young looked over his shoulder. With his bayonet poised to plunge into the lieutenant's back, a Japanese soldier came running as fast as he could with his head bent down.

For a second, Young stared as if he couldn't believe his eyes. The man had to be crazy or at the least out of his mind in some way. By reflex, Young fired his pistol and dropped the man only ten feet away.

Eventually, the counterattack ended, and the Japanese faded. Young led his men back down Hill Seven to where they'd begun.

Young kept muttering that the enemy were sacrificing everybody in sight to push us off that hill.

The sergeant agreed.

Young asked how many the Japanese had lost.

The sergeant shook his head. They'd had thirty-two casualties.

Company I had better success with their drive to take the same area. Their men had wound their way through terrain lined with pillboxes and caves. The Japanese had holed up in some of the tombs the Americans had encountered earlier.

Hanging on to every piece of ground they took, I Company had been able to surround each pillbox until someone tossed in a grenade that killed the resistance. The tombs proved more difficult, but the men with flamethrowers eventually cleaned out the enemy. The work was slow and tedious, but they kept advancing.

By the end of the day, they had reached the southern tip of Tombstone. Still under heavy fire, they were able to connect with L Company and start back up Hill Seven. The Japanese had already spent themselves in the push on Young's men. I Company kept coming. As the sun began to slide toward the horizon, K Company made a breakthrough and got to the top of the hill. For all their bizarre self-sacrificing, the Japanese had not prevailed. We had at last taken Tombstone.

31

Clearing the Crags

The ridge we called the escarpment cut the island in two. The high cliffs were long and pocked with caves and holes. As it turned out, the Japanese had cut passageways everywhere through the escarpment. The task was to take this one area honeycombed with Japanese tunnels and hideouts. Once we got over the summit, we'd be in the home stretch, but that's like saying once you've climbed to the top of the Empire State Building with your bare hands you'll be a real winner. Really? Forget that! The Tanabaru escarpment couldn't but turn into slaughter alley before the struggle was over.

The men knew we would be vital in the assault to take the escarpment. My artillery unit fired sporadically, and of course, we couldn't actually see our shells crash into the enemy, but the shaking of the ground confirmed the hits. Sergeant McQuiston kept the men supplied with proper coordinates, and we pounded the enemy. The problem our infantry faced would be the assault coming down from the Crags.

The Crags were jutting pinnacles that provided the enemy with excellent shooting positions. These hunks of rock had earlier proved to be a towering menace. Sooner or later, this position had to be taken out. It wouldn't be easy.

Finally, the guns went silent. We worked feverishly to build up our artillery stockpile. Every now and then, we fired at the Japanese to make sure they remembered we were out here. Finally, the Second Battalion went to work on the Crags and prepared to attack the Tanabaru escarpment proper. H Company started moving into contact with the enemy.

A guy named Lieutenant John Farnsworth moved into position to direct the fire of one of the tanks. Japanese machine guns opened up on the Sherman. Their blasts didn't slow old John down any. Farnsworth crawled up on the tank's turret and started directing where the tank should aim. Instantly, the Japanese machine guns opened up on him and the tank. Farnsworth didn't move but shouted for the Sherman tank to take aim on the enemy. Enemy fire only intensified.

Farnsworth screamed to keep firing without moving off the turret. Shooting was incessant, bullets flew past him, but he didn't move.

The tank's blast rocked it with such a jerk that Farnsworth sailed off the back of the Sherman, smashing into some bushes. The tank fired a second round.

Lieutenant Farnsworth crawled up on one knee and dusted himself off. The slamming jar of the tank's cannon fire had saved his life. The Japanese machine guns went silent.

"Got 'em!" Farnsworth shouted. "Yeah! We knocked the bastards out!"

Around noon, the First Battalion of the 381st started to move against Nishabaru Ridge. This time there was no artillery barrage to cover them. Silently creeping forward, the battalion caught the Japanese by complete surprise. Two of their companies were able to set up mortars with direct fire on the enemy. We were making real progress when another company started to move up Hill Seven, our old nemesis Hill Seven.

A lethal round from that location stopped the company in their tracks. This one location had earlier halted the 382nd and now they were doing it again. Company A swung around to engage the enemy, but the commander Lieutenant Kenneth Aakerhaus got hit in the exchange and died, leaving only four surviving officers.

Kakazu provided a cover that allowed the Japanese to stop all movement in their direction. In an effort to break the situation open, soldiers of G Company would have to make a dash for it. The commander looked at the field and estimated they had to cross 250 yards of open space. The troops were about to enter one killer of a marathon race. They certainly would be exposed.

The men looked back and forth at each other but said nothing. G Company raced into the open field. Machine-gun fire immediately opened up on them. Men fell left and right. Mortar fire spattered over the field, blowing holes around the soldiers.

The commander yelled not to stop and crumpled over from a bullet strike in the face.

Only two of the nineteen in the Third Platoon made it. Six more stayed pinned down in the field. Even though the deadly fire didn't stop, they eventually crawled across to the other end of the grassland. Four were killed and six wounded when a spigot mortar landed in their midst.

By the end of the day, we had five companies that had made it to the top of Nishabaru Ridge. The 382nd had knocked out a major objective by conquering Tombstone. Nothing about any of these accomplishments proved to be pleasant because our losses had been heavy, and the Japanese didn't stop firing. As night fell, they kept up their bombardment.

Our artillery unit had not been used with the massive forceful- ness it had in the past. Darkness began to settle, and it was time for one of those wonderful gourmet delights of such delicacies as C rations, which were precooked, ready-to-eat canned goods with such wonders as Spam. (Some poor pig had given his best for the army.) Of course, there might be K rations that were supposed to pep you up. Actually, the D rations were chocolate bars filled with goodies like nuts, which were the only item worth tasting. How- ever, after a day in the field jumping from ditch to ditch, you'd eat the bark off a tree and not mention it was on the dry side.

We ate silently and finished by tossing the empty tins away in the bushes. The truth was that we were just glad we were still in condition to eat. Too many weren't.

32

Going On

When you look around and see dead soldiers, their spent lives slap you in the face with questions, thoughts that still rumble through your mind long after the war is over. When night falls and none of the enemy appear to be creeping around, you think about these haunting enigmas. Were all those men heroes?

Some of them wound up with Bronze Stars or a Distinguished Service Cross. Silver Stars were given out and a few received the Congressional Medal of Honor. Unfortunately, those are often given posthumously. Such medals are symbols of the gallantry and bravery that saved our war effort. But I still wonder, weren't all those men heroes?

Out there crawling through barbed wire and machine-gun blasts takes more guts than one could have thought possible back in those days in boot camp. To my way of thinking, they all should have received a medal for just showing up for duty.

As I listened to McQuiston and the men talk, I didn't detect that anyone ever thought that we'd lose the war. The issue was whether they'd be around to see the end of it. The Japanese were fools to have started the clash. Once they bombed Pearl Harbor, their days were numbered. That wasn't the problem. The struggle that my men faced was whether they would go marching down the street in a victory parade or end up in a graveyard on Okinawa.

After a day of fighting for the Crags, the problem intensified. We'd lost many good boys taking that hill and the Japanese were still on the reverse side. Sure, we'd knocked out obstacles in taking Tombstone and now had five companies on top of Nishabaru Ridge. Trouble was the Japanese hung on to the downhill side. They didn't even let up when night came. Took a real hero to keep on going!

———————

April 21 came drifting in with clouds that seemed to warn another dark day was ahead. The Japanese had never let up: kept fighting like crazy to capture Nishabaru Ridge. The town side of the Crags still had enemy dug in. The men in my artillery unit kept firing and our objectives remained the same. We were aiming to take the town of Nishabaru, but we hadn't got the job done. One hell of a conundrum!

With all of that struggle boiling, we witnessed another display of heroism for sure. M Company moved into position and started up the steep slopes of the ridge with the big machine guns. The only way to get the guns up the incline was by dragging them, and the men had to pull the load. Not only was the weight of the iron choppers a problem, but moving such equipment left men exposed. The enemy didn't stop firing.

A lead soldier at one of the guns shouted for the two at the back to push harder, but the damned thing still couldn't get traction.

One of the two soldiers at the rear yelled they were pushing as hard as they could and to keep your pants on!

The lead man demanded more muscle to get the big blaster in place.

The three men had only gone a couple of yards further when the enemy opened up with constant machine-gun fire.

The lead man screamed, twisted, and tumbled backward into a clump of small brush.

The man at the rear leaped to one side, rolled, and crawled over to his buddy. He howled that the lead man had taken three shots in the chest.

One glance told Sergeant David Dovel he didn't have time to set up his machine gun on the tripod. If he didn't do something quick, they would be blown away. Grabbing the sixty-two-pound gun and holding it against his hip, Dovel began firing.

He screamed at his men to look out. The machine gun blasted instantly.

Dovel kept jumping back and forward, constantly changing positions so they couldn't get a bead on him. The Japanese kept sending knee-mortar fire, but nothing hit him. Completely exposed, he kept the rapid fire exploding in all directions.

Sergeant John Arends's machine gun got knocked out of action while Dovel was firing. Arends grabbed his automatic rifle. Motioning for Lieutenant John Stevens to join him, the two men charged the Japanese, firing those automatic rifles in the midst of a hail of machine-gun fire.

Stevens yelled to try a grenade or two. Leaping forward, he rolled and tossed a grenade straight in front of him.

The blast shook the group, but the enemy's machine gun stopped. Arends and Stevens kept charging up the hill, hurling grenades in front of them and constantly firing their rifles. At the risk of their lives, the two men wiped out a truckload of Japanese.

―――――――――

We knew how critical the assault had become because we were getting low on ammunition. The howitzers had fired without ceasing. If we ran out of shells, the Japanese might figure out we quit firing because of running low. They'd quickly come swarming in. Heaven help us! Couldn't have any of that!

Sergeant McQuiston shouted in my ear. "Ammunition bearers are hauling in another load. They also got to get ammo up to the front. They keep saying that they are getting close to running out."

I nodded. "Keep firing till we hit the bottom of an empty box."

McQuiston hurried away.

One of the guys that saved the day was Lieutenant Colonel Franklin Hartline. The West Point man had been a big-time football player at the Academy. He ended up in this fight becoming the battalion commander. You would have thought old Franklin was out there trying to earn his college letter.

The lieutenant colonel was hopping around, going from position to position, shooting any kind of gun that was lying there. Then Franklin switched and started hurling hand grenades like he was throwing a pass. He kept yelling at the mortar guys, directing where they should fire. Hartline turned up all over the battlefield and stopped for nothing. Must have scared the enemy to death.

Everyone in the encounter had been worn to the bone. I figured the Japanese would crater, but they didn't. Around three fifteen, the enemy mounted another counterattack. Our walkie-talkie rang.

"Hit the front line with all you got!" the voice on the other end shouted. "The Japanese are coming at us with everything but the kitchen sink. We will keep feeding you the coordinates. Got to stop any counterattack!" They hung up.

I handed the phone to McQuiston. "Keep your ears open for a call giving us coordinate information. I'm going to do a little reconnaissance. Don't let up unless ordered to do so."

McQuiston saluted. I took off.

Didn't take long to discover that battalions of the 383rd and 382nd were forging across the eastern end of the gorge that separated Tombstone and Nishabaru Ridge. The day before, the 382nd had taken a small hill and held it. What they didn't know was that the Japanese were playing possum, waiting for the right opportunity to come out of hiding and start the fireworks. Abruptly, machine-gun fire opened up and the firefight was on. With binoculars, I could see the men hitting the ground but not stopping.

While this action unfolded, G Company pushed their way to the edge of the village, but as soon as it looked like a breakthrough, the Japanese cut loose with a torrent of mortar fire. The boys in G found themselves getting pounded from both sides. Being exposed from their two ends made them particularly vulnerable. In short order, they lost thirteen soldiers.

"Got to get out of here," the soldier screamed in his walkie-talkie. "Give us immediate smoke cover. Now!" He slammed the phone down and started shooting.

Within minutes, airplanes zoomed in dropping smoke bombs. The curl of white smoke quickly created a ground cover that hid the soldiers.

"Get the hell back," someone yelled. "We got to blow out of here."

The men carefully beat a retreat, leaving the village behind. Hard to believe thirteen men had died there.

———————

By the end of the day, the losses had not been for naught. With the heavy loss of their own lives, our soldiers had still taken Nishabaru Ridge except for the extreme western part. The grim shadow of Kakazu still hung over that end.

As night fell, the men of the 361st Artillery unit stepped back to allow the cannons to cool. No one was sad to see the sun go down. The day had been almost unbearable.

I thought about what we had all experienced and endured. Not one of our men had been spared the agony of the day. Yeah, in my book they were all heroes.

33

The Escarpment

The Deadeyes had done quite a job. The men of the 381st and 382nd had taken a big dose of hell and given it all back special delivery airmail. The Japanese had to know they weren't dealing with Donald Duck and Mickey Mouse. However, a price was paid for every inch of ground we took away from them. The cost remained high.

Hill Seven had been a problem from the beginning. That particular hill seemed to carry a curse. While it wasn't big, the damned hunk of dirt remained fierce. Well, who should they call up but our old friend Lieutenant Hoss Mitchell. Hoss and L Company were assigned to clear out the Japanese. Taking two platoons with him, Hoss started up the hill.

Sergeant Paul Lemons crouched close to Hoss and asked if he'd seen any of them yet.

Hoss shook his head.

Lemons slipped back but kept walking. The silence became eerie.

Rifleman PFC Ed Mitchell stood at the rear. He commented that it bothered him that they hadn't heard from the enemy yet and hoped this wasn't a setup.

The man next to him nodded but didn't answer.

The unit kept moving. Abruptly, heavy mortar fire rained down on them.

Hoss called for everybody to drop down.

Rapid machine-gun fire drowned out any other conversations. The men didn't move until the roar settled.

Hoss screamed for an attack and rushed forward.

L Company eventually got to the crest of the hill and hunkered down. The Third Platoon never made it. Heavy mortar fire kept them pinned. When they could no longer move, they walkie-talkied to Hoss. No one was sure what to do, but Hoss thought they ought to wait until it got dark.

With their guns ready to fire, the men marked time. Late in the afternoon, the Japanese counterattacked. Bullets flew like hail. The soldiers kept firing back.

When the sound of battle slacked off, Hoss called the unit on the phone.

The unit reported it had been a tough one. Really tough. But they'd stopped the enemy. They had no idea how many were killed, but the bodies were all over the ground.

Hoss Mitchell thought about it for a moment and asked how many had come up the hill.

The soldier answered ten. Nine were wounded. He was all that was left.

At the same time, the men of I Company struck the Japanese on Hill Nine. Lieutenant George Weiner commanded the soldiers of the Second Platoon. As they approached the hill, Weiner knew they needed more information on what might be ahead.

Weiner told the sergeant that he was going to crawl further and get the lay of the land. He needed cover.

The sergeant nodded.

Weiner cautiously worked his way ahead of the platoon. He'd gotten about fifty yards up the hill when ten machine guns opened up from the main ridge to the south. Weiner's body jerked violently before he tumbled over backward and rolled down the hill.

The sergeant moaned that they got the lieutenant. He ordered the soldiers to start backing away.

The men quickly beat a retreat. The sergeant rolled over and grabbed the walkie-talkie to report that the enemy had just killed their platoon commander. They'd caught him from both the left and right sides. The sergeant called for the artillery people and the antitank guns to blast this area all to hell. They would be out of there within minutes.

The platoon kept retreating. Almost immediately, the artillery barrage covered the area with shells. The Japanese got Lieutenant Weiner, but we ended up wiping out the entire batch.

No matter where our men turned, the Japanese kept slugging it out. Some units had to retreat, but our men fought well even if, tragically, many died. We had cut through some of the toughest territory in the entire war, but our guys kept going. Fundamentally, the defense of the Tanabaru-Nishabaru line was broken.

───────────

By the end of the day I suspected we would gather the commanding officers as well as the executive officers and maybe the operations officers in the command tent to hear what General James Bradley and General Claudius Easley planned to do next. I walked in and nodded to a number of the men I knew who were already there.

Stretched across the front of the platform were maps of our next confrontation. Routes had already been marked out for where the 382nd Infantry would come pouring in across from Tanabaru Hill and keep marching straight ahead. Another set of lines marked the 381st coming out of Nishabaru and aiming at a place called Maeda. Obviously, careful thought had been given to this attack.

General Bradley walked to the podium and all talking ceased.

"At ease, men," Bradley began, and then stopped to clear his throat. "The last four days have been as difficult as any of us have ever faced. Even with incessant mortar and artillery fire, we have still worked our way forward. At every turn, the Japanese counterattacked. As difficult as it has been, we held them off. Nevertheless, the cost has been high. In addition to the ninety-nine men killed, we have ninety-nine who are missing. We all know what that probably means. Moreover, six hundred of our finest soldiers have been wounded. While no comparisons can be made, we killed thirteen hundred of the emperor's warriors at the same time. While you may not have felt it during the struggle, we have won a highly important victory."

A hush settled over the room. Surely, everyone appreciated the achievement, but losing eight hundred soldiers took one's breath away. The raw figures left their mark.

Bradley turned back to the large map. "We are now positioned for the next big hurdle. The escarpment is a fierce line of cliffs that cuts the island in two. That's where we are headed tomorrow."

I didn't think General Bradley even needed to say the word *escarpment* because everyone in the room knew what this ridge meant. Running almost completely across Okinawa, the escarpment had been well equipped to be the enemy's major line of defense. Whatever we had faced previously, the escarpment would be a much worse experience.

"I have six battalions on the line for a coordinated attack," General Bradley continued. "Two of Colonel Halloran's battalions will attack from the south atop Nishabaru Ridge. Kakazu will be assaulted by one battalion from both the Twenty-Seventh and the Seventh Division. We're calling this group Bradford's Task Force. Other units will be deployed in additional configurations. Are there any questions?"

Hands began going up as various leaders had their own personal questions. Commanding officers wanted more details on where to position their units. Executive services and operations officers had procedural questions.

General Bradley concluded by noting that Japanese artillery had been relatively heavy during the night. "Under the cover of darkness, we believe they have been retreating to a new position. The big guns have been a camouflage for troop movement. They are repositioning themselves to the Maeda escarpment."

As Bradley walked away, General Easley took the podium. "This recent movement and return to a new defense line reveal the truth about the enemy. We are not fighting a banzai-minded group of maniacs. We are faced with well-trained, informed, and skillful generals. Once more, we must defeat a highly competent foe."

I guess so, I thought to myself. *We're going to take another trip through hell with the cannons booming and the Japanese screaming. Here we go again.*

34

One More Hill to Climb

I walked away from the Command Center thinking about what was ahead the next day. Frankly, I had to give accolades to the men. They had physically endured the most difficult conditions with virtually no grumbling. Well, not many of us were excited about eating Spam, but the guys bit their lips or joked about having leg of pig for supper. The 381st and 382nd were one tough bunch.

The smell of war hung in the air. The constant firing of cannons sent a wave of acidic smoke that burned your nostrils. Gunfire, antitank firearms, relentless shelling with grenades or mortars blended into an aroma of destruction. And of course, the scent of death, of decaying bodies, turned your stomach. Nobody talked about these awful odors and we sure as hell didn't write home about it, but the stink stayed.

I got into my jeep and turned on the ignition. Even the jeep had a barbecued petroleum smell. As I prepared to pull out, a

memory came to mind. Hadn't thought about that odorous experience for years.

I must have been around nine years old when my stomach
started aching with a steady, dull throbbing sensation. As boys
will, I ignored it, but the hurting didn't stop. That particular
morning, I started my usual walk to school, but I only got a couple of blocks when I crumbled to the ground. I couldn't walk any
farther.

The best I could do was to crawl back to our house. I pulled
myself through the doorway and sprawled on the floor.

"Lord, help us!" my mother nearly screamed. "What's happened?"

I moaned. "My stomach's killing me."

"Get in here in that bed." She picked me up and carried me over
to their soft bed.

I tried to catch my breath, but the agony made it hard even to
breathe. Even the cat walking across the floor felt like old Tubby
made the bed shake. I couldn't stand it, but I could hear my mother
talking on the telephone.

"Yes, Dr. Seibert. Get right over here. Art's hurtin' real bad."
For a few moments, she was silent, but then she bellowed. "I mean
right now! This minute. Art's in trouble!"

I heard the receiver click as she hung up the phone attached to
the wall. I didn't want to move.

"Doctor's on his way," my mother said, hurrying around the
bedroom. "Don't you fret none. He's comin'."

When Dr. Seibert arrived, he immediately started poking
around on me. In a few minutes, he stood up. "Beulah, I'm taking
this boy to the hospital. We got a big problem. I'm sure his appendix is about to rupture. We can't waste any time."

"Oh, God help us!" Mother looked up at the ceiling and grabbed a blanket to throw around me.

Off we went in Dr. Seibert's old Ford. When we got to the simple country hospital, they wheeled me into the operating room without even hesitating at the door. They told me later the rest of that little adventure.

Apparently, when the doctor began to operate, my appendix burst. The smell was so foul some of the nurses had to leave the room. The stink of that ruptured appendix sent everyone running for fresh air.

Of course, penicillin hadn't been invented yet. Mother was certain that I would die and apparently the doctor seemed to agree. I guess I didn't, but for a while I thought I preferred a quick exit from this world. I have no idea how I survived, but I was sick for a long time.

Dr. Seibert and I saw each other so often that we became fast friends. The doc was always chewing on a stogie. Watching him chew on the stub taught me to smoke. Loved the smell. Strange how different scents affect you.

And bring back memories.

The time had come to jump off. Colonel Cyril Sterner took the Second Battalion of the 382nd up the hill. To our amazement, in forty-five minutes the entire battalion reached the top of the Tanabaru escarpment. At about the same time, the Third Battalion encountered eleven Japanese with two machine guns. In short order, they took them out and marched quickly on to the Tabletop area east of Hill Nine. Anyone acquainted with the previous struggles had to be surprised.

Bradford's Task Force discovered the same lack of resistance. As the day wore on, our soldiers kept moving forward. The town of Tanabaru fell to us. The Second Battalion captured Hill 143. Taking this hill, which dominated the surrounding area, was important. We were now in a position to observe the flashes of the enemy's big guns and could accurately hit that target.

By afternoon, we had a different picture. The Japanese cranked up the heavy artillery again and the war was back on.

So far, we'd had a day of sweeping, significant gains, but the area in front of us was formidable enough to chill the blood. The Maeda escarpment had been given another name by the soldiers on the field. Some called it Sawtooth, others Hacksaw Ridge. Those were the kinder names among a host of profane descriptions of this death trap.

The ridge abruptly rose five hundred feet above sea level before being topped by a fifty-foot precipice. Climbing up this sheer wall was possible but only with great difficulty and only at the western side. At the other end, a sheer tower of granite that we called Needle Rock shot straight up in the sky. Small hills stood scattered around the outcropping. Everyone knew we were looking at Dracula's Castle.

General Easley showed up at an observation post and declared the ridge needed "softening up." I immediately got the call from headquarters to target the ridge. I gave the coordinates to Sergeant McQuiston and told him to have the men start blasting the entire area. We began blasting a long section of the escarpment. Our objective was to pound every gun position that forward observers could locate. They would send the coordinates to Command Central and in turn the big boys would call them on to us.

The face of this high cliff was covered with machine guns that had excellent observation positions to cut down everyone in front of them. The Japanese really knew what they were doing when they fortified the front of the escarpment. Thirty-six artillery pieces blasted away with what was about the equivalent of 1,616 pounds of ammunition. In response, Corsair aircraft dive-bombed the southeast corner with twenty-four five-hundred-pound bombs and a similar number of hundred-pounders. The Corsairs proved to be one of the greatest fighter aircraft of all time. Pilots used these fast and powerful planes to help turn the tide of the Pacific War. By the end of the war in August 1945, they had knocked out over 2,140 Japanese aircraft. The American pilot kill ratio was eleven to one. The Japanese took it on the chin.

The ground shook, but the enemy kept firing. Any observer could see that we were truly up against a wall. Their rock fortress appeared to be an impregnable defense that somehow we had to figure out how to scale. As our artillery kept firing, I began to realize another dimension to this new confrontation. The enemy's leaders didn't seem to care how many soldiers they lost.

35

Onward and Upward

During the assault, the performance of some of the men stuck in my mind. Everyone gave their all, but some of the guys fought with extraordinary skill. For example, PFC Bill Reeder had been a professional baseball player before the war and had quite an arm. He looked like a World Series pitcher when he started throwing grenades at the Japanese. A couple of mortars opened up on his unit, and that sent Bill into action. He threw an entire box of grenades with such accuracy that the Japanese and their guns stopped like a truck at a stop sign. Bill was in E Company, which needed to take Needle Rock. His aim proved to be so deadly on target that the company took their objective because of his throws.

Another man that stays in my mind was PFC Lee Moore, the flamethrower. After E Company got to the top, the Japanese started a counterattack. As the enemy came rushing up the hill, Moore grabbed an automatic rifle and ran straight at them. Firing from the hip, Lee dropped the enemy like a swamp dweller swatting mosquitoes. Recognizing that they were still coming, Moore climbed on top of the rock and fired down on them right and left.

In the fray, a few of the Japanese dived into a cave. Lee saw them go in and picked up his flamethrower. Charging that cave like a mad mama bear, he turned the fire machine on full blast. Laying the nozzle down, he started throwing grenades into the cave. Lee Moore had made himself so vulnerable that it was amazing no one had shot him. When the attack was over, he had killed twenty-four Japanese. His bravery ended up being recognized with a Distinguished Service Cross.

Hard to say what makes a man stand up in the midst of bullets flying in every direction and charge the enemy. Obviously, that was taking your life in your own hands. Anyone who charged the foe with such gallantry had to know they might well be gone by the end of the day. They weren't fools and they understood the cost. I think they had to believe in something that was more important than themselves. They had families of great importance to them. These heroes made their stand because they loved their kin and country more than their own lives. That's what makes a hero.

When the assault began, I Company was immediately blocked by machine-gun fire coming from a cave on the face of the escarpment. We began to realize that the Japanese had turned that entire area of the cliff into a fortress. Their fire proved to be so fierce that the company was quickly pinned down. One of their men shared their conversations with me.

"We've got to get closer to that cave," leader Lieutenant George Weiner said. "Can we get a flamethrower up there?" He looked around at the squad.

One man raised his hand. "I've got the blaster, sir. Count me in."

"Okay. We'll give you all the ground cover we've got. You'll have to crawl up that steep slope to get close enough to have a decent shot. We'll do our best."

The man nodded, picked up the heavy unit, and slipped the pack on his back. "Ought to do the trick," he said, and picked up the nozzle. "This one can send a stream of fire that will bounce off the walls and ceilings. Gets into unseen space. I'll smoke 'em out."

The men nodded their appreciation and he started working forward.

"Alright, men," Weiner said. "Open up on that cave. I don't want any mistakes that jeopardize our man."

A barrage of gunfire aimed at the cave's entrance slowed the Japanese while the squad watched the flamethrower inch his way upward. The Japanese obviously had no idea he was coming. In short order, he got within a few feet of the entrance, then stood up and rushed to flatten himself against the megalith wall. The flamethrower exploded with a blaze of fury. The soldier waited a second and then crammed the nozzle into the entrance to the cave. Smoke roared out.

"Stay poised, men," Weiner said. "We'll charge forward as soon as we get the chance. Keep your eyes open and your heads down."

Suddenly, three simultaneous explosions sent rock and debris flying out of the entrance to the cave. Fire roared out, followed by a bellow of smoke. The flamethrower dropped to his knees and covered his head when the ground shook.

"My God!" Weiner exclaimed. "What in the hell did we hit?"

I Company rushed forward. For several minutes, the smoke continued to roll out and then finally receded.

Lieutenant Weiner crawled up next to the flamethrower. "You think we got 'em all?"

The man laughed.

"Okay. Lead us in with that zip gun of yours." Wiener waved for the rest of the men to follow.

Fire had blackened the walls and the ceiling, leaving a charcoal look to the interior. Two mangled machine guns lay broken on the rock floor. Bodies of four dead Japanese had been virtually roasted. Smoke continued to curl up from their remains.

Weiner peered into the blackness. "This cave doesn't end quickly," he mused. "Looks like the lair just keeps going. Give me a flashlight."

One of the soldiers handed him a light.

"The flamethrower must have ignited a box of ammunition," the lieutenant said. "Be cautious, but keep walking."

The cave went back about fifty feet and then veered to one side. Scratches and scrapings on the wall left the impression of pick-axes that had once extended the cave. The men kept following the winding tunnel.

Abruptly, they could faintly hear chatter. Pressing their ears to the wall, the men quickly realized Japanese were on the other side.

Lieutenant Weiner stopped and shook his head. "My God!" he said softly. "The Japanese have hooked all these caves together through a series of tunnels. We're faced with a more serious problem than we ever dreamed of."

———————

The battle raged through the day. The entire 383rd had their hands full as they discovered the reverse side of the slope swarming with Japanese. When the men of E Company discovered the openings to the cave beneath their feet, they poured crude oil and gasoline into the openings. The soldiers set the gooey mess on fire and waited for the Japanese to get smoked out. They didn't have to wait long.

Japanese came rushing out the entrance right into the path of our machine guns and mortars. They were like sitting ducks in a carnival. We were making real progress.

By the time the sun began to set, we were firmly in position on the escarpment. In addition to our losses, we had learned a considerable amount about what we were facing. Their pillboxes were made of reinforced concrete and positioned on the cliff, making them impervious to gunfire. We had discovered that the entire escarpment in front of us had tunnels and caves running everywhere like an ant den. No matter which way we turned, the Japanese would be there. Even when we hit them aboveground, they could still be beneath and behind us.

One tough predicament!

36

Deadly Deadeyes

On the morning of April 27, the 381st started to move out. After a good night's sleep, the Deadeyes were ready to rumble. Patrols started marching and the big artillery stood ready. I watched my men loading the shells and preparing for a constant barrage when the attack began. We knew that what happened during the next ten hours could prove crucial.

The Second Battalion took off with G Company and F Company coordinating the approach. The plan was for these two units to join in a unified front. As soon as they started up the escarpment, they ran into trouble. Their plan started going up in flames.

G Company called in on the walkie-talkie that they had a pill-box in front of them and the enemy was firing like crazy. They weren't sure they could move.

F Company responded that they had the same problem and it looked like the enemy was cutting a swath between the two companies.

A blast of rapid machine-gun fire cut the conversation short.

Lieutenant Owen O'Neil crawled over to F Company's Sergeant Elias Hill to ask if they could move at all.

Hill didn't think so. The damned pillbox was dug into the cliffs. They couldn't get to it without being out in the open and that was committing suicide. While they sat here trying not to get killed, the Japanese had a perfect view of their every movement. They were trapped.

O'Neil noted that F Company and G Company had the same problem. He wasn't sure they could do anything right then except dig in.

The sergeant agreed. As I listened, I knew we had to respond effectively in some way.

On the right, Lieutenant James Ruth tried to lead G Company against the pillbox fortress.

Lying flat on the ground under a hail of bullets, Sergeant Jim Crowder pulled out a pair of field glasses and studied the situation. For a full minute, Crowder watched the shadowy outline of Japanese movement.

Crowder concluded that if they got any closer than thirty yards, they were dead. The boys back there on the ledge just weren't gonna get any closer.

O'Neil thought it impossible to get out of there ourselves till nightfall. He thought the rest of the men should stay put.

O'Neil spoke softly but rapidly, telling the men to keep blasting those caves lining the escarpment. There was plenty to do keeping the enemy from making any kind of counterattack. He didn't know when they would get out of there. Might be dark. Just keep shooting. O'Neil hung up and scrunched behind a boulder.

While the frontline action unfolded, another dimension rolled out with the 763rd Tank Battalion. These soldiers had been reinforced with flamethrowing tanks and looked awesome. But when they started rolling out, they hit marshy ground.

Captain Merrill Baker slung the steel door open and stuck his head out of the tank's turret and wanted to know, "Why aren't we moving?"

Lieutenant Leon Andrews was already standing on the ground. He roared that they were stuck in this shithole of soggy soil. Had to have assistance to get out.

Baker demanded they order it.

Andrews called in to get the Ammunition and Pioneer Platoon up there. The tanks had plowed into a hellfire marsh and were stuck in the mud. He hung up and stood there smoldering.

Captain Baker growled, "Somebody screwed up and they're fouling up the entire operation!"

Andrews glared at him but said nothing.

While they were waiting, the infantry seized a hill in Maeda. Captain John Byers found Japanese in every crack in the ground. They were everywhere, as well as snipers firing out of the heavy undergrowth in a village in front of them. To make matters worse, American machine-gun bullets were ricocheting from our own units on the escarpment. The Japanese were bad enough without that added attraction that could kill you just as dead.

Finally, some progress was made on getting the 763rd Tank Battalion moving. By midafternoon, two tanks and a flamethrower pulled out.

The three tanks roared forward. For the first time, the Japanese on the south slope of the escarpment were in a position where they weren't hidden in the caves and trees. The setting fit the tank battalion's objectives to a T.

Andrews ordered into his intercom to hit 'em with everything they had.

The flamethrower tank roared forward, throwing a stream of fire that fried everyone in its path. The 763rd blasted everything in front of them. When the confrontation was over, they had killed around three hundred Japanese and knocked out fifteen to twenty machine-gun nests and four mortars.

Not a bad day's work.

On the extreme left, the Third Battalion attacked against moderate resistance and drove four hundred yards. They were now in an excellent position to attack the town of Shuri, which was less than a mile away. No one had advanced further than the Third Battalion did that day. The problem was that everybody else ended up hog-tied by the bitter resistance of the advance on the Maeda escarpment. Hordes of Japanese appeared everywhere we turned. Incessant fire came from the front, the back, and the flanks. That's hard to escape.

One of the big breakthroughs came when Captain Bollinger gambled that he could set up F Company in a different position from the usual. As darkness was falling, he knew that the night before the men had found it impossible to dig adequate foxholes in the rock and coral that surrounded the Needle. This problem allowed the counterattacking Japanese an open range on our men during the night. Bollinger decided he would scramble how the game was played.

Leaving the foxholes behind, the captain placed the men on top of the huge boulders that dotted the area and they waited. Sure enough, in the dark the Japanese came creeping in with their bayonets fixed. With a scream, they descended on the foxholes, jabbing away at what turned out to be nothing.

The men on the boulders started firing. The Japanese who came to kill were slaughtered. When the assault was over, the boys in F Company had killed forty-seven enemy.

The day had been tough and long . . . but much longer for the Japanese.

37

Endless Struggle

On April 28, the sun rose like any other morning and so did the Japanese. The enemy had to realize we were knocking them out like a fox cleaning out a henhouse. Still, they continued to be formidable. K Company 28th found that out for sure. Having discovered a number of barracks southwest of the escarpment, the soldiers set out to clean house. The result? The roof fell on them.

Lieutenant Albert Strand and thirty-six men immediately got nailed by gunfire from the barracks and the southern slope of the Maeda escarpment that the men called Sawtooth.

Strand yelled to fix bayonets and get ready for one hell of a fight.

Soldiers dropped to their knees and ducked behind a boulder or a fallen tree.

The lieutenant shouted to the men that their objective was to take that barracks. He pointed to the building nearest them and said they needed to capture that rockpile. The enemy wasn't going to throw in the towel.

No one said anything, but the men prepared for the worst. Inching their way through the thick brush, the company kept firing at the barracks while the enemy fired back just as steadily. Finally, the men weren't but yards from the building nearest them.

Strand said in a low voice that they were going to rush the side of the barracks. When he swung his arm forward, they were to run like hell right at it.

The Japanese fired a few more rounds and then stopped. Sounded like they might be reloading.

Strand shouted and rushed forward. The men followed.

The lieutenant knew that they'd be coming out quick. He lifted his rifle.

A Japanese soldier ran around the back of the barracks. One of the men fired and he fell backward. A couple more came through the open window, and then the barracks emptied out a group of them. Men were swinging their rifles forward like lances.

A couple of Japanese had long officer's samurai swords that they swung like baseball bats. A swordsman caught one of our men across the throat and virtually decapitated him. Another soldier screamed and plunged his bayonet into the stomach of the attacking Japanese. The enemy screamed and grabbed his belly, dropping the samurai sword.

A soldier yelled to Lieutenant Strand and fired. Strand looked over his shoulder just as the enemy sank to his knees and dropped.

A Japanese came through the window opening and jumped on one of our men. Before the soldier could turn, the enemy plunged a bayonet into his back, pushed him to the ground, and stomped on his head. Before the Japanese could raise his rifle, a soldier caught him in the side of the head with the butt of his rifle. The Japanese bounced off the side of the barracks. The soldier rammed a trench knife into his heart and stabbed him twice before the Japanese could move.

The fight went back and forth for several minutes until the last Japanese had been killed. In the sudden quiet, a few of the men stood around with faces turning white, saying nothing. Others kept rubbing their blood-red hands and holding on to their helmets. Never had any of them seen such fierce hand-to-hand combat. Of the thirty-six K Company attackers, only twenty-four remained alive.

The walkie-talkie rang.

It was Colonel Daniel Nolan calling to check on how they were doing.

The report was about as bad as it gets. They had just got through going at the enemy with bayonets and trench blade knives. A really tough struggle, indeed!

Nolan asked slowly about what was next.

Lieutenant Strand said he could see more Japanese in front of them than he had men of his own. Still, Strand said he thought they could advance.

Nolan said God bless you and hung up.

The lieutenant told the men to hang on and take the other barracks.

The men dropped to their knees and started inching forward. They had barely turned the corner when Japanese appeared to be coming out of everywhere. The men fired constantly, and the enemy fell constantly. The exchange continued unabated, but after exchange upon exchange, it appeared there were a million Japanese to replace every fallen American.

The sergeant crawled next to Strand and told him they couldn't stand this assault must longer because they were going to run out of bullets if the enemy didn't overwhelm them first.

Strand nodded and rang up the walkie-talkie, calling Colonel Nolan.

He told the colonel there were just too many snakes in the grass. They had to back out of there. Could they drop smoke on them?

The colonel said it would take a few minutes, but it was on the way. Major Howard Miles would execute the order.

Strand hung up and told the men that smoke was on the way. As soon as the planes dropped the canisters, they were getting out of there.

The sergeant crawled away.

The roar of airplanes came even faster than Strand expected. Diving in and out, the Corsairs attacked the barracks and surrounded the area with a thick fog.

Strand ordered the men to get the wounded out first. "Keep firing back, then get the hell out of here just as we came in."

In short order, the remnant of K Company beat it back through the bushes, carrying the wounded and dying. The smoke bombs provided adequate cover for the men to get out of the range of fire. When they reached the rear, Colonel Nolan and Major Miles were waiting.

Nolan congratulated them on putting up one hell of a fight. He wanted to know how many were left.

Strand shook his head. They were nearly wiped out and didn't have a count on how many could still walk. They were near the bottom.

Colonel Nolan nodded and said he was sorry, so sorry. He

guessed they would have to combine with I Company to have enough men to function.

Major Miles shrugged and said, "I doubt if we got seventy in a combined company."

Nolan shook his head. "I know it's a bad deal."

The lieutenant saluted, looked down, and walked on.

For a moment Nolan watched him drag away. Then he said that Miles was one good man. A fine soldier.

———————

During the morning, Captain Louis Reuter took the G Company on an exploratory mission. They could see ahead of them the entrance to a large cave. Reuter halted the men.

He took two of them to make a preliminary search. They needed to know what was in that cavern.

The men nodded and aimed their rifles at the cave. The three men cautiously inched their way forward. For whatever reason, no Japanese fired on them.

The captain instructed the two men to follow him. He would creep in first to see what the enemy was hiding in there.

Reuter cautiously slipped around the side of the entrance but to his surprise found no one inside. Looked like the locals had exited out the back door and taken a little stroll down for teatime.

The men kept moving slowly and cautiously down the passageway but found no one.

Then one of the soldiers pointed ahead at a slight beam of light.

The men crept closer. They found themselves in a large room that had been carved out of the rock. Three tunnels ran in different directions. A hole cut in one of the walls opened to the outside world.

Reuter was shocked to see that they had a complete view of the landing beaches and the terrain we had sweated blood getting across. They could study every move the army made.

The Japanese might have hidden an army in here, one soldier observed.

Another soldier had the feeling that they could have lived indefinitely in this den. Tunnels went every which way.

Reuter held up his hand and told them to listen.

One of the men leaned against the wall. The sound of gibberish echoed faintly from the other side.

Japanese were on the other side of that wall. It couldn't be very thick if the Americans could hear them. The enemy had no idea they were there.

The soldiers recognized they were gonna have one hell of a job cleaning out these tunnels.

"Yeah, without them killing us," Reuter added.

38

Digging In

The discovery of caves and tunnels proved to be a stifling development. The more we uncovered, the more dread we felt. The Japanese had probably concluded they could hold out forever shooting from these clandestine locations. We didn't have forever.

Sergeant Harlan Stretch and his platoon had spent the night on top of the escarpment. Strange sounds and sights had erupted that proved disconcerting. With no idea what was going on, the platoon became part of the investigation into what the Japanese had created in the caves.

The next morning Stretch talked with Captain Louis Reuter.

Stretch reported that a weird thing had happened the previous night. Reuter looked askance at him as if he knew what he was going to say. The captain asked if the Frankenstein monster had walked through his camp.

While they were sleeping, Stretch reported, they'd started hearing voices. Bizarre sounds. Goofy. He swore it sounded like

Japanese gobbledygook. Then every now and then strange beams of light popped up. Just as suddenly, they disappeared.

Reuter stiffened and asked if it sounded like it was coming from underneath them.

Stretch brightened. It was exactly like it was coming up out of the ground! Was that spooky or what?

Reuter nodded and told him he was not crazy. The sergeant had heard the Japanese going back and forth in tunnels right underneath him.

Harlan Stretch swallowed hard. The Japanese were roaming around under the ground?

Reuter explained how they had discovered the facts yesterday when they explored one of the caves. The Japanese had built tunnels all over the damned escarpment. The Americans were not just fighting the enemy out there ahead of them, but those under the cliffs as well.

Stretch rubbed his mouth nervously and wondered what they were gonna do.

Reuter said they had no alternative but to find those sonofabitches and cut their friggin' heads off. The men should pay attention to what was under them.

The sergeant shook his head and moaned that if it wasn't one thing, it was another. He walked away shaking his head.

The captain stood there for a minute thinking about the situation. Obviously, discovering a swarm of soldiers under their feet would be unnerving to the men. Moreover, who knew what kind of gimmick the enemy might come up with that would shoot up through the ground. The entire situation was bad.

Captain Reuter reached for the walkie-talkie and called Colonel Nolan.

The gruff voice barked.

Reuter reported the big problem of tunnels running every-where across the escarpment. "It's like they have a subway down there. We better face it before we get bit in the ass."

Nolan paused for a moment and asked what he was suggesting.

"We need to rustle up some barrels of crude oil and gasoline."

Sergeant McQuiston approached me while we were waiting for orders from Command Central. "The men are ready to fire the artillery. When do we start?"

"I got word that the Japanese are dug in those caves and tunnels that line the escarpment," I said. "We can't blast them because they're underground. All we'd do is knock our men off the top."

The sergeant rubbed his chin. "We got to do something."

"Right now, we can only wait," I said. "I'm afraid we got to depend on the right answers coming down the pike."

McQuiston shook his head and walked off.

While we were waiting, F Company had hunkered down on Needle Rock. They were expecting relief from another company that would allow them to climb down. While they were waiting, someone started warming up some coffee. The men sat around waiting for the next crew to come in. I had already communicated with them.

Suddenly out of nowhere, a Japanese officer stood up in plain sight and started waving a saber over his head and screaming something or the other in one of their battle cries. The enemy came flying out from behind every rock and tree. F Company had been so surprised that coffee flew everywhere as men dashed for their rifles.

Captain Bollinger began yelling commands. "Those bastards are coming in. Shoot 'em! Damn it! Shoot!"

After a couple of minutes of shooting, a sergeant crawled over to say they couldn't stop them. As fast as they knocked one enemy down, two more popped up.

Bollinger grimaced. He could see the situation. They had no choice but to retreat from this godforsaken Needle Rock. The men should back off.

The sergeant scrambled through the maze of gunfire, shouting, "Retreat! Leave the worthless hill to those damned Japanese. Get out of here!"

Hand grenades flew like snowballs. A Japanese set up a machine gun in the middle of the hill and started blasting.

Bollinger screamed, "Shoot the guttersnipe! Get him before he gets you!"

Two soldiers fell backward with wounds in their legs. The Japanese started to adjust the sight to shoot higher, but one of our men got within a few feet and shot him dead. I could see this was a critical situation.

The sergeant yelled that they were all over them. They had to do something.

Bollinger called our artillery unit. "Shaw! You've got to blast the Needle. They're killing us."

I listened carefully. "You got the coordinates?"

Bollinger barked them over the phone.

"Hey, isn't that where you are?"

"Yes," the captain said factually.

"We'd be dropping bombshells on you."

Bollinger paused. "We're probably not going to get out of here any other way. We'll have to take our chances. Get on with it, Major Shaw." He hung up.

As the artillery rounds fell, PFC Lundman got trapped on a high ledge. When he realized the Japanese were prevailing, he dropped to the ground like he was dead, but he could watch the enemy overrunning the camp. They grabbed American cigarettes off dead bodies and started puffing away. A few finished off the coffee still simmering in a pot over a campfire. The private watched in agonizing silence and didn't move.

Finally, F Company's Sergeant Lloyd Dodd realized that Lundman had been left behind on that precarious ledge. He knew what they had to do.

They couldn't leave Lundman. They had to go back and get him even though enemy were all over the place. Dodd knew how treacherous the return would be, but they had to kick ass big-time.

The men charged up to the crest of the outcropping of rocks and came firing like assassins from hell. Caught by surprise, the Japanese started running. This time the enemy beat a retreat.

Dodd bent down over the private and asked Lundman if he was okay.

He had a couple of shrapnel wounds from our own mortars but thought he was okay. He asked the sergeant, "How many did we get?"

Best that Dodd could see—fifteen dead Japanese.

We knew tunnels ran all over the escarpment and had to be dealt with and cleaned out. Many of the passageways broke off from single tunnels dug straight down through the cliff like endless chimneys. Trying to climb into one of those holes exposed our men to being shot on the next levels below. The best idea was the one from Captain Louis Reuter, who'd suggested we pour drums of oil and gasoline down the shafts inside the rock fortress and then set them ablaze with flamethrowers. When we got through, the Japanese ought to be running for their lives.

The men started pouring black oil in openings. You could hear the goo splash clear down to China. Tanks of gasoline were emptied last, coating the walls with stinky old Texaco brand X that would explode like a volcano. One of the men with a flame-thrower stepped up to the hole and blasted the raunchy mix. Fire shot everywhere. Smoke filled your nose. The enemy's security tunnels turned into their own private death traps. No telling how many Japanese had died in the blast.

Smoke came pouring out of even fairly remote caves some distance from the top of the cliffs. Far from going out immediately, the steam rose and the fire burned for a long time. The Japanese wouldn't be attacking us from inside the escarpment anymore.

Job done.

39

Making Do

I wouldn't say that I was a fatalist who believed my death would come in some way over which I had no control. Of course, it would be true. When the final train pulls out of the station, I'll have no say over when I take my ride out of this world. However, out there in Okinawa, I just tried to hang on. Religion of any kind wasn't really any part of it.

One morning I watched Chaplain John Reagan saying Mass for the 383rd Infantry. Father Reagan had his hands full administering comfort and final rites because so many men were wounded or killed. Walking around without a pistol was a tough assignment out there where the Japanese would kill you for no other reason than you were standing there.

Father Reagan wore one of those long white albs and a chasuble with a bright-colored strip down the center. The men were kneeling in the dirt around a makeshift altar that was actually only a wooden table pulled out of somebody's tent. When the priest held up a gold chalice, many of the men leaned forward with their faces close to the ground. I had no doubt they were sincere. When you know you could be dead by the end of the day, earnest fervor comes easy.

I appreciated those men and their devotion. The problem was that I just didn't live there. Wasn't my thing. My head was into staying alive and keeping those around me in the same boat. In addition to the Catholics, we had a few Jewish boys. I knew virtually nothing about them. Actually, I didn't know much about religion at all. I hadn't grown up doing the God business.

That morning I just walked away from the service. The truth was that this war was a night-and-day operation. The Japanese were just as likely to come tiptoeing out of the dark as they were in the broad daylight. I figured that I had to keep my mind on business if I was going to survive.

Up there on the front line, the 383rd weren't neglected by the Japanese at night. One time, out of the blackness of evening, a mortar barrage opened up followed by everything from grenades to spears. The bad boys came charging out of the trees and up Bald Hill like hungry wolves. In the dark, they could get to us faster than we could see them coming. They hit G Company particularly hard.

PFC Charles Starr dropped to the ground when a bullet grazed his helmet. All around him men were falling. He knew he had to do something.

The soldier next to him warned that if he stood up, "They'll blow a hole in you the size of Chicago."

But, the private replied, if they didn't hit 'em back, they were dead anyway. They couldn't let them prevail.

The other soldier didn't answer. When he looked again, Starr discovered he had been hit square in the forehead.

Starr rose up on one knee and started firing his Browning automatic rifle in every direction. After a round or two, he placed the rifle on the ground and started throwing hand grenades. In rapid succession, he went back and forth between the gun and the explosives. The enemy attack stopped.

Someone shouted that tanks were coming up on the back side. No hair was growing on Bald Hill that night.

The roar of tanks became deafening. Blasts from the big tanks shook the ground and roared around the hill. Charles Starr put another clip in his BAR and started shooting again.

When Starr next looked around, he quickly realized that not many of their men were left. With mortars flying overhead, he had no time to reflect on what he couldn't avoid seeing. He kept shooting.

The roar of the tanks grew louder while the fire from the Japanese diminished. Starr watched one of the Sherman tanks roll into their area. A big headlight illuminated everything in front of the massive killing machine. The steel turret door popped open and a man wearing a football-type helmet stuck his head out.

The tank driver asked where the rest of the company was.

Starr fumbled for the words. He finally said, "Gone."

The tank driver's mouth dropped.

They'd started out with thirty men. Now, Starr said, he could only count nine. Of course, it was too dark for accuracy.

The tank driver groaned and paused for a moment. He said, "If numbers offer any consolation, I expect between us we killed about three hundred Japanese." The steel lid fell shut and he drove off.

Starr watched the tank crash through low brush and disappear into the night.

I later discovered that an L Company platoon experienced much the same problem, but not without hitting the enemy in the face. The assault proved to be particularly brutal on most of our men. In the exchange, the platoon leader had been killed along with every commanding officer. PFC Everett Chittenden looked around and realized he was all that was left.

One of the men said, "You're all we got. We just elected you the chairman of the board. Let's go."

Chittenden shook his head and groaned: it was a sorry mess.

The unit plunged into a return attack on a strong Japanese unit. The fire back and forth remained heavy. Chittenden leaped into action, hitting the Japanese that had previously killed their men.

Without saying a word, the private rushed toward the Japanese sitting behind a machine gun. Apparently, the gun had jammed, but before they could clear the chamber, Chittenden shot them.

A Sherman tank rolled into the clearing and Everett jumped on the back, scrambling up to the top and warning that enemy were on the left. Turn to the left!

The tank pivoted and fired. Chittenden had to hang on for dear life.

The private ordered, "Straight ahead!" and the tank roared on.

Chittenden quickly recognized that snipers were firing at them from behind trees and had to be taken out. If they didn't stop the assault, the Japanese would just keep picking off soldiers.

The PFC ordered the surviving men to knock out the lousy bad news bears. He charged into the bushes with the men behind him.

Chittenden caught the first sniper loading his rifle and cut him down. Without slowing, the private turned in the direction from where he could see a rifle firing. Dropping to a knee, he watched for a moment. Forty yards ahead, a face peered around the trunk of a tree. Everett nailed him on the spot.

Chittenden called to his men to clean them out.

The unit had walked a short distance when another sniper dropped one of the men. Before the Japanese could retreat, Chittenden struck.

The men broke through the trees into an opening and cautiously looked around. They thought they had cleared the area and rolled the enemy back.

A rifle shot cracked from a ridge in front of them. Chittenden swayed for a moment before falling face forward. The men pulled him back into the trees, but it was too late.

PFC Everett Chittenden posthumously received the Distinguished Service Cross.

That's what was on my mind day and night. Watching good, valiant men die eats away at your sensitivities. God talk just seemed on another planet somewhere far beyond us. Our eyes were fixed on making sure we didn't fall like Everett Chittenden did.

40

Plowing Ahead

On May 11, the Tenth Army threw four divisions at the Japanese. The Ninety-Sixth took the extreme left side of the attack and the Seventy-Seventh went to the right. Into this action, the US Marine Corps sent in their First and Sixth divisions. The Ninety-Sixth charged for the high ground that guarded the town of Shuri. The main thrust went to the 382nd against the entire Shuri area. The high ground around Shuri had to be taken for us to make real progress. The charge was on.

Not much has been said so far about the marines because I didn't have much contact with them, but they were out there doing their regular outstanding job big-time. Some of the stories of their success filtered back through the lines. One of the Marine Raiders was a guy named PFC Ollie Faye O'Dell who was rumored to be one tough son of a gun. His buddies called him Digger O'Dell.

O'Dell and another marine had been dispatched across an open field covered with high grass. They'd gotten about halfway across when they realized they were surrounded by Japanese hiding in the grass. The two men had walked into a trap. PFC O'Dell instantly shoved his buddy down on the ground to avoid his being hit. Swinging in every direction, O'Dell's automatic tommy gun fired like a machine gun. O'Dell kept blasting while he put one boot on his buddy's back to keep him from getting up. When he quit shooting, O'Dell had killed fifteen Japanese and saved the other man's life. That's a pretty accurate picture of the kind of men the marines were. Tough bunch of guys!

The road to Shuri took the 382nd through new terrain. The sheer rocky escarpment had blocked any forward advance because the caves and superior position of the cliffs gave the Japanese leverage. Cleaning out tunnels and winding escape routes had been an arduous task. My artillery howitzer cannons had shelled the cliff face constantly, but had often made little more than a dent in the rock. Only by pouring oil and explosives down those holes in the escarpment had we been able to dislodge the enemy.

Our path to Shuri was on much flatter land. Ahead of our advance were clay hills and ridges with caves. Trees dotted the slopes. Two major hills with the code names Dick and Oboe stood ahead on either side of our path. The commanding officer of the 382nd Infantry, Colonel Macey Dill, figured that these hills would make an excellent jumping-off location for the big push to finish the Japanese war machine. They had to be taken. But first we had to get there, taking smaller hills as we went.

When the men moved out, the First Battalion launched a mortar that knocked out the machine-gun nest sitting on the top of a hill and made it much easier to advance. Unfortunately, B Company tried to reach a draw between hills and got pinned down by heavy fire. They couldn't see any way out.

That's when Lieutenant Seymour Terry went into action. Before the war, the lieutenant had been an executive in a dairy in Little Rock, Arkansas. An ordinary American guy, Terry had extraordinary courage. He could see a cave and a trench at the other end of a draw, and realized that's where the Japanese were shooting our soldiers from. Grabbing a phosphorous grenade, he hurled the explosive into the cave. When phosphorous sprayed the cave, the enemy had to come out. Terry stood there with his rifle picking them off when they rushed out. He threw more grenades in another cave, but the Japanese started tossing them back. Grabbing satchel charges, he crawled near the entrance and threw the explosives in. The blast finished off the resistance.

But there was more. Terry found five additional caves filled with Japanese armed to the teeth. Inching his way from cave to cave, he kept slinging the satchels. Eventually, Lieutenant Terry wiped out the entire enemy squad. He had killed at least thirty Japanese through nothing more than courageous effort.

He didn't stop there. For the next three days, the lieutenant continued to exhibit fierce courage. His daring attacks cleaned out resistance to our forward progress. Finally, Terry paid the ultimate price and fell on the battlefield. What he had accomplished proved to be so significant that when the war was over, Lieutenant Seymour Terry was posthumously award the Medal of Honor, the highest honor given by the country.

The Japanese were anything but happy about our progress. From one of the few caves they still held, the enemy dragged out a 75mm artillery piece ready to wipe us out. Fortunately, one of our companies saw the cannon being positioned for action and knocked it out. The Japanese mounted a counterattack in virtually every direction open to them. Firing continued through the entire afternoon. By eight o'clock that night, the soldiers had killed 122 Japanese with only twelve of our men deceased.

While this assault unfolded, I Company fought another ferocious battle coming up the east slope. A rain of fire poured down on them. No one was sure which way to turn. Finally, Sergeant James Mason confronted the Japanese head-on.

Mason yelled to give him a grenade and shouted that the bastards were right in front of him.

A soldier crawled over and handed him one.

Mason screamed and slung the explosive.

The grenade exploded, but the Japanese hurled another one back at him. The sergeant grabbed it and threw it straight back at them. The explosion was deafening.

The soldier lying next to Mason asked how far they were from the enemy.

The answer was about a hundred feet: the enemy were on top of them. Mason hurled another grenade.

Once more the Japanese answered with a return grenade. Shrapnel flew everywhere.

Mason stood up and hurled one more grenade. The ground shook.

Machine-gun fire opened up, forcing Sergeant Mason to roll next to a boulder sticking up out of the ground. Mason listened carefully. The machine gun kept firing, but it revealed a location. Mason pulled a pin, counted to three, and hurled another grenade directly at the roaring sound. Once the blast and smoke from the explosion died out, it was clear he had hit the gunners.

The exchange continued for the next thirty minutes and then ended. Sergeant Mason had wiped out the Japanese.

By the end of the afternoon, the 382nd had put in a good day's work. They had greatly improved their position and stabilized their situation. The sacrifices and bravery from men like Lieutenant Terry and Sergeant Mason, as well as from all the units, had pushed the Japanese back. However, the problem was that the enemy had set up on hills Oboe and Dick and had unimpaired observation of what we were doing and where our troops were moving. Oboe was the highest hill in the Shuri area, once again giving them a superior position to fire at us. A critical survey of the situation demanded tanks. They were necessary to first knock off a hill called Zebra.

C Company started around the west end of Zebra and nearly had the area contained, but the going continued to be rough. PFC George Ault recognized that the Japanese had a machine-gun nest that had to be wiped out if any more progress was to be made. Moreover, they were taking out too many of our men and something decisive had to be done immediately. Ault jumped up and knocked out two Japanese in the first foxhole he came to. Not far ahead had to be the pocket of machine gunners. George rushed at them and leaped into a trench where eight Japanese had three machine guns. Before the enemy knew what hit them, Ault wiped out the entire unit. His extraordinary action cleared the way for the rest of the soldiers to surge forward even if a few caves remained occupied by the enemy.

Still, the deadly fire didn't stop, and good men were getting wounded. Smoke bombs were dropped that allowed the tanks to move forward. The situation demanded that the tanks start evacuating the large number of wounded soldiers. Two tanks kept roaring through the smoke and picking up our guys, but C Company kept taking it on the chin. Sergeant Bill Ballard, who had been leading the charge, got hit in the leg and went down. Even with this injury Ballard wouldn't allow himself to be rescued until all the other men were out. Finally, PFC John MacKennis Jr. had to take command. No noncommissioned officers were left.

On the morning of May 11, the tanks returned to clear a path, but mines were everywhere and soon two were disabled. By the end of the day, six tanks had been hit. The battle went back and forth, and artillery screamed through the air. The battlefield felt like a hurricane season of bullets leveling everything and everybody in sight. The enemy had become well entrenched and weren't giving up or retreating easily. Not much ground was taken, but by the end of the day almost 150 Japanese had been killed and a large number of caves sealed. Their position had been seriously weakened.

41

Disaster

Strange how you can get on each other's nerves. Seeing the same guys day in and day out tends to wear on one. You end up liking or hating 'em. At first, you don't think much about it, but with time their unique peculiarities get under your skin. Everybody's got 'em. Doesn't have to be something big, just repetitious. Like Hans Goins would sit around eyeing people and figuring out who he could gig next. Day after day, he'd keep it up. Lieutenant John Hayes was forever saying, "You got it?" Almost after every sentence, he asked, "You got it?" Made me want to respond, "Say that again and you're going to get it." Sergeant McQuiston constantly scratched his head. You didn't notice it at first, but after fifty scratches you wanted to ask him if he needed hair oil. Add the pressure of thinking this might be the day you got killed, those small annoyances could almost make you reach for a club.

I had to keep my mouth shut and pay attention to taking care of the men in the 361st unit. Being the operations officer meant I had the responsibility to keep everything running smoothly. I had to swallow those small irritations. No matter how annoying they might be.

May 13 looked like another one of those "blow 'em all to hell" days. We'd been told to stand ready for the order to start firing. The men didn't appear nervous, but you could never tell. Once we fired up the big howitzers, anything was possible. The roar could make you deaf without earplugs in. My guess was everyone had to be a little on edge.

Corporal Hans Goins stood there with that mischievous grin that meant he was getting ready to needle somebody. Goins sidled up to Swinging Bill Arnold. "Is it true your mother was a monkey? 'Cause you sure look like one."

Arnold didn't even hesitate. Almost by reflex, he swung at Goins, missing his chin only by an inch.

"Hey! Just kidding," Goins said. "Back off."

"You sonofabitch," Arnold growled. "I'll teach you to—"

"Okay, boys." McQuiston stepped between the two men. "Let's not start something that will end up putting one or both of you in the brig."

Old Swinging Bill crouched down. "I don't care," he hissed. "I'm gonna knock your damn face off."

"Yes, you do care." Lieutenant Hayes grabbed Bill's arm. "We got too much goin' on for this kind of nonsense." He turned to Hans. "Now, keep your big mouth shut before someone cleans your teeth with their fist."

The corporal shrugged, nodded, and walked away.

"Alright, Arnold," McQuiston said. "Cool off. You know Goins just likes to get a rise out of anyone he can. The fool doesn't know when to quit."

I could see that Swinging Bill's eyes were almost dilated with anger. Hitting the mother button pushed him into a state of extreme agitation. Goins was lucky Arnold didn't swing a knife. I waited a minute before I walked over to him.

"Goins got to you," I said. "The man's an ass for doing that sort of thing, but he didn't mean anything about your mother. He was just tryin' to get under your skin."

Arnold looked at me with an intense stare. I wasn't sure what the look meant.

"Your mother *was* a fine person."

Bill's face shifted from an angry glare to a softened, hurt look. He didn't say anything and walked away.

Hans Goins had gone over to one of the cannons and was standing there smoking a cigarette. I walked over to him.

"You enjoy being a loudmouth jerk?" I said. "'Cause you were one today."

The corporal twisted his eyebrows and looked away.

"I'd suggest you leave Corporal Arnold alone, and you might get a new writer for those lousy jokes before someone stuffs a shoe down your throat."

Goins nodded. "Look. When we just sit around here doing nothing, it gets old. A little levity loosens everyone up. You know how it is, Major. We all get a little tense."

"Insulting people doesn't provide relief. Got me?"

Goins nodded but didn't say anything.

Yeah, this was going to be a "blow 'em all to hell" day for sure.

After that little episode, the men wandered off into a discussion about what we were accomplishing. A few guys weren't sure.

Lee Lewis shook his head. "All I do is toss shells into those huge barrels. They're hot as a firecracker. Wonder they don't melt down. I hope we're doing something good."

George Morris agreed. "All I do all day is fire at invisible targets. Can't help but wonder if we're really doing any good."

The men fell silent.

———————

The next move was to take a ridge with three main peaks that Command called hills. For strategic purposes, the area was called Dick Baker, Dick Able, Dick Right, Dick Center, and Dick Left. The officers knew this piece of land had to be taken. The First Battalion had the assignment to capture Dick Baker. Tanks were in place and would be used to evacuate casualties. The Seventy-Seventh Division would stay adjacent to the First Battalion. The units were in ready position for the assault.

Colonel Macey Dill ordered Colonel Charles Johnson's First Battalion to take the field, so they started up the Dick Baker incline. B Company found themselves in a surprising position, taking the hill in record time with almost no resistance.

Captain Seymour Terry asked Colonel Johnson what he made of it.

Johnson didn't know. He knew that usually taking the high ground like they just did in such an easy jaunt meant something bad was waiting on the other end.

Terry said he'd make sure the clip was in place in his gun. When he was hurling hand grenades at the Japanese, at least he knew where the bad boys were. Right then he wasn't sure about anything. He couldn't believe the enemy had just abandoned the hill.

Johnson said to tell the men to be extra careful. They couldn't ever tell who might be hiding under a rock.

The captain started walking from man to man. Over and over he repeated for them to keep their eyes open and to pay attention. They had to watch out for a trick, he warned them over and over.

Johnson told Terry that he must have been through some heavy shit: he seemed unshakeable.

Terry laughed. He had once run a dairy barn that produced milk that was delivered all over the state of Arkansas. He had milk become sour and trucks turn over, but they just kept on rolling. He figured this run was of that order. "We just keep producing regardless of what occurs."

Johnson laughed. "I wouldn't say this was exactly like milking cows, but I like your spirit."

Terry observed that the British would say "Keep a stiff upper lip! Cheer up, old man, and queue up."

Johnson kept grinning and said, "His Majesty, King George of England, would be proud."

Suddenly the entire hill shook from the explosion of 90mm artillery fire that rattled everyone's teeth.

"Stiff upper lip, hell," Johnson said, and dived for the ground.

Another artillery shell leveled trees with a follow-up shock.

Captain Terry shouted for them to take cover.

Explosions happened everywhere. One after another, 90mm blasts became deafening. First Platoon had virtually no place to hide from the bombs that kept dropping. Three more 90mm smashed into the platoon.

Terry realized the enemy had just been waiting for them to climb the hill. They had walked into a bushwhacking trap.

Colonel Johnson screamed for retreat.

A 150mm bomb dropped in the middle of the squad. The over-whelming force sent Johnson flying backward into the bushes.

The assault changed. Knee-mortar shells began bombarding the platoon, flying in from all directions.

Terry shouted before one of the mortar shells caught him square in the chest. Company Commander Seymour Terry was gone.

The soldiers tried to scramble backward, but most of the men were hit by the bombardment. Finally, B Company had to aban-don their position. Two men reached the bottom of the hill. A Company's Lieutenant Woodrow Anderson rushed over to them.

One soldier looked up with a trickle of blood running down the side of his face. He said they'd started out with fifteen men and only had two left.

Anderson cried out for God's help.

———————

The truth was that in the midst of the losses of Johnson's unit, we actually did well that day in our overall strategy. Naval fire from the ocean and the artillery of the 361st and the 362nd flattened the enemy in ways that no one could immediately see. A column of Japanese had been moving up from Shuri when we got our sights set on them. The entire unit ended up blown all to hell. When the First Battalion surged forward, more than four hundred Japanese bit the dust. The 383rd Infantry stormed up to the top of Conical Hill by wiping out all opposition in their path.

That day the Deadeyes gained a foothold in the hills of ines-timable importance to the forward advance of our soldiers. The Japanese knew the importance of this strip of land. Trying to keep us out, they had sacrificed over a thousand men that one day. Their sacrifices were to no avail because we had now gained the upper hand.

Even though the staggering losses of B Company cut to the bone, we had driven nails into the Japanese coffin. They knew—we knew—they were being driven back and couldn't stop us.

The 361st Field Artillery Battalion fired throughout the entire day. Sergeant McQuiston had been a slave driver, keeping the men at the job. The day proved to be long, but there was nothing boring about hour after hour of shelling.

Around eight that evening, McQuiston approached me. "Major, I think we settled the question about whether we were doing any good or not. Artillery made all the difference today."

I nodded. "McQuiston, these men can be proud. They may not have seen the destruction actually happen, but they did blow the Japanese's legs off."

42

Conical Hill

Conical Hill consisted of rambling spurs and ridges around a con-
ically shaped peak. The top of the massive peak shot up almost
five hundred feet and dominated the terrain around it. Anyone as-
sessing the formidable sight knew this would prove to be a tough
one to capture. Conical Hill certainly was strategic, because the
port city of Yonabaru was only a thousand yards to the south. The
third-largest city on the island faced the Chinen Peninsula across
Yonabaru Bay. From that perspective, the Japanese had been able
to see everything we did. The entire area would be highly important to whoever captured or lost it.

The hills approaching Conical had been labeled with code
names Easy, Fox, Charlie, and King. The Second Battalion was
sent to strike in the south, while the 763rd Tank Battalion came
from another direction. In the shuffle, the commanding officer of
the tank battalion, Lieutenant Colonel Harmon Edmonson, had
gone out to check the forward movement of the unit. Mortar fire

caught Edmonson and killed him. The loss shook everyone. Taking those hills and finally Conical was obviously going to be as difficult as suspected, but the race was on.

A Company was given the job of taking the crest of Easy Hill, where the Japanese had an excellent position at the top and could rain grenades down on anyone trying to make it up the hill. I had to listen carefully to understand where the artillery should fire.

Sergeant Ben Tlougan quickly sized up the situation for us. "We're not going to be able to do much of anything till we clean out that hilltop."

"I can see that," the soldier next to him said. "But I don't see what we can do about it."

"I do," Tlougan said. "Cover me."

The sergeant jumped up and ran ahead of the platoon. He hit a grassy area and rolled under a fallen log. The Japanese opened up on him, but Ben was ready. When the rifle fire stopped, he started firing grenades at the top of the hill. The Japanese responded in kind.

Tlougan didn't move but kept hurling grenades ahead of him. After several rounds were exchanged, he stood up and started firing. The Japanese appeared unready for such a bold move. A few enemy shot back, but most got up and started running. Almost single-handedly, the sergeant had taken Easy Hill.

In a short while, A Company moved on and took Fox Hill. What had been defended by twenty to thirty Japanese fell before the relentless drive of men like Tlougan. A Company had made a good start in sweeping toward Conical Hill.

While this action unfolded, F Company attacked the coastal side, aiming at the town of Gaja. Just short of Conical, they started up a draw when fire opened up. Three men fell immediately, and the platoon stayed pinned down for three hours before they were forced to retreat. The problem wasn't new. The day before, F Company had encountered the same problem in trying to get up the rear slope of the Gaja Ridge. This time Command called in flamethrowing tanks. The killing machines immediately blasted the caves and hiding places. The enemy rushed to escape being roasted alive. Once they were in the open, they made an easy target. For once, our soldiers were on a ridge where we had a perfect vantage when the Japanese came running out of hiding; they were mowed down. By the time our attack was finished, we had cleaned out the area. However, heavy fire coming down from Conical Hill kept us from taking and occupying the town of Gaja. Time to bring in the big boys.

The tank flamethrowers had an awesome capacity. The operator could remove the machine gun and insert the flame gun in a minute or two. The flamethrower could fire one gallon of fuel per second to an effective range of 25 to 30 yards with oily fuel, 50 to 60 yards with thickened fuel. The flamethrowers with fuel capacity of 50 gallons were employed for M4 Sherman tanks. The weapon used compressed carbon dioxide gas to propel the fuel, had a fuel capacity of 290 gallons, a range of 40 yards with oily fuel and 60 to 80 yards with thickened fuel.

When the oily substance hit a cave or the enemy, the compound stuck, and the flames couldn't be put out before they were finished burning. We knew the tanks would be particularly effective in such circumstances.

Company G had been able to take advantage of a draw between King Hill and the northern hogback of Conical. While the ground gain wasn't large, the soldiers were in an excellent position to strike the next day. Colonel Ed May was directing the fight from the front lines and could see the advantage that had been gained. He reported that the new position should allow them to reach the crest of Conical the next day.

The Corps headquarters had set up in an ancient castle. Nakagusuku Castle became the working quarters of General Hodge, who carefully studied the report from Colonel May. Seeing the possibilities, he reached for the phone to call the top.

General James Bradley took the call.

Hodge thought the Second Battalion was in a position to really do some good. He wondered what the general's opinion might be about Colonel May making the big push up Conical tomorrow.

Bradley chuckled because he believed if anybody could pull off an attack, it was certainly Colonel May. Bradley said to send him forward.

General Hodge hung up with a grin on his face.

Hodge turned to his chief of staff and said that he thought they just might have the key to unlocking the Shuri line, and they might have the right man to try. They would hit the enemy in the morning.

During the night the Japanese beefed up the town of Gaja. They must have figured we'd be coming that way. The job of breaking through went to F Company with Lieutenant Robert Muehrcke leading the charge.

Muehrcke told the platoon to see how fast they could clean out the area. They were on the move and he wanted to keep it that way.

The men nodded, picked up their rifles, and started down the road. They had not gone far when one of the scouts sent out ahead came running back with the report that the hills were covered with pillboxes. They had to knock them out before the unit could go further.

Muehrcke pulled out his field glasses for a hard look. He turned to the platoon and said that they were going to split up and take both sides of the trail. They had a truckload of pillboxes to knock out.

The soldiers moved quickly, firing rifles and mortars straight ahead.

Muehrcke's walkie-talkie rang.

Colonel May reported they had platoons of tanks pounding the Japanese dug in on the north slope. He wanted to know, "How's your platoon making it?"

Muehrcke reported that they were about the business of knocking out pillboxes. "Don't know how many are left, but when they're gone, we're on our way."

Colonel May said excellent and the phone went silent.

Muehrcke and his men kept pushing against the pillboxes, which fell quickly. The Japanese were on the run. The lieutenant called Colonel May and reported that they were ready to march on the town.

May asked, "How many pillboxes did you have to take out?"

"Eleven."

At eleven o'clock, Colonel May decided the hill had been softened up sufficiently for the infantry and tanks to move out. The Japanese weren't about to give up without a real fight. The artillery went back and forth, and soon the infantry came out on top of the crest of Conical. When the Japanese realized what had occurred, they sent an entire company to attack our new position. They came pouring in like wild animals.

Sergeant DuNiphin wasn't going to relinquish this hard-fought-for new position. Grabbing his rifle, he boldly stood up and unloaded the clip at the Japanese charging at him only ten feet away. When he ran out of bullets, the sergeant picked up an M-1 and kept firing until he had emptied it.

The soldiers around him responded to such a brave example, and no one gave an inch. The Japanese weren't able to dislodge DuNiphin's men. The leader of the Second Platoon, Lieutenant Richard Frothinger, realized an assault was on to knock Du-Niphin's men off the crest. He immediately led his men in a hell-for-leather onslaught into the teeth of the machine-gun nest supporting the counterattack. The Japanese were so astonished that they turned and ran. Throughout the afternoon, Colonel May continued probing the defenses surrounding Conical Hill. His approach paid off handsomely.

The day's assault had found the soft spot in the Japanese line and capitalized on the discovery. The Japanese had simply not used their dwindling manpower well. The battalions under May's guidance had defeated them soundly in taking the Conical area.

General Buckner called the work of the Second Battalion a brilliant example of small-unit tactics. The Japanese would never recover from their losses that day. They were not yet beaten, but the fatal wound had been delivered.

43

No Chivalry Left

"Who's your favorite movie star?" Sergeant McQuiston asked me.

"I don't know," I said. "Ingrid Bergman is a good start." I leaned back against the howitzer cannon to see what the other men standing around smoking would say.

Lieutenant John Hayes laughed. "Make mine Veronica Lake. Man! The peek-a-boo girl! Is she ever a sultry dame!"

"Too smokin' hot for me," Hans Goins said. "I want 'em on the cool side. You know. Like a Donna Reed variety." He took a big puff on his cigarette. "Now there's a beauty for you."

The ground shook from an explosion far enough away that we felt it only with our boots.

"You guys are wandering down dreamland road," I said. "Come on. We're fighting a war."

"Yeah, but you can still dream," Swinging Bill Arnold said. "No law against that."

"For me, I'll take Maureen O'Hara any day," McQuiston said.

"Now, that Irish lass has eyes and lips meant only for the likes of me. What a beauty!"

Hayes snorted. "She wouldn't touch you with a ten-foot pole if they carried you in wrapped in Christmas paper."

The men laughed. We all knew we needed to stay in touch with home, and movie stars were one enjoyable way to do so. We were all just blowin' smoke and killing time until the day's orders came in.

The walkie-talkie rang. "Yeah," McQuiston said.

"General Bradley's ordered you to hit the Japanese with full force. We want the 361st Artillery Battalion to fire constantly. Hit 'em with all you got."

"When do we start, sir?"

"Right now. Be extra cautious if you see any Japanese running out of the bushes toward you. Last night the First Battalion killed sixteen Japanese charging toward them. When the bodies were examined, they discovered that the uniforms had been soaked in a flammable substance that might ignite when they were hit. Looks like the Japanese have come up with a new, gruesome approach to the old kamikaze trick. They tried human torches as a new way to get us. Hasn't worked, but you don't want one of those fireballs dropping in on you."

"God almighty!" McQuiston said. "We don't need that one for sure."

"Here's your coordinates. You're going to be firing at Conical and Dick Hills to help maintain the toehold we've gained."

McQuiston scribbled the numbers down.

"It's important for you to soften up the area. Tell your artillery personnel that they are preparing the way for the infantry. That's it." The phone became silent.

"Okay, men!" McQuiston shouted. "Gather around. I got the numbers."

———————

The various companies began moving out. The Japanese knew we were coming and started hitting us with everything they had. B Company quickly worked their way up Dick Able hill even though the day before they had been hit with everything but the garage door. C Company attacked Dick Right.

By late afternoon, C Company had been whittled down to only forty riflemen. Nevertheless, the forty proved to be the toughest guys around. With a remarkable show of strength, they made their way to the crest and dug in just below the skyline. To get to that point, they had killed twenty-five Japanese and knocked out two machine-gun emplacements.

Once they were on top, they discovered a cave about two hundred yards away. The enemy had been firing from there.

Captain Newell knew that the caves were loaded with Japanese. He told the men to throw a couple of satchel charges in and see what happened, and to have their weapons ready to fire at whatever came out.

PFC Frank Jones crawled cautiously on his belly until he was close enough to throw the satchels in. He didn't move when the explosives shook the ground.

C Company watched the smoke roll out of the cave. Abruptly, a long stick was extended with a white flag tied on it.

The soldier standing next to Newell asked if that flag *really* meant anything.

Newell shook his head. He knew those boys had killed some of our men with that little tactic. They probably were wired with explosives. When they got close enough to the Americans, they'd pop the cork. Chivalry had died a long time ago out there.

The soldiers opened up on the eleven men waving white flags, dropping them where they stood.

The only hill that remained under Japanese control was Dick Left. Colonel Macey Dill and the 382nd Infantry knew they were sitting on a hot area and didn't want to move. As the sun began to set, the fighting escalated. Grenades went back and forth. A supply line sending up hand grenades to our doughboys continued to work through the night. The First Battalion poured more than a thousand rounds of mortar fire on the enemy. This time the Japanese wouldn't give. By morning the exhausted American soldiers were forced off the hill.

The First Battalion had been so seriously mauled in the exchange that their efficiency had been impaired. Company E moved in and quickly faced the same battle, keeping the grenade exchange continuing. Sergeant Gerald Sisk tried to move the unit forward, but in ten minutes seven men were hit.

One of the soldiers asked what they were going to do.

Try not to get killed, Sisk guessed.

The grenades kept flying.

Fire went back and forth. Machine guns raked the troops, and there didn't appear to be any way to get at the Japanese. The men stayed in position, shooting at anything that moved in front of them. They couldn't see that their returned fire made any difference.

Finally, Sergeant Sisk got the company commander, Lieutenant Charles C. Renick, on the walkie-talkie and reported that they were pinned down and didn't know which way to turn.

After a long pause, Renick said he didn't think they had much to lose by rushing over the crest of the hill. The Japanese weren't expecting it. If the unit stayed where they were, they were going to see more and more men die.

Sisk shuddered and asked if he meant to charge right at them.

Renick saw no other way.

Sisk hung up the phone and made the sign of the cross on his chest.

He told the men what Command wanted. They should go over the crest and shove their guns down the enemy's throats. He jumped up and charged forward. The men fell in behind him.

PFC Clayton Orr became the first man to go over the top. Sergeant Garfield Arnsdorf followed along with PFC Aida Amdahl. When PFC Clark Butler came next, he was instantly killed. Platoon leader Lieutenant Neal Bridenbaugh directed the men to settle into defensive positions. Intensive fire knocked Bridenbaugh to the ground and Sergeant Michael Schneider had to take over.

Twenty-five men fell in their attack, leaving only fifteen to defend the crest. The situation was precarious to say the least. Men in the Second Platoon suffered fourteen casualties. The survivors started digging foxholes while lying on their bellies.

On May 16, the company's mortar section set up at the base of the hill. For three days, they fired 1,400 rounds a day. Actually, they were shooting 120 rounds a minute. Case after case of grenades and ammunition were lugged up the battle-worn hill. In turn, twelve bodies were carried back down and forty wounded men came back from the crest. As terrible as the price had been, we had gained an observation position that the Japanese had previously used against us. We could see them just as they had once watched us.

Late that afternoon, we discovered Japanese marching up the road from Shuri. As our soldiers watched, another group came swinging down the road like they were going to a Sunday-school picnic. The company called us at our station.

"Major Shaw, we want your artillery unit to zero in on a road leading to Shuri. I'll give you the coordinates. We think you can wipe out a couple of squads of the enemy."

"Okay," I said. "Give 'em to me."

As soon as the officer got off the phone, I informed the men. "You've wondered what difference we make. Right now, we're going to blast a good-sized group of the enemy all to hell. Fire up, men."

When all the cannons fired at the same time, the ground and everything else in sight shook. We kept firing until I got the last phone call of the evening.

"Your doughboys did it, Major Shaw," the voice said. "You wiped them out."

44

Monsoon Season

The rain came down by the bucketful morning, noon, and night. The roads turned into two-foot-deep mud, causing jeeps to sink in halfway up the tires. Road depressions around the camp turned into ponds. Soldiers found it impossible to stay dry. I can candidly tell you that there's nothing like fighting a war with soggy socks.

Sergeant McQuiston entered the tent I had the men erect for planning purposes. "How long is this torrent going to last?"

"As long as the gods of rain decree," I said sarcastically. "Hell, I got no idea."

"Sure eats on you," McQuiston said. "Washes your enthusiasm right down the drain."

I nodded. "Do I ever understand."

"The downpour's got to affect our overall planning."

I nodded. "Right now, I'm going up to Command if I can get my jeep to drive through the mud. I'll bring back some insight. Tell the men to sit tight."

"Sit tight in a mud puddle?"

I laughed. "Try finding a little better shelter than that."

McQuiston left and I started the jeep. My poncho helped, but my boots had been through the waterworks. Most of the way, I tried to drive on the side of the road and stay out of the tracks. I could see that if I dropped off into one of those old ruts, the trail might turn into a riverbed and I'd be stuck for hours. Made driving go slow, but eventually I got there.

Men stood at attention as I slipped into the back row. Standing in rigid posture, my toes felt like they were swimming in my combat boots. General James Bradley already stood at the podium.

"At ease," the general said. "Please sit down."

We sat on ramshackle field chairs someone had dragged in from heaven knows where.

"The constant rain now presents us with a field problem," the general said. "Of course, I know that your men are faced with significant discomfort, but that's only a minor problem. If the monsoon continues, the tanks won't be able to move, and we will lose the critical support they give us. Without tank support, we would soon be faced with disaster." Bradley turned to the large map behind him and pointed out the terrain to be faced.

"We must control these areas to stay on the move. The city of Shuri is not that far away as the crow flies, and the time has come for us to sprout wings. I do not believe we can wait for the skies to clear. We must strike even if it is in the rain. Is that understood?"

The officers around the room nodded their heads.

"On the twenty-first of May, I am asking you commanders to make a supreme effort to deliver a knockout blow. To start us down that road, the 382nd Infantry will assault the Oboe Hill area. We must hit them hard and fast, even in the mud." Bradley looked over the heads of the men straight at me. "The 361st Field Artillery will soften the area first and then support their strike with heavy artillery. Major Charles Johnson's First Battalion has just had a five-day rest and should be ready to move out and hit Oboe direct. The Second Battalion has the task of working on those little side hills Hen and Hector."

General Bradley stopped and took a deep breath. "I know, I know. We are asking a great deal in this weather, but if we don't succeed now, we will pay a high price later. Is that clear?"

Once again, the officers voiced their affirmation.

"Thank you, gentlemen," the general said. "Let's go get 'em."

The officers quickly headed for the door. I fired up my jeep and started back the way I'd come, trying to avoid disappearing in a mud hole ten feet deep. Not far in front of me a convoy had gotten stuck in the mud. Big trucks were trying to pull the front jeep out of a quagmire so they could get moving again. A two-and-a-half-ton 6x6 truck had a chain on the jeep's bumper and was trying to pull him backward. Another Mack NW military truck stood ready to join the effort. Obviously, I wasn't going to get past this mess if I stayed on the same road.

I swung off the road and started a bouncing, bumpy drive over a rocky shoulder. I kept praying the tires would hold. Since I wasn't a believing or praying man, the situation certainly had to be exasperating. Somehow, I kept going.

Sergeant McQuiston was waiting for me when I pulled into our camp. He had the usual poncho pulled over his helmet and looked relatively miserable.

"What'd you learn . . . sir?" he asked.

"The party's about to start," I explained. "You need to get the men lined up to fire the cannons. We've got to provide support for the 382nd Infantry. Even with the precipitation, we're about to attack big-time."

McQuiston blinked. "Really?"

"What'd I just say?"

The sergeant rubbed the rain off his face. "I guess it don't matter none that we're about to drown."

"Don't turn into a soap opera on me," I said. "Let's get the men hustling. The attack on Dick Left Hill is about to begin."

McQuiston saluted and took off.

Actually, Lieutenant William Stock's First Platoon of Company F had already started up the hill. As they got near the top, the Japanese greeted them with those inevitable grenades. The platoon quickly discovered they couldn't shoot at what they couldn't see. The Japanese had camouflaged themselves so well, the men weren't able to find a target.

The men put their M-1 rifles down and started throwing grenades. The twenty men hurling the bombs at the Japanese eventually slung more than three hundred pounds of explosives over the crest. They had dropped five hundred hand grenades on the enemy, and that took its toll. The Japanese began to pull back as their men fell left and right.

We opened up with our howitzers and aimed at the top of the hill. By one o'clock we had literally blown off the crest of the hill. Our shells had made mincemeat out of anybody still up there. The First Platoon picked up their rifles and marched forward. The battle for Dick Hill was finished. The Japanese had lost again.

Meanwhile the First Battalion charged against Oboe Hill, fighting oppressive odds and waiting for us to show up. Lieutenant Colonel Ed List and his men came rolling in with bullets flying past them like angry mosquitoes.

Major Byron King thought the enemy must have fifty machine guns firing at them. They had to stay on the ground. Captain Hugh Young knew they couldn't stop. If they stayed put, they would eventually be blown away.

They had to stay moving targets on a steep slope.

For a few moments, the men were silent. Then Major King stood up and ordered them to annihilate the goofballs. King charged straight ahead shouting for the men to hit the bastards.

The deadly bullets of terror only increased. Almost lying on the ground, the men didn't stop creeping onward. But the torrent of death didn't stop. Eventually, the small group of survivors got to the top of the hill. The Japanese must have been confounded trying to explain the kind of enemy they faced. They had just been overwhelmed by one of the most heroic groups of men in the war.

At dusk, fifty Japanese charged up a gap between C and L Companies. While they were turned back, A Company and part of B were knocked off the hill. Lieutenant Al Wilson wouldn't let matters stand: he started a counterattack. The Japanese kept up their assault and endlessly rained machine-gun fire on the men. But Wilson's men wouldn't quit and kept pushing back. For six hours the battle raged.

Japanese artillery fire opened up on A and B Companies. Once more C Company came under assault. A few Japanese broke through and set up machine guns, firing in every direction. All through the night, the combat continued, but when morning came the dough-boys had hung on. The big punch General Bradley wanted in the rain and mud had been delivered. Most of the men had become so exhausted that they were virtually asleep on their feet.

No matter what else had occurred, the Japanese had been cut to ribbons. The monsoon hadn't stopped us.

45

The Lost Platoon

May 15 became the night of rain.

Seemed like no one would start out or stand in the downpour, much less launch an attack. Wrong. The Japanese sent a crew up the reverse side of King Hill with the usual deadly intent. Their exchange with M Company's heavy machine guns suggested that staying inside under a warm blanket had certainly been the better idea. Through the trees, M Company knocked out at least sixty Japanese in that little foray.

For the moment, Command Center had not been asking for artillery support from our unit, so we could wait out the rain under water-repellant cover. No one complained about that opportunity. However, we knew the situation for Company G had to be different. They had been given orders to make another run at the western slope of Conical. The task would not be easy, and the rain only intensified the struggle. Nevertheless, Colonel Dill sent the men into action.

G Company quickly discovered they were confronted by a battery of caves and pillboxes. There was good reason why that side of the hill had proved so obstinate. Our soldiers were not deterred by such a formidable defense system, but the advance proved to be costly. PFC Robert Coy recognized the problem and rushed one of the machine-gun nests.

"Teki!" the Japaneses screamed. *"Teki!"*

Though he was completely exposed, Coy kept firing his BAR. A surviving Japanese soldier rushed him with a trench knife. Coy's bullet hit the assailant square in the forehead. He fell backward in the grass, his blank eyes staring emptily at the dark sky. Another Japanese popped up and fired a pistol, but Coy left him sprawled on the ground.

G Company kept moving, but as they were almost to the crest, artillery fire increased. Mortars were falling every four square feet. Dust and debris flew in every direction. The men did not flinch and kept crawling forward. Even under those adverse circumstances, the platoon did not stop.

Six men tried to hook around the Conical peak, attempting to tie in with the Second Platoon. Sergeant Denton Jackson led the men upward. PFC Clifford Tschoepe made it to the top. Suddenly a machine gun opened up on them, hitting all six. The hill was so steep that they all rolled seventy-five feet to the bottom. Amazingly, they all survived.

Company G kept pounding. The rain and the mud did not stop them. By the end of the day they had established a front line that wound around the area and hooked up with C Company on Charlie Hill. Conical peak remained a problem, and a gap still existed between Conical and King Hills. Still, the gains were important even if they occurred in the deluge.

———————

The next day, the 382nd's new objective was Love Hill. The area turned out to be a low, barren ridge that ran into the southern spur of Conical. Once we held that area, we'd be in position to knock out the Japanese entrenchments that still existed on the southwest slope of Conical, as well as support the ongoing attack on Oboe Hill.

Sergeant Hilton Stults was to lead the direct assault on Love Hill. He and a platoon of twenty-six men were to hit them with full force.

Signaling for the platoon to follow, Stults started forward. He knew Japanese were to the rear and that they were alone in this attack, but he didn't hesitate.

One of the men asked how far they were going.

The sergeant answered they were charging all the way to the top because they had to take the Love Hill area. He warned the men to stay low and pay attention because they didn't seem to be encountering the enemy. He knew that was not a good sign.

The platoon kept moving. Occasionally, rifle fire cracked through the air, but no enemy appeared.

One of the men grumbled that he was as wet as an old hound dog in a storm. The bushes were about as dry as a swimming pool. The ground felt like mush.

Another soldier growled that it was like being assigned to take a bath with your clothes on.

The heavy rain became more of a drizzle. The climb wasn't steep, so the men didn't struggle with the ascent. In record time, the platoon reached the top of the hill.

A soldier remarked, "That was easy." He couldn't believe they'd just moseyed up the trail like they owned the place.

Sergeant Stults kept looking to the right and left. He mumbled to himself that it was too good to be true.

A roaring thunderclap of cracking guns opened up on the exposed men. Over fifty machine guns fired at once directly at the men standing in the open. Hidden guns from Charlie, King, Conical, Oboe, and Love Hills fired simultaneously. The squad fell right and left. Stults tumbled over on the ground. The shooting didn't stop as man after man of the trapped platoon dropped to their knees or fell on their faces. The killing didn't stop.

From the valley below, the American soldiers watched in horror. Nothing could be done to save the stranded twenty-six soldiers. The Japanese continued firing until no one moved on the top of Love Hill. Finally, the barrage stopped. The platoon had been wiped out.

Firing went back and forth throughout the entire day. The rest of C Company could only glance at the men still lying all over the top of the hill, men whom they could no longer reach or assist. The situation left the company horrified by the extent of the loss. The day ended, and by eight the night was black.

Sergeant Stults raised his head slightly and asked if anybody was still alive.

One voice answered.

Another answer came from the far corner.

Someone said that two of them were there.

Stults said in a low voice that only six had survived, but they shouldn't move yet.

Another soldier called out that he was alive but wounded.

Stults said they had to crawl off the top of this hill quietly. Possibly they could hide in one of those caves.

Stults started inching his way between dead soldiers until he got to the edge of the clearing and called in a low whisper for the men to join him. Four other men crawled toward him.

They knew that they all had been hit in one way or the other.

Stults told them to be careful because the Japanese were watching. He started leading them down.

The wounded men made no sounds but kept their pain to themselves. In the dark, the trail still had broken limbs and jagged rocks than made the slow descent even more difficult. The men slid some of the way. A couple of the wounded could barely walk.

One of the soldiers spotted another of the island's tombs. They could hide inside.

The men hurried to the entrance and pulled away a rock covering the opening. The soldiers dragged the two badly wounded men in with them. Sitting in the pitch-black cave, they caught their breath. At least they were alive.

————————

Four days later in the early morning, a bright red flare pierced the sky. Two soldiers on duty saw the trail of fire streaming across the sky and thought it could be a trick of some kind.

As they watched, two figures seemed to be walking out of the bushes.

The figures kept waving, and the first one was shouting "Don't shoot! Hold your fire!"

The first guard drew a bead on them and was ready to fire if they tried anything funny.

The second man shouted that they *really were* Americans. They had two more back in a cave and needed help.

The two guards rushed forward. Each man put his shoulder under one of the wounded men and walked them back into their camp.

The guards said everybody had been talking about the lost platoon. It was assumed they were all dead.

One of the men confirmed he was Sergeant R. D. Turner. They had spent three nights and days holed up on Love Hill.

Private Kenneth Boynton and Turner tried to get out. However, the Japanese had a machine gun fixed on the tomb. For some reason, they seemed satisfied to keep the Americans holed up so they couldn't get out.

A guard asked how they survived.

Private Keith Cochran said that the second night an old man and an Okinawan woman came into the tomb with a girl about ten years old. "The old coot must have been ninety. No kidding. We didn't know what they were doing, but there were two rooms in the tomb, and we hid in the second."

Private Bill Schweneger added, "They turned out to be right friendly. Cochran communicated with them in sign language. The girl went out and filled two of our canteens with water. We put halazone tablets in and could drink the water even if it looked dirty."

Cochran said that the Okinawans stayed with them all day and even cooked food for the soldiers. "We just couldn't believe that they would treat us so good." The unit rested during the day waiting to see what would come next.

Turner explained that on the fourth day a big air strike hit. "We guess our own airplanes thought Japanese had holed up in the tomb. Artillery went off and the ground shook. They almost thought an earthquake had hit. Charlie Company started pounding the cave with machine-gun fire. Bullets were flying everywhere. Our own artillery opened up on us and blew one of the rooms all to pieces. Looked like our own side would wipe us out."

That night Cochran sneaked out to one of the shell holes to get more rainwater. He saw a cave not that far from them that had a campfire burning in the entrance. He listened carefully and realized the Japanese were singing. Women were laughing. It sounded like they were having a big-time party.

When he got back to the men, he shared what he had seen. They decided the time had come for a now-or-never break. The men took off their shoes and left everything behind, even their rifles. They knew they couldn't afford to make a sound and had to help each other because a couple of them were badly injured. The survivors didn't stop before they got back to our side of the line. Boyton helped Schweneger because his foot had really gotten mangled.

Boyton said that they prayed all the time they were there. With only one Bible, they took turns reading it.

The guard pointed and saw another soldier coming through.

Sergeant Donald Williams hobbled in, leaning on a tree branch for a crutch. Color had faded from his face: he appeared pale. He exclaimed that they were a sight for sore eyes. Then he slumped onto a fallen tree sprawled out on top of the grass.

One the guards recognized that he needed a medic.

Willliams agreed. He and a buddy had gotten pinned down in a depression on Love Hill. The two of them got hit three times apiece. "The Japanese were floating around after the artillery barrage they put on us, so we had to play dead." Williams stayed there with his buddy from four to seven that night and didn't move. When it got dark, he carried his friend down the hill. Eventually, they found a cave and crawled in, exhausted and bleeding. During the night, Williams crawled out and started looking for water. He found the body of a dead American soldier with his canteen still half full. The man obviously couldn't use it again, so Williams took it back to the cave. Just before morning, while it was still dark, he tried to carry his buddy out. Unfortunately, the injured man was so weak that he fainted, and Williams had to return to the cave.

"The Japanese never saw us, but they were out there. We could hear them walking around and talking. Thank God they never entered the cave. We settled in for the night but kept watching the entrance to the cave and didn't sleep. The next morning became the real nightmare. Artillery blasted everything around the cave and one of our airplanes even hit the area with rockets. Somehow, we made it through the day with explosions constantly pounding the area. When night came again, I crawled out and went looking for water. This time I found a full canteen and brought it back."

The guard asked if it came off a dead soldier.

A glazed, faraway look swept over Williams's eyes. His voice quivered when he said yes.

The camp guard understood.

Some Japanese must have seen him crawl back into the cave. Williams could hear them approaching outside. "I don't know where they got it, but the Japanese had an America bazooka they fired into our cave. We guessed the explosion must have knocked me out for a few moments. The concussion was awful, but that wasn't enough. They tossed in a grenade and the explosion show-ered my buddy with shrapnel. Everything felt blurry, but I could see two Japanese fixin' to come in. I had a Japanese pistol taken off a dead officer some time back. I aimed.

Donald Williams stopped and began coughing. He mumbled and took a deep breath. "The cave was a small tomb . . . maybe eight by ten feet at most. The two Japanese bent down to come in. I shot the first one right through the head. The second guy took off and I never saw him again. All night and the next day, we waited, hoping we'd be found by our soldiers, but no one came."

Williams took another deep breath. He explained that he knew by this time that after all he'd been through, his friend was dying and would never make it back. He himself had not eaten in three days and had given most of the water to his buddy. "I had become so weak that I doubted I could make it back by myself. All I could do was try."

Nobody said anything. The camp guards and the four other survivors just listened.

"I staggered out of the cave in the dark and started down the hill. At the bottom, I found a shell hole filled with rainwater. I fell on my face and drank like a thirsty horse. Forget those damn tablets, I felt like I was dying. If a flare went off, I would flop on the ground and play dead. Eventually, the moon came out and it stopped raining. I found a hole and must have slept for four hours. When it started getting light again, I woke up. Didn't take a moment to know I had to hotfoot it back to our lines. Along the way, the Japanese fired a couple of mortars at me. I'd hit the ground and play dead. Once a Japanese walked by only a few feet away. That's when I finally got up and made it back to our lines."

The story got around about the "lost platoon" and the few men who ended up surviving the ordeal. When the intelligence officers interviewed the survivors, they received invaluable information on the position of the Japanese weapons and mortars. The soldiers looked weary beyond fatigue. Each man's eyes were sunken, and their cheeks drawn. Their bodies were covered with flea bites. Fleas had settled in, leaving them with a constant irritation. Sergeant Turner and PFC Schweneger were immediately taken to the hospital. The remainder went to the rear for extended rest and recovery.

Surprisingly enough, in a few days PFC Cochran, Sergeant Williams, and Private Boynton were back in action. The war went on.

46

Air Strikes

At the least, the downpour had significantly dwindled. We hoped the rain had stopped. Our men hated walking through the mud that was everywhere in our camp. We had covered some of the firing mechanisms of the howitzers with tarps, and nothing appeared to have been damaged. The men were ready to roll, but no orders had come through for where to aim.

G Company still struggled to hang on to their position on the crest of Conical Ridge. They were having a rough time doing so. The fight continued morning, noon, and night, which of course meant no sleep for the soldiers. Finally, we got orders to shoot the big guns. Turned out the Japanese had been ordered to make a stand and indeed they did.

The enemy had dug in halfway between the crest and the ridge base so we couldn't get at them. Even the howitzers couldn't pry them loose. The Japanese had dug a tunnel through the ridge that was actually a death trap for anybody who tried to enter it. Our adversary had truly burrowed in for the winter.

On the night of May 16, a company of Japanese came charging in led by an officer in polished black boots, white gloves, and the works. This commander looked like something straight out of the movies. With a stiff, high collar and officer's coat that hung nearly to his knees, he wore a military hat encircled with a red band, and at his side dangled a samurai sword. Standing out like a flashing light in a dark night with American soldiers charging at him, the officer was inescapable and a perfect target.

Machine guns were firing everywhere. When the enemy tried to set up a nest on the ridge, one of our soldiers shot the Japanese and stopped that action. Another rifleman took aim and knocked the commanding officer off the ridge. In the midst of the attack, the black boots and white gloves went flying over the crest.

Eight of the Japanese commander's men went after the body and we promptly knocked them off. We weren't sure why the Japanese officer wore the prom-night dress getup, but something must have been going on. Here were our men in uniforms that hadn't hit a washing machine in what seemed like years, and the other side came out like a prince going after Cinderella. Whatever . . . he was now dead.

All in all, the engagement actually wasn't bad for us. The other side lost forty-five Japanese now sprawled all over the top of the hill.

When this skirmish was over, General Hodge wanted to send a good number of men down the coast to get behind the defenders of Shuri. General Bradley knew the 383rd had lost too many men to be in a position to pull this off. A considerable amount of arrangement and readjustment would be necessary to complete such an operation. To get some sense of what was ahead, Major Leon Addy sent a twelve-man patrol into whatever remained of Yonabaru. Sergeant Reeder, who had distinguished himself in the fight over Sawtooth Ridge, would lead the patrol. The sergeant rounded up his men and started down the road to see if they could take the city.

Yonabaru had been the island's third-largest city. We had "softened" the town (if that's the right word for what artillery did to the city): we'd blown the town into a mass of broken rocks, crumbled cement, and destroyed buildings. Trees had become toothpicks stripped of all leaves. The barren pile of rubble was depressing to see. The population had disappeared.

Three soldiers from another unit decided that they'd be the first in and see what souvenirs they might find in the rubble. They strolled in like conquerors. Immediately, Japanese took aim. Although the three men had been drinking and had to be on the slightly drunk side to saunter into such a vulnerable area, they instantly sobered up when bullets came flying past their helmets. All three hit the ground and wriggled behind a large chunk of broken concrete. Tucking their tails between their legs, they beat it back out the way they came in.

The truth was that we couldn't afford to lose anybody. Even the three idiots crawling out of Yonabaru had an important place in the military assault. The First Battalion of the 383rd had hung on to Charlie Hill but sustained such losses that the unit had reached a grave point. The battalion had witnessed C Company being wiped out, and that left a mark. They knew the Japanese had not lost the ability to direct lethal cross fire against any of our attempts to move forward. We had made highly significant gains, but the Japanese were far from out of the game.

By May 20 we had lost more than three hundred men struggling to take Charlie Hill. Tanks had been disabled. Air support had not been called in because our lines remained so close to the Japanese. At best, we were only a hundred yards from the enemy, and still trying to defend Charlie Hill. An airplane attack would drop bombs on our own men.

Colonel Ed May had become frustrated with our inability to break free of this struggle but remained perplexed about how to proceed. Lieutenant Charles Hymer had an idea.

Hymer began by explaining that he'd been flying every day over the Charlie area in a small cub airplane. "I've come to know the area like the back of my hand."

Colonel May studied the lanky pilot and waited.

"The sky," Hymer went on, "gives one an unusual perspective, and looking down on the entire area of conflict, I've watched both sides move their men around."

May began drumming his fingers on a map lying in front of them as if this conversation were going nowhere.

"I'm convinced that I could direct airplane strikes to the exact target they must hit without endangering our soldiers a hundred yards away.

May stopped drumming and leaned forward. Could he be sure of the exact target?

Hymers said, "Our dive-bombers function differently from artillery because we come down out of the sky. I'm suggesting a 'backward' air strike against Hill Charlie. I've flown over there so many times, I could direct it in my sleep."

May wanted to know how he would suggest they proceed.

Lieutenant Hymer knew they had a relatively light force on Charlie. He would begin by withdrawing them for a short period. "There's such a small Japanese force there, we could get away with a temporary retreat. Then I would send in eight carrier-based navy planes and probably about four marine torpedo bombers. I'd have them come straight in just above ground level and then swing straight up after releasing their bombs. I'll fly in the lead airplane and direct the attack from the first plane that strikes. I think that could finish off the Japanese presence."

Colonel May sat there staring at Lieutenant Hymer. Eventually, he spoke: he believed they had something! "Excellent. We can do it!"

Lieutenant Hymer flew in with Captain James Nauss, a marine pilot, at an altitude of only fifteen feet. When they came over the Japanese, Nauss released a five-hundred-pound bomb and then they zoomed vertically straight up to avoid crashing into the hill. Each of twelve airplanes made a similar approach, dropped a bomb, and then flew straight back up. The ground shook with the explosions.

As the airplanes flew away, the infantry immediately came back in. Captain John Van Vulpen led two platoons of B Company back in to take over. Suddenly, hellfire broke loose. Five men were killed and four disappeared somewhere on the battlefield. Smoke bombs had to be called in to cover their retreat. The bombing had been a great idea, but it simply didn't do the job. The Japanese remained in control of the position where they could fire on us.

However, as the infantry had advanced covered by tanks, E Company discovered a Japanese soldier they decided had to be the most durable man of the war. When our air strikes hit, the guy holed up in a cave. After it was over, he came out and started down the road. The machine gunner on the lead tank saw him and opened up on him, but the gun jammed. The guy kept running. The tank gunner got the gun open and fired, blowing the soldier into the air, but he landed on his feet. A second blast once again sent him flying, but he landed right side up and kept running. The third round got him. Whoever he was, he deserved an award for endurance.

It certainly seemed like Love Hill was the wrong name. Something more like Dreaded or Slaughter Hill would have been more appropriate. Company G hung on to the western slope of Conical Hill, but the Japanese attacked constantly. In assault after assault, the enemy had been mowed down, but they kept coming. In four days, G Company killed 153 of the bad guys.

Trying to assess what was unfolding, General Claudius Easley stood on an observation post erected on Conical Hill to obtain a clear view of the unfolding conflict. General Easley had gained a reputation for being an amazingly accurate marksman with a rifle. He demonstrated his skill standing on the platform.

One day Easley saw something that needed to be fixed. He lowered his binoculars, pointed to the field, and asked the sergeant to loan him his rifle.

The aide handed him a rifle.

General Easley watched a Japanese soldier moving five hundred yards away, aimed, pulled the trigger, and the enemy slumped to the ground.

The sergeant gasped. The target was five football fields away.

Easley shrugged and winked. "That's how you get to be a general."

47

Stalemate

The rain didn't stop.

The downpour actually picked up and increased with a continual drenching, drowning precipitation. On May 22, the entire
Tenth Army ground to a halt. Deteriorating roads became impassable swamps. Even bulldozers ceased to be able to pull trucks
out of the mud. We called the M29 cargo carrier a Weasel. On
Leyte, the Weasel had been invaluable yanking any size vehicle
out of the mire and getting it going again. No longer. The thick,
oozing, adhesive mud impacted the wheels and stuck to the sus-
pension system. Eventually, muck even worked into the motor
and clogged everything. Even when some wheels got traction,
the extreme dragging effect on the motors pushed strain to the
point of destruction. Roads were lined with vehicles with steam-
ing engines and radiators boiling over. Finally, even the M5 trac-
tor no longer hauled heavy artillery through the mud. Nothing
worked.

In order to maintain a steady supply of food, water, and ammunition, already overworked soldiers carried supplies on their aching backs. Men were sliding, slipping, sinking into the mud pits that were so ubiquitous no one could avoid them. Mud covered the men from head to toe, bending strained men to the ground.

During this ordeal, no slack was given on either side. The life-and-death struggle continued unabated. The two sides were separated by only a few yards, and the fighting never let up. The hot war had become a wet war.

By the evening of May 21, Command could see that the Japanese defenses around Shuri were crumbling. The Japanese were running out of men to man their guns. Unfortunately, our soldiers could not take advantage because of the weather. Plans for attack were drawn up and orders issued that were almost as quickly canceled. Any forward progress could be no more than inch by inch.

Two days later, the 381st made an advance on two hills southwest of Sugar and Conical Hills. Two platoons of E Company worked their way through a small village, but the constant firing from Sugar and Conical forced them to retreat. Possibly encouraged by the withdrawal, the Japanese mounted a counterattack on Sugar Hill. Around one hundred Japanese surged against F Company. Only five hundred pounds of accurate targeting repelled the assault. The war had not even missed a beat.

While this activity was unfolding, A Company of the 383rd made a repeated assault on Love Hill. Colonel Ed May, knowing the assault could be highly significant, sent Company A to see what could be accomplished. Nothing had changed, and the Japanese unleashed another torment straight from hell.

Sergeant George Smith started up the hill with his men. The terrain proved to be rough and arduous to overcome, but A Company kept creeping up the hill.

The corporal said he couldn't see or hear any Japanese.

Smith warned, "Don't slow down. They're most certainly out there."

The men kept working their way forward.

Smith called out that the enemy was just in front of them.

The soldiers stooped lower to the ground.

Smith began to make out the horizon line of the crest of the hill ahead of him. They couldn't be that far from the top. Abruptly a machine gun opened up on them. The men hit the ground, but the explosive fire didn't stop.

A soldier close to Smith rolled over on his back. Gravel had skinned his face, leaving streaks of blood on the ground. The man groaned that they'd got him. The words slowly stopped.

Smith screamed for a medic to get over there.

When he looked back in the soldier's face, blank eyes were staring aimlessly into the sky. A bullet hole near the center of his body had started turning red but stopped bleeding. Smith knew the man was gone. The image burned in his mind.

The sergeant started firing in the direction that the machine-gun fire was coming from, but even though he kept shooting, nothing changed.

A mortar exploded in the midst of the platoon with a deafening roar. The sergeant realized that he no longer heard anything. A low-level buzzing filled his ears, but he wasn't really hearing any voices.

The sound of one of the men screaming only slightly echoed

in Smith's ears. Suddenly a Japanese soldier ran out of the bushes with his bayonet fixed. Smith stared, unable to decide what to do. One of the soldiers on the ground tripped the Japanese. Before the enemy could recover, the soldier jumped up and grabbed the man's hair. With all the strength he had, the soldier pounded the enemy's face back and forth in the dirt. The man's lips broke open and blood pulsated out of his nose before he turned limp. The soldier slammed a trench knife in the man's back.

Smith watched, unable to move. His head felt stunned, empty, unresponsive.

The soldiers kept firing at the Japanese rushing out of the bushes, but soldiers were still falling before the rampaging enemy. Sergeant Smith's head seemed to swirl around and around. He could no longer think or respond. Smith began to count the men lying around him. At least a dozen were on the ground not moving.

Nothing any longer made sense. Smith knew the men for whom he had responsibility were being annihilated. He couldn't stand the thought that he was responsible for at least a dozen men dead on the ground. The entire unit was being wiped out. Smith wasn't about to crawl away from the deaths of his buddies, but his thoughts blurred. Nothing made any sense.

Sergeant Smith finally grabbed his rifle and stood up recklessly, exposing himself in the exchange. He took one step before a machine gun cut him virtually in two. The remaining men began running back over the hill. They knew the assault had been another disaster.

As night fell, Lieutenant Harold Weingartner quickly recognized that the Japanese were beginning another assault on his men. Some Japanese set up a machine gun only fifteen yards away. The sudden blast blew the top off PFC Jim Duncan's foxhole.

The machine gun stopped, and Duncan reasoned they must be changing clips. Grabbing a portable flamethrower, Duncan rushed the enemy nest.

The astonished Japanese looked up from the machine gun just as Duncan pulled the trigger on the flamethrower. Three Japanese screamed as fire engulfed them. Flames leapt up from their uniforms and their hair became human torches.

"You bastards kept us up all night!" Duncan kept swinging the flamethrower back and forth, yelling that those bastards wouldn't keep them up all night again.

G Company kept firing and at least forty-two enemy fell dead. One soldier was so exhausted that after pulling the safety pin on a grenade, he dropped off into sleep. Only the pressure of his grip kept the grenade from exploding in his hand.

All through the night, the Japanese kept coming. Shortly after midnight, the enemy rushed Company C once more and grabbed three key foxholes. By 3:30 a.m., a full company of enemy were attacking through a gap between C and L Companies while another two platoons assaulted A Company. PFC Donald Schiever had stayed in the foxhole next to where the Japanese had settled in. Even though he was wounded, Schiever kept firing at the three occupied foxholes. He had held ground single-handedly and kept the Japanese from moving forward.

By five thirty, C Company had taken back the three foxholes. At dawn, supplies started coming in again. The challenge of getting across completely impassable roads had nearly brought the relief drive to a halt. However, an even larger problem threatened to wipe out the entire company. An air strike that was supposed to be canceled came flying in with a five-hundred-pound bomb. The blockbuster went off on the other side of the hill but was only twenty-five yards from our soldiers. Swooping planes strafed the Japanese and took a heavy toll.

C Company sat there with their rifles ready and their teeth chattering.

The following day, General Bradley sent the Third Battalion of the 383rd to hold the east end of Oboe Hill. Whoever screwed up on the orders caused naval gunfire to fall short and killed fifteen of our men. As far as the First Battalion was concerned, they were down to such a small number of men that antitank platoons were sent in as reinforcements. The usual three rifle companies had been so depleted that there were only enough men left to make one platoon. Colonel Johnson could rustle up barely 188 men, the normal number for one company. The situation began to look grim.

On May 26, Command recognized that the men who had sustained this struggle had to be relieved. Heavy machine gunners were moved into the line as riflemen. Even drivers parked their vehicles and shouldered rifles. We were throwing everything we had into the conflict. By five thirty that evening, the struggling infantrymen got the first signs of hope.

One of the scouting planes observed that a thousand Japanese were going south from Shuri. This was the first sign that the Japanese were abandoning the Shuri line and might be in full retreat. The enormous sacrifice and struggle appeared to be paying off. The First Battalion had lost 410 men fighting for Oboe, Zebra, and

Dick Hills. Only by the most persistent heroism had they been able to hang on, and now the struggle appeared to be over. The soldiers endured, hoping against hope that such was a fact.

A couple of days later, the sun came out for the first time in ten days. Maybe, just maybe, that was our rainbow.

48

Rolling On

Change was in the air. For reasons I couldn't quite identify, a shift in the war had seemed to settle in my bones. By May 26, a new quietness floated through our camp. The sounds of cannons and rifles were no longer ringing in our ears. Bombs weren't exploding. We'd all seen *The Wizard of Oz* and hoped that we had landed somewhere on the other side of Dorothy's rainbow.

"Major Shaw," Sergeant McQuiston asked, "you ever get the feeling that the anchor's been pulled up and the boat's about to move?"

I laughed. "Hey, you've gone navy on me."

"No, I mean it. My skin is taking a new reading on what's going on. Something's different."

"Well, Sergeant, the word I'm getting from Command is that the Japanese appear to be retreating. I got a hunch that they're running out of men. We've killed a truckload of them and that's got to be bringing their show to a halt."

I looked around at our crew. The men seemed unusually relaxed. The usual pressure and nervousness weren't there. Maybe . . . maybe, we had come to a new turn in the road. We'd discovered that the fierce resistance that we had faced had actually come from well-placed pillboxes and machine-gun nests that were run by a relatively small force. The actual situation became clear when Lieutenant Colonel John Williams led the 381st in the capture of Sugar and Cutaway Hills. Williams had taken the place of Colonel Halloran, who'd contracted a severe case of the flu. When the 381st marched into no-man's-land, they found the hills littered with Japanese bodies. The Japanese made an attempt at resistance on Charlie Hill, but the defense turned out to be more a suicide action. During the remainder of the day, the Third Battalion encountered only slight opposition. We were definitely on the move.

However, that relaxed movement didn't mean all resistance had vanished. We still had work to do. The Second Battalion of the 382nd Infantry had to clean out Hen and Hector Hills. On the back side of Hen Hill, the Japanese had a six-foot trench and were still tossing grenades over the top. G Company and PFC Clarence Craft walked into the encounter.

Craft was a California boy from the town of Santa Ana. Usually a mild sort of guy, he ended up right in the middle of the struggle to take Hen Hill.

The sergeant called out that the enemy were directly over the hill right in front of Private Craft.

Craft said he knew that they were just on the other side of the ridge.

The sergeant warned that they were slinging hand grenades at us.

Craft yelled back that if our boys would keep the explosives coming, he'd lob them over the hill.

So the sergeant lined up four men into a supply line, which handed grenades from man to man until they were in Craft's hand. In turn, he hurled the grenades over the hill. The explosives kept shaking the top of the ridge, but the Japanese didn't give. Eventually, Private Craft hurled three cases of grenades at the enemy. Abruptly, a Japanese stuck his head up and peered over the hill. Instantly, the private grabbed his rifle and hit the Japanese square in the forehead with the rifle butt. The man sprawled on top of the ridge.

Craft dropped back, reloaded the rifle, and leaped over the top of the hill. A dozen Japanese were lined up in the trench in front of him.

Craft yelled "Surprise!" and started shooting.

Most of the Japanese were so stunned, they only stared. A couple fired at him, but he shot them.

The private charged into the trench, killing all the Japanese nearby. At the other end, ten Japanese grabbed bamboo spears and charged straight at him.

Private Craft hissed and shot all ten.

By himself, Private Clarence Craft had cleared out the trench. But he wasn't done. Without stopping, he jumped out of the trench and saw that, not far in front of him, the Japanese were setting up a machine gun. Without breaking his stride, he threw a grenade straight at them and hit the ground.

The explosion sent shrapnel flying in all directions. When Craft looked up, the three Japanese were humped over the barrel of the machine gun. Dead.

Musing out loud that he was slowing them down, Craft got back on his feet.

Ahead of him, the private recognized the outline of a cave. No question but that Japanese were in there. He grabbed a satchel charge and slung it at the entrance. Craft waited. Nothing happened.

Fearlessly crawling to the cave, he saw the explosive sitting inside near the entrance. Apparently, the firing mechanism hadn't gone off. Craft stood up, walked in, pulled out the satchel, and adjusted it. He threw it back in.

The explosive shook the ground. Smoke rolled out of the cave. The mortar had done its job. The private walked in. Lying on the ground was a Japanese officer. Craft paused only to pick up his ceremonial swords.

By this time the rest of the Second Battalion had started over the hill. The men had stood on the back side staring when Craft took off on his own. His example had spurred them forward.

The soldiers couldn't believe what this private had done on his own. He'd killed the enemy like a one-man army. Fellow soldiers began gathering around Craft.

A sergeant observed that he'd wiped out the bandits all by himself. He had an unusual sound of respect in his voice.

One soldier noticed that he had picked up a sword.

Craft said he knew that if he didn't get it first, the guys over there in the Ninety-Sixth would pick the area clean of all souvenirs. "I just wanted to get mine before they came hopping in."

The men laughed.

Craft urged the men to keep moving onward.

Over seventy Japanese had been killed in the attack. PFC Clarence Craft had killed somewhere between twenty-five and thirty of them. A few months later, he received a presidential summons to come to Washington. President Harry Truman placed the Congressional Medal of Honor around his neck. His valor had not gone unrecognized.

On May 31, the 383rd found no resistance as they approached the town of Shuri. For days, this elusive objective had seemed almost impossible to reach. Artillery had pounded the entire area, but the Japanese persisted in their efforts to hang on to it. Now we walked in from one end and the marines came in from the other. Artillery fire had turned the town into a pile of rubble. The emaciated bell tower of a Christian mission stood like a ghost above the surrounding town, where the remains of the wooden buildings looked like toothpicks in a sea of broken concrete and split rocks. The Japanese had once made their headquarters in the ancient Shuri Castle. Now all that stood was the skeleton of three remaining walls towering over hunks of twisted steel and slabs of cement. About the only entity still recognizable was a network of tunnels underneath the castle's remains. The Japanese had used another escape network to get out of the city.

The cost for our soldiers to walk in so casually had been the lives of 2,074 of our boys. However, the Japanese had lost 8,500 at least, trying to defend this area. The only way we marched through was that heroic fighting men had laid their lives on the line day after day.

49

The Big Apple

Sergeant McQuiston had walked through the ruins of Shuri and knew the city had been virtually destroyed by our artillery attacks. He had seen the smoked hull of Shuri Castle and knew well that everything would have to be rebuilt . . . if there were any Japanese left to do the rebuilding.

"Why don't they give up?" McQuiston asked me.

"Looks like they would," I said. "I heard down at Command that ol' General Mitsuru Ushijima believes in that old Japanese idea that they keep fighting until the last man is dead. Intelligence believes he is right now organizing for a last stand, so they can all go out together. Our boys are breathing down his neck."

"Why, that old bastard!" McQuiston said. "Hope someone shoots him along the way before he takes any more men with him. He deserves a graveyard."

"Appreciate your sensitivity." I grinned. "The truth is Ushijima has already lost an entire division. His other division was chewed to pieces in the battle over Shuri. The rest of his army is fairly well gone."

McQuiston shook his head. "Bunch of crazies," he muttered. "I want to go up to the front and watch it wind down."

"I don't think I'd do that," I said. "There's still plenty of war going on with bullets flying."

McQuiston shrugged. "I still want to watch it happen up close."

"I'm tellin' you that's a good way to get killed."

The truth was that the average Japanese soldier had already figured out where all this struggle was going. The army we'd faced right after we landed and battled across the island had a fanatical mind-set that if they took some Americans with them, getting killed was sacred martyrdom. What was left of their army appeared to have jettisoned that idea. When they saw us coming with tanks, artillery, and mortars, these remaining enemy took off in the opposite direction. Seemed like this remnant were more discreet than their dead comrades.

Don't get me wrong. The war wasn't over, and we knew it would take the full force of our men to annihilate what was left of the Japanese. No question about it. Our men were on the move. From the first of June to the sixth, we made steady progress. The Deadeyes were quick to roll over the opposition, but it was still dangerous business. Colonel Ed May's troops encountered brisk resistance as they plowed forward. However, time after time, we were knocking the Japanese dead in our inevitable march to the finish line.

The rain had let up but then returned with that continuous drip, drip, drip that slowed our vehicles to a halt. Much of our movement of supplies and wounded men ended up coming by ship through the ocean port of Yonabaru. Of course, roads were constantly getting washed out, and that really gave us problems.

The 383rd kept pushing forward under wet circumstances. The Second Battalion descended on the road junction of Iwa, an important site. Natives stood around watching. The number seemed unusually large, but when the soldiers started checking, they found a number of soldiers wearing civilian clothes. Apparently, the enemy had seen what was coming and ducked out the back door. When they started out again from the Iwa junction, the Second Battalion ran into Japanese with considerable fight still left. The encounter turned as savage as any previously experienced. Nevertheless, the First Battalion broke through the heaviest resistance and five hills fell into their hands. We discovered a squad of Japanese digging in a new position on another hill and killed fifty-three of them.

The day's victories were overshadowed by a death that stunned everyone. Colonel Ed May had been one of the most gallant soldiers in all of the skirmishes. His pattern of observation had remained the same: Colonel May always watched the front lines from a forward observation post. One day as he was standing there, a Japanese gunshot hit him in the chest with the bullet going through his heart. The men of the 383rd were stunned.

When the report reached General Bradley, he said, "He was the finest soldier I have ever known." Colonel May had always been an exacting commander who was a master of the military arts. No one could question his bravery. His men trusted him and followed his example of valor and courage. The men of his regiment made a small monument to mark the site of his death. Posthumously, Colonel Ed May was awarded the Distinguished Service Cross.

The next big step came on June 10. The Big Apple Hill and Ridge had to be taken to keep the show on the road. Colonel Halloran directed the 381st Infantry's effort to take this objective, which the men knew had to be one of the last of the Okinawa invasion.

Two companies were suddenly pinned down in rice paddies at the base of the hill. The situation was quickly becoming critical.

Captain Philip Newell, leading C Company, realized immediate action was needed. He called in smoke bombs to cover their tracks. The Japanese assumed our soldiers were retreating. Wrong.

"Major Shaw?" the voice on the walkie-talkie boomed with authority.

"Yes, sir," I answered.

"We have a situation that needs your attention. The Japanese have erred in assuming C Company is retreating because of the heavy smoke. With the white fumes still covering the ground, they sent a hundred soldiers into a building on the escarpment where the enemy are changing into civilian clothes right now. We believe they're getting ready to attempt an infiltration."

"I see," I said slowly. "You're suggesting that we need to put a stopper in their bottle."

"You got it. We want your artillery crew to bombard that entire area until we've scared the pants off the Japanese."

"Gotcha," I said. "When do we start firing?"

"We're observing the Japanese right now. Get ready and we'll give you the signal. Hit 'em with all you got."

"Yes, sir."

I called McQuiston over. "Tell the men to load the cannons and stand by."

McQuiston saluted and began alerting the men. When the order came, we fired everything we had. We kept firing until the walkie-talkie rang again from command.

"Major Shaw, tell your soldiers they can cease firing."

"We got 'em?"

"Sir, you made mincemeat pie out of those jokers. Ain't gonna be no slipping into our lines today."

———————

While we were pounding the enemy pinning down C Company, G Company ran into a fascinating situation. The men were approaching a cave that they expected would hide Japanese. As they listened, they could hear noises inside. No question that Japanese were in there.

One of the men whispered to the sergeant that maybe they ought to toss in a smoke bomb. The Japanese seemed to have become wimps. Maybe they'd just walk out with their hands up and wouldn't be putting any of our guys in jeopardy.

The sergeant sounded cynical when he asked if the soldier wanted to play Tarzan and try it.

The private thought about it and finally decided to give it a try. Did they have any smoke bombs?

The sergeant yelled for one of those buzz bombs to blow a little smoke up the enemy's dress: he wanted some real fog to come rolling out of that cave.

Jones stayed low but quickly came over with the fireworks.

The sergeant put the canister in the private's hands. He told Tarzan to go swinging in there and see what he could scare out of that cave.

The private worked his way to the entrance. He paused, pilled the safety pin, and tossed the device inside. Gray, curling smoke immediately covered the opening. The soldier aimed his rifle, half expecting a shoot-out to follow.

"Hawaii! Hawaii!"

The soldier mumbled, "What in the hell is going on?"

A man's voice kept repeating "Hawaii."

A stick with a white cloth emerged out of the smoke. The Japanese soldier came out waving the stick with one hand and just waving with the other. Out of the fog a second figure appeared. A woman.

The woman's traditional kimono had a large cummerbund around the waist. She was strikingly beautiful with carefully made-up features and artistically shaped eyebrows to match the grandeur of her face.

"Hawaii!" she began to repeat, imitating the man.

The soldier rolled over and found the sergeant behind him. "I think that's the only English word they know. I can't shoot no damn women."

The sergeant nodded and decided to ship the prisoners back to detainment. The private motioned for the pair to come forward. The man and the woman kept bowing as they slowly approached the soldiers.

The sergeant asked if they spoke English.

The man nodded his head enthusiastically and repeated, "Hawaii."

50

The Home Stretch

I was standing beside one of our cannons ready to receive instructions from Command. We knew the infantry had been moving forward rapidly on all fronts, but our artillery unit had remained in a calm mode. For a change, all reports coming in were good and the Deadeyes were making significant progress. Much of the war had been a roller-coaster ride with wild swings because the enemy kept charging and then retreating. We pushed ahead and then often traced our steps backward. Up and down, up and down. Nevertheless, we knew our artillery had greatly shortened the war.

"Major!" McQuiston called. "Got a question."

"Sure."

"Since our assaults have slacked off, I was wondering if you had any objections to my running up to the front to take a look."

"Objections? Sure I do. I've told you how dangerous the no-man's-land can be."

"Well, you've been going back and forth doing reconnaissance. I just thought that—"

"You thought you'd love to tell the folks back home how close you were to the killing. Right?"

The sergeant shrugged. "Just wanted to see the action up close."

"Okay, McQuiston," I said. "Just remember that I told you to watch out."

A smile broke across his face. "Yes, sir. I'll trot up the road and see what I can. I won't be gone long."

"Yeah, you do that."

The sergeant took off like a jackrabbit.

Seemed like every aspect of the infantry was charging forward. Companies A and B attacked through the Ozato area, but the forward surge was not without problems. Company A's Second Platoon experienced heavy machine-gun fire. Lieutenant William Harp reorganized and started back up to the top to grab the ridge. Machine-gun fire caught him racing up the hill and it was all over. For the moment, the A Company could not overcome constant fire and had to camp out for the night just where they were. Nevertheless, the 383rd kept plowing ahead.

Three small hills east of Yuza continued to be a problem. Consequently, Company E received orders to assault Yuza Ridge, which was covered with pillboxes. The unit reached the top of the hill but came under mortar, grenade, and rifle attack. No foxholes could be dug because the ground was hard rock. The men were exposed, and the casualties mounted.

A knob on Yuza had gone unnoticed until Company G started

through the area. To the surprise of leadership, the seemingly insignificant rise turned out to be riddled with tunnels and pill-boxes. Because of the interconnectedness of these tunnels, the hill became difficult to take. The Japanese had not given up yet.

That night Colonel Dill moved his antitank company to the top of Yuza Ridge, only to discover that it was swarming with Japanese. No one was sure how such resistance had developed. As the fight developed, a tunnel was discovered that connected the ridge to Hill 167: it was 2,200 yards long. The enemy were able to run men back and forth without our seeing them. Different companies experienced machine-gun fire that took a toll. While the 382nd knew the Japanese were beaten, that insight didn't slow down the enemy. There was no surrendering because their leadership at the top was committed to the bitter end.

Misunderstandings didn't help us. Colonel Halloran sent I Company to fill a gap that had developed between the First Battalion and the Seventeenth Infantry. The ground was exposed and night was coming on. The Third Platoon found themselves completely in the open, the most dangerous possible place to be. Messages between the different platoons got confused and no one was certain what was going on or who was exposed. Colonel Halloran couldn't determine where the units were and what should happen next. Around two thirty in the morning, a tremendous explosion blew up our heavy machine-gun emplacement. At least twelve men were wounded. No one could determine where the blast came from.

We got the next phone call in the late afternoon. "Major Shaw, get your men ready," Command said. "We're going to have a big blowout momentarily."

"What do you mean?" I said.

"Japanese have been located in the town of Makabe. We've seen 'em walking around and figure there must be a sizable number over there. That's where we want to open up on those babies."

"Just us?" I asked.

"Oh, no! We're going to use the marines' artillery as well. We're firing ten army and ten marine units at the same time. I think we're about to set off the biggest blast in the Pacific war."

"Hmm," I mused. "Okay, we'll be ready."

"I'll call in the signal to fire."

"Gotcha." I hung up.

The 361st Field Artillery unit had been ready to detonate for some time before the call came. The men stood around smoking and chewing the fat. Some of the men, including Hans Goins and Swinging Bill Arnold, appeared to be locked in an intense conversation. John Hayes and Lee Lewis sounded like they had some sort of disagreement with George Morris. Just a typical killing-time situation while the men waited to fire the howitzers.

The walkie-talkie rang.

"Major Shaw," I said.

"Fire!" the voice on the other end demanded.

"Done," I answered, and hung up.

"Okay men," I shouted. "The orders came through. Fire at will."

The ground shook as every cannon blasted away. We kept firing on the Makabe target for at least forty-five minutes. Finally, the phone rang again. "The 361st can let up," the officer said. "Appears that we have destroyed the town. At least two hundred sixty-four blasters made pulp out of the place. The Japanese were annihilated."

I hung up slowly, thinking that once again, artillery had made the difference and saved some of our men's lives.

Our big field howitzers had been capable of firing murderous rounds during the entire conflict. Someone figured out that all of these cannons together fired at least 302,581 rounds during the battle to take Okinawa. However, the Japanese had equally used their artillery in a highly effective fashion. Antiaircraft guns had been significant. Their 320mm spigot mortars had a highly demoralizing effect. We were amazed when those flying boxcars came raining down on us. The craters they left could measure thirty to forty feet across and might create a hole fifteen feet deep. Those blasts left many men so disoriented that they wound up in special wards created simply to deal with the men who cracked under the strain of disorienting explosions and a head-rattling roar that could leave them deaf, sometimes for long periods or permanently.

Still, the effect on the Japanese from our artillery fire proved worse. Constant blasts morning, noon, and night nearly drove many of them crazy. Once they became disoriented, they inadvertently made themselves easier targets to hit. Our artillery units had made a tremendous difference in the entire campaign.

Generals Bradley and Easley knew we now held all the dominating hills and ground on the entire island. There were a few pockets still to be cleaned out, but not much was left. We would lose some more American lives, but the heavy fighting was finished. The Japanese had nowhere to go.

As our cannons cooled, I realized that Sergeant McQuiston was not around.

I grabbed Bill Arnold by the arm. "Where's the sergeant?"

Arnold shrugged. "I think he took off quite a bit earlier, before we started blasting. I believe he went to the front line."

"He didn't tell me!" I said indignantly.

Arnold raised his eyebrows but didn't say anything.

I looked at the sky. The afternoon was disappearing. I thought, *McQuiston better get his butt back before the sun goes down.* Wandering around out there in the dark could be suicide. The Japanese still had the capacity to infiltrate, and many a soldier would fire first and ask questions later.

The men broke out their K rations for the evening feast of Spam. Not exactly what we were looking for after a day of battle, but what the hell, we had no alternative. Quiet settled over the camp and a few of the men continued talking.

Around nine, the walkie-talkie buzzed.

"Yeah," Captain Lorne Martin answered the phone. "What's up?"

I listened and wondered what Command might be ordering at this hour of the night.

"Oh!" Martin said. "Yes, we have a man by that name." After a long pause, he mumbled softly, "I see." After another long pause, he hung up. The captain looked at me and then stared at the ground.

"What's going on?" I asked.

"They found his dog tags and knew he came from us," Martin said. "Sergeant McQuiston got nearly to the front and was hit by friendly fire from behind." The captain stopped and took a deep breath. "Sergeant McQuiston is dead."

51

The Final Battle

As the news of Sergeant Art McQuiston's death spread through the 361st, men fell silent. You never get used to death, but in a war, you know that it is going to happen. After the grueling struggle we had endured on Okinawa, some men distanced themselves and avoided making friends. The pain becomes too great when guys you have shared your life with are suddenly killed. Many soldiers just did their job, curled up in a ball at night, and said little to the other men.

I had really come to care about my sergeant. Men like Bill Arnold, Goins, Morris, and Lewis were fixtures in my life. McQuiston had led the parade and now he was gone. With the end of the war in sight, his death felt too personal and tragic to reflect on. No one wanted to talk about it.

He was gone.

A few towns were left that had to be taken. Aragachi and Medeera turned out to be more of a task than one would have expected.

Leaders of platoons and commanders sometimes fell. The enemy weren't throwing in the towel just because we came rolling over them. The village of Ozato turned into a hamlet from hell. Whatever the Japanese had told the residents had apparently soaked in before we came marching through. When they saw us coming, the locals started committing suicide. A wave of death swept through the town. One of our units discovered a dozen women and their children had holed up in a lair in the ground. As our soldiers forced them to come out, they began falling on the ground. Later examination by a military doctor revealed they had taken strychnine. Our medical team had their hands full trying to save whomever they could. Some survived, but many didn't.

Ozato started to be overrun with civilians. Japanese citizens seemed to be coming in from who knows where and converging on this city. Even though the town was in ruins, they kept coming. These civilians became more and more of a problem. Of course, they were Japanese, but the human nature of the American boys was to care for them regardless. The doughboys felt compassion for these poor civilians who had not received good treatment from the Japanese army and were pushed around like stray cattle. Caught between their army and our artillery, many had fallen.

The 305th Infantry of the Seventy-Seventh Division kept rolling and crossed the Yuza Ridge. Pockets of resistance appeared and were wiped out. The army had to fight its way across these areas. Even though they were defeated, the Japanese didn't capitulate. Often, they committed *hara-kiri* but no one surrendered.

On June 18, we ran into another of those experiences that will forever stay in everyone's mind. General Claudius Easley had been the eyes and ears of General Bradley. Easley's routine was to maneuver back and forth up and down the front line, watching everything that happened. His acute sense of observation in battle settings made him an invaluable forward observer. On this day he had crawled to the summit of a small hill to direct artillery fire on the enemy. Somewhere out there, a Japanese machine gunner had taken aim on that particular hill and already downed an important aide. When General Easley looked out over the edge of the hill, the gunner shot him in the head and instantly killed him.

Claudius Easley had been the spark plug of the division, and his death shocked the entire unit. His demise proved to be a staggering blow to the Ninety-Sixth. The men built a monument to mark where General Easley had so tragically fallen.

As the month of June wound down, our soldiers finished cleaning out any remaining enemy troops. I knew that the Japanese officers would not surrender. On June 11, American airplanes dropped surrender invitations on the Japanese command center.

Of course, they were ignored. Five days later I took Swinging Bill Arnold with me and found an observation post from which we could follow the final act in the drama. We were watching with binoculars as the curtain came down on the Japanese war effort. Military officers stood at attention waiting for General Ushijima and his chief of staff, Lieutenant General Isamu Cho, to come out of their tents.

Swinging Bill leaned over. "Think anybody can see us up here?"

I shook my head. "Before I started up, I checked with Command. All that's left is finding the Japanese that are hiding in caves. They know their army is finished."

"I don't want to end up like Sergeant McQuiston did with a Halloween-style surprise."

I only nodded. I didn't want to talk about it. I pulled up my binoculars and focused on the scene.

Ushijima and Cho came out at almost the same time. The two generals faced each other and bowed. With an aide armed with a *samurai* sword at each man's side and white gloves on their hands, they looked like something out of a textbook. Both men wore the tropical uniform with their white shirt outside the uniform's high collar. A red-sash belt had been wrapped around the waist. The traditional belief was that the sash brought good luck and immunity to bullets. Fat chance that was true. The uniform was a light-green khaki color, probably because of the hot weather. The three-quarter-length trousers came to the knee. Each general wore a green tropical tunic with a *shin gunto*, a small sword hanging at his side that was both a weapon and a badge of rank.

"What's the scoop on what these guys are doing?" Arnold asked.

"*Hara-kiri* is an ancient form of the ultimate surrender in the Japanese art of war," I said. "They fight to the death, and rather than be captured, they kill themselves. Goes way back."

"Hmm," Swinging Bill mused. "You mean these two jokers down there are going to kill themselves in front of all those soldiers?"

"Afraid so. They'll probably stab themselves in the belly and then draw the blade upward. Something like that. It's a form of having honor even in defeat."

"I think I'd prefer our way of being considered a nice guy."

"I imagine Ushijima and Cho are going to take the big sleep because of the defeat of their army in this struggle, but that's just a guess."

"Look!" Bill pointed. "Can't believe my eyes!"

With a quick swing of his arm, one of the generals plunged the dagger into his own stomach. For a moment, he wavered back and forth and then fell to his knees. The soldier behind him abruptly swung his *samurai* sword like a baseball bat, lopping off the general's head with one swipe. The other general followed suit and did the same. The man's head bounced a couple of times and rolled to one side.

"Oh, my God!" Arnold gasped. "Awful."

"Yeah," I said. "Awful like this whole war."

We slipped away from our observation area and started back. We didn't say much. We'd seen enough.

When the final calculations were made, the totals said that the Deadeyes had killed 37,763 of the enemy. The 361st Field Artillery Battalion had played a crucial part in knocking off a well-entrenched foe. Some pockets of resistance remained, and they had to be cleaned out, but the Japanese knew they were beaten and the war was over for them.

The code the Japanese followed remained a "to the death" resolution. While many of the soldiers would have probably given up by then, officers like General Amamiya forced the survivors to stay behind. The result was that many of the caves where they were hiding had to be blown up and sealed shut. At night, Japanese survivors tried to escape in the dark and board the underground railroad hurrying north. They didn't get far.

By July 1, the struggle was finished. The bitterest and most significant battle of the Pacific was over.

52

The Bomb

As the final days of the Okinawa struggle wound down, the rain began to slack off. Almost overnight, it felt as if someone had turned the faucet off. Abruptly, we were once more back on dry and dusty soil. Almost made you want the monsoon back.

With the end of the military conflict, the entire Ninety-Sixth Division had been loaded on a fleet of LSTs and shipped over to the gray beaches of an obscure island called Mindoro. This hunk of nothing floated out there in the Pacific Ocean without any apparent meaning or purpose except to keep us happy. Called "the Rock" by the men, Mindoro was the holding tank for our impending attack on Japan proper. We knew what was coming.

Every single person who had survived the battle for Okinawa knew they were lucky to still be alive. Sitting out there on the Rock, the men understood they were still faced with only two alternatives: life or death. The odds were decidedly in favor of death.

We didn't talk about the gruesome fact much, if at all, but we understood that the Japanese would fight to extinction no matter what. Sure, we'd win, but what a price to be paid! And every man knew that the same old story of devastation and death would start all over again once we hit Tokyo. I didn't want to think about the men I had lost. The memory of those deaths remained a painful path I didn't want to walk down. As best I could tell, I wouldn't recall much of what I had seen on Okinawa for decades.

One day on Mindoro, Swinging Bill Arnold sidled up to me. After Sergeant McQuiston was killed, Arnold had taken his place as my go-to guy. Bill had come to the army with some serious problems, but he had overcome his struggles in a significant way. Like a youngster growing up, Bill had left behind the fears from his childhood and turned into a man I could count on. He had supervised loading the howitzers when we broke camp. I saw him coming toward me. I immediately recognized that quizzical look in his eye.

"Major, we're hearing lots of rumors. Dark rumors."

"Yeah," I said. "Like what?"

"We're hearing that women and children with bamboo spears are going to meet us on the beaches when we land on Japan proper. Is that possible?"

"I was never much on gossip," I said. "Rumors are rumors. Nothing more."

Swinging Bill scratched his head. "You're avoiding the question. Could we end up fighting a bunch of women?"

"Okinawa demonstrated that the Japanese would rather get killed than stop fighting. I'm afraid that's an attitude we'll probably run into head-on when we hit their beaches."

Arnold swore violently. "We been giving chocolate bars to the kids we find on this island. In my wildest imagination, I can't see myself shooting some little boy running toward me with a bamboo stick. No sirree! I can't see that happening any way, shape, or form."

"Well, Arnold, you been praying to survive. Now you can change those prayers. Start praying we don't have to kill women and children. I think that would make a decent prayer."

Arnold only shook his head and walked off.

He never told me what had happened on Okinawa to change him, but I could read change in his face and his actions. We had been surrounded by dying and dead men. Bodies of Japanese were scattered everywhere and some had been left lying there in the grass for several days. The horror and stench had been overwhelming, and I knew Swinging Bill had seen the gore. Possibly for reasons I'd never understand, the gut-wrenching sights had had a reverse effect on him and somehow or the other broke the spell of that childhood scene that had so severely haunted him.

Strange how it all works. Sergeant McQuiston had been a real buddy, while Arnold was weird. Now McQuiston was gone and old Bill turned normal. Would never have expected such a thing.

———————

I'd gone down to Command to see if any news had come in about what was next. I knew the men were worrying about the struggle facing them, and I wanted to have some tidbit to tell them. When I walked in, I was surprised to see such a disorderly scene. Usually men stood at attention or made virtually no noise. Soldiers were standing around in small groups talking while the generals huddled together in private conversations down there on the platform. A group of men had gathered around the communications officer, sitting there like a rock, listening with a headset glued to his head and picking up the latest reports of whatever was coming in from abroad. Obviously, something unusual was going on. I saw Colonel Avery Masters standing by himself. Masters was the commanding officer of the 361st Artillery Battalion and I knew him well.

"What's the deal?" I asked him.

"You haven't heard?"

I shook my head. "Just got here."

"Big story has been coming in. Just getting pieces of it. Apparently, the Air Corps dropped some kind of a brand-new bomb on a city called Hiroshima. One bomb blew the entire municipality all to hell. Killed thousands in a single swipe. Happened earlier in the week. We're just now getting the report."

"You're kidding."

"Nope. They're calling it an atomic bomb."

I frowned. "Never heard of it."

"You haven't heard of it?" Avery laughed. "Hell, the generals never heard of it. The whole project's been top secret, but man alive! Have we ever got a dandy of a bomb. Blows every friggin' thing in its path to smithereens. Everybody's trying to figure out what comes next."

"Could this shorten the war?" I asked.

"Hard to say. Them Japanese don't seem to be too bright at figuring out when to quit. If I was in charge, it sure as hell would. I guess this A-bomb was dropped several days ago, but it's got to make a difference in how the enemy are thinking. Shoulda scared the living shit out of them."

The man at the communications desk jerked off his earphones, jumped up, and ran toward the cluster of generals. He handed one of them a piece of paper. Silence fell over the room. After several moments of talking among themselves, a general went to the podium.

"We've just been informed that another A-bomb has been dropped on Nagasaki with similar results. One bomb took out an entire city."

The men cheered and clapped. Soldiers slapped each other on the back. We had knocked the ball out of the park again. No telling how many of these new bombs we might have, but the Japanese had to know we could take them out one city at a time without even one infantryman stepping ashore. My men would be excited about the prospects for a quick end to the war.

It wasn't until much, much later that we learned those two bombs left the Japanese high command in complete chaos. Strongly divided factions couldn't agree on whether to immediately surrender or to keep fighting to the death. A coup almost occurred within their ranks as well as against the emperor. In the end, the emperor voted for surrender and the reluctant generals folded.

When the report came that the Japanese had finally, completely, unconditionally surrendered, the men went stark raving nuts. Carriers and battleships anchored in the Pacific shot off their giant guns continuously. Men ran up and down the roads firing their rifles in the air. Every machine gun in the army endlessly pounded away at nothing. Men screamed and hollered. The entire military complex on Okinawa had a conniption fit. After years of struggle, the battles were over, and we were still alive.

The war was over.

Men like Swinging Bill could stop praying. They would not be faced with women in kimonos rushing at them with kitchen knives while small children charged with bamboo spears sharpened to a flimsy point. The killing was finished.

The war was over.

I thought about the many men I'd known now buried in the Ninety-Sixth Division Cemetery on Okinawa. Little American flags and white wooden crosses dotted each grave over good men, decent men, patriots to the end. Wherever they were now, even the deceased surely had to celebrate.

The war was over.

Back in the United States, our wives, girlfriends, families had to be weeping for joy. Their loved ones had not become memorial gold stars on a small banner hung in the living room window to commemorate the ultimate sacrifice. Parades could start to march and bands play. People would dance in the streets. Churches would fill with people offering thanksgiving for victory and the cessation of hostilities. Mothers and fathers would weep in relief and for joy.

The war was over.

53

The Road Home

The ships taking us to Tokyo now had a new task. We were going home. Sounded simple, but nothing was. The soldiers were ready to board in the morning—the morning that did not come for weeks or even months for some of the men. The rumor floated around that we might end up doing occupational duty in Korea, but then a switch came through on that idea. The Deadeyes were going to be sent to Japan proper to take over the country and serve under the Sixth Army. Men who wanted to see Japan while waiting for discharge didn't mind the endless delays.

Going to an occupied Japan sounded like one big vacation, and the men began tearing down tents as well as burning and destroying the wooden kitchens on Mindoro. The entire area was quickly checked out to make sure we left it in tiptop condition—for who? The monkeys and lizards? Seeing a conquered Japan certainly beat coming in as invaders. We were ready to roll—and then the new orders came through.

The trip was off.

The men were angry and disgusted. We were literally left with nothing to do, and emptiness weighed heavily. Twiddling their thumbs after fighting night and day made men agitated and bewildered. Waiting was not a science we were trained in.

To offset the chronic boredom, the army started offering courses in everything from algebra to zoology. Athletic programs and events popped up. The movies even got better, and the food improved. (Of course, when the movie projectors broke down, the men went bonkers.) Even bottles of beer came floating in from who knows where. The Red Cross erected what they called Fatigue Junction centers with everything from Ping-Pong to billiards along with bingo, Cokes, and cookies—with women running the place. Recordings of the Glenn Miller orchestra and the Andrews Sisters filled the air. Men could swim at the beaches, but how many days can you lie out in the sun when you actually want out of a place? For most of the men, Mindoro felt like a one-way ticket to the nuthouse.

Somewhere along the way in this mess of poor organization, someone got a bright idea. A newspaper called the *Deadeye Dispatch* was started to keep the men informed about what was going on in the outside world and gave a little touch of "this and that" to help them feel like a real world was still out there on the other side of the Pacific. Someone came up with the idea of nominating a pinup model for the "Occupation Girl" of the Deadeyes. The ravishing beauty would be our official symbol of victory. The contest got off to a roaring start as nominations poured in. If nothing else, the movies let us feast our eyes on the beauty queens of Hollywood. One of those beauties would work just fine.

The front-runners were movie stars like Olivia de Havilland,

June Allyson, and Yvonne De Carlo. Then the contest took an un-expected turn. Somebody came up with an entry without even a touch of glamour and the sex appeal of a carrot. There were no pictures in a swimming suit of a voluptuous woman modeling expensive lingerie. The dark horse candidate was Marjorie Main.

She had been around Hollywood in raucous, two-fisted movies as a "just for laughs" type. In a movie with Wallace Beery entitled *Jackass Mail*, Marjorie Main *had not* been the Hollywood beauty queen. Later she became Ma Kettle in a hillbilly role. Ma and Pa Kettle became the laughs of the movie industry. Her supporters in the 361st Infantry argued that Marjorie Main was just what we needed to represent the rugged, knock'em-dead values that had led us through the toughest battles of the war. Along with my 361st Field Artillery group, we took on the challenge to elect none other than Marjorie Main as our model of the year.

Once the voting began, we dumped several hundred ballots into the box, supporting our dynamic candidate. We came up with slogans like "A Fighting Girl for a Fighting Division." The joke caught on and the idea took hold. The men came to champion her cause. Musicians in the division band began writing songs to proclaim her as our ideal woman. Men started painting slogans on the trucks and tanks saying "As Main Goes, So Goes the Divi-sion." Then there was "Remember the Main" and "Reminds Me of Mom." Even colonels and generals got in on the act, and Marjorie Main led the pack of nominees.

By the time the voting was over, Marjorie Main had won by six thousand votes over all her bathing beauty competitors. When the division's public relations office got the news, they had a field day publishing the results across America. Before long, the average man on the street knew more about the Deadeyes—not because of their extraordinary bravery so much as their eccentric taste in pinup girls.

The news left Marjorie Main speechless and overwhelmed. She quickly signed autographed pictures that were sent off to General Bradley and promised to meet the men when they came sailing into the harbor. As promised, when the first of the division sailed in, she was there waiting for them. Wearing a cowboy hat, leather gloves, and an ornate gun belt and holster, she swung an old-fashioned six-shooter in the air. The men hoisted her on their shoulders and carried her around the ship. Marjorie Main strolled around, shaking hands and talking with the soldiers. She even made a trip to Camp Anza near Los Angeles to be with "her boys." Rather than just have lunch with the soldiers, she insisted on putting on a white chef's cap and serving the men as they came by. The rumor was she had to be taken off the serving line because she was giving each man two steaks and they were running out.

The month dragged on without any clear instruction or direction as to when soldiers would be leaving for home. Getting back to the USA became an obsession. As the sounds of battled faded, the men became more and more homesick. Eventually, a point system was devised for determining the order in which soldiers would be shipped back to American shores. However, there had been so many disappointments that many soldiers didn't take the promise seriously.

With disappointment and tension growing, the army needed some alternative to keep soldiers happy. Special service officer Captain Clarence Ashcraft came up with the idea of creating a Deadeye Bowl, an amphitheater with continual entertainment.

Stage shows and swing bands popped up and the big show was on. The crowds grew to six thousand men and even movies were shipped in. The problem of getting home remained, but attitudes took a swing for the better.

Time continued to drag by, but by early December genuine directions for returning to the USA fell into place. The Deadeyes sent 6,599 men to Leyte on converted Liberty ships for the first leg of their trip back to the States. Not long after Christmas, the next 1,800 officers and men moved out. For those remaining, the Christmas season wasn't easy, but there was a light on the horizon. The Red Cross tried to cheer everybody up with makeshift parties. For New Year's Eve another celebration was planned. The report was that they cooked 4,500 hamburgers, 400 pounds of french fries, and passed out 14,400 bottles of beer. Now that's a party!

And then the party was over.

The remaining soldiers boarded the *General Langfitt,* an army transport ship. Fifteen minutes after the last man stepped on board, they pulled up the anchor and the last soldiers were on their way home. Without a band playing, a crowd cheering, or speeches being made, the final wave of men silently and unceremoniously left behind the worst fighting of the Second World War.

The hard part was leaving behind the buddies and pals buried in the division's cemetery on Okinawa. The fallen would forever remain as silent guardians of an island that was the final battlefield of the most savage war the world had ever known. Their silent witness still stands as a tribute to the valor of everyday American boys who laid down their lives for their family, friends, and country thousands of miles away.

As the last soldiers sailed away, a world so different from their own disappeared into the sunset. Every man had been severely tested by the constant threat of death. Bombs, artillery, machine-gun fire, and even, for some, hand-to-hand combat had faced them at every turn. The awful, grim Specter from the grave had lived among us day and night. The dead had not fallen to his blade without resolve and valor. We would never forget them.

Back home, we wouldn't want to talk about what we had seen. Most of us wouldn't speak of the war for decades. The horrendous memories remained more than could be digested, sometimes in a lifetime.

But for now, it was over. We were going home.

The ships began arriving, including the *General Langfitt*, an eighteen-thousand-ton army transport, that was the last vessel to leave for home. At 2:00 p.m., January 17, 1946, the transport pulled out of the harbor headed for San Francisco. We left behind the silence of buddies now gone who would never leave the island. The hush of windswept beaches we would forever remember. We believed we had achieved the hope of a better world for our children and families.

Being an officer, I found myself in what certainly seemed like luxurious accommodations after what I had lived with all those months on Okinawa. I felt like I had hit the jackpot. I didn't realize that because of my rank I would get first-class treatment. Somewhere out there crossing the ocean, the captain announced there was a change of plans. We were going to Los Angeles. Whatever. I just wanted to get home.

When the ship pulled into the L.A. harbor, huge crowds were there waving and shouting. The newspaper called it the most tumultuous welcome ever given returning troops in the Los Angeles harbor. Who should pull alongside in the army greeter boat, the *Snafu Maru*, but Marjorie Main wearing a ten-gallon cowboy hat with revolvers hanging at her side. She was there to welcome "her boys" home. The Los Angeles Musicians' Association Orchestra and an army band blared their patriotic marches as we came tramping down the ship's ramp.

I immediately called my wife, Joan, and told her I would meet her in Kansas City as soon as I could board a train. I had no idea what time it would be other than "as soon as possible." We had a child I had never seen. Did I ever want to hold her! The world of constant explosions and death was gone, and I was stepping into the normal world of what most Americans called "everyday life." I couldn't wait to take the plunge.

As the miles flew past, the clattering of the train wheels against the rails beat out a steady rhythm that sounded like a melody of promise. We roared out of California into Arizona and then on into New Mexico. Even a night in the sleeper car seemed heavenly after months in foxholes.

When our train came rolling into the Kansas City station, the passenger car came to an abrupt halt. For some reason, we were disconnected and left as a lone coach sitting on a side track. After months in the hot, tropical South Pacific, I thought we'd freeze to death. Finally, I climbed out and walked up the track to a small hut where a yardman appeared to be throwing switches.

"Sir, for the last several years, we've been fighting your country's battles in the South Pacific. Now we come home and sit abandoned out here in your freight yard. Can you help us?"

The man blinked several times. "Soldier, you can damn sure bet I can. You go back to that passenger car and I'll have a locomotive down here in minutes to pull you on in. Thank you for what you've done for America."

I saluted and hurried back. True to his word, we were quickly pulled into the station. I rushed through the terminal and grabbed a cab, handing the driver a piece of paper.

"Can you get me to this hotel?"

The cabbie looked at the name. "Young man! We are on our way." Off we blew through the streets like I was a celebrity going to the White House.

———————

I had not seen my wife in two years. Of course, we had corresponded as much as possible and she had struggled through having a baby by herself. That day my little girl, Sharon, only knew me as a picture on the wall. I wondered what those many months had done to all of us. Two years. Think about it. Two years! What would it be like to return to my family?

The cab pulled up to the curb. "Well, sir, here we are. That's your hotel." He stopped by the revolving doors, which were swinging around as people came and went.

"Excellent." I reached for my billfold.

"You don't owe me nothin'," the cabbie said. "It's an honor to help a man who has served our country so well. No, sir, thank you for riding with me."

I didn't know what to say. I solemnly shook his hand and got out. "Thank you, kind sir. I appreciate that good word more than I can say." The gracious cabbie drove away.

I quickly walked through the lobby up to the registration desk. "I need the room number for Joan Shaw."

The clerk looked askance at my army uniform and frowned.

"We don't arbitrarily give out that information. I'll call and see if that is agreeable to Mrs. Shaw."

I shrugged and waited.

"She said to send you up," he finally said, and smiled. "Room three twenty-eight."

I got on the elevator and started up. A glance in the mirror said my tie was straight and I looked fairly decent for having traveled day and night across the United States in a train car. Months in the tropics had turned my skin so dark that I almost looked like an Indian. The elevator door opened. In front of me was another door with 328 on the front.

I knocked. Almost instantly the door opened.

Joan just looked at me.

I don't know how long we stood there, saying nothing, looking, struggling for words, remembering who we had been, who we still were, husband and wife.

"Come in," Joan finally said, and held the door open.

We sat down in two comfortable chairs across from each other and just gazed.

"It's been a long, long time since we've seen each other," I said.

"Certainly has," Joan said.

We started talking, and talking, and talking. Time had no meaning. Somewhere in the wee hours of the night, we realized for the first time that we had talked for hours.

Finally, I said, "Joan, I'm back."

She said, "I can't possibly begin to tell you how glad I am." She reached for my hand.

54

Morning Comes Again

The decades passed with their own peculiar but incredible speed. I tried to put the memories of the war behind me. Unfortunately, those images seldom stayed put. Most people didn't notice that soldiers almost never spoke of what had happened. Climbing imposing cliffs with machine guns firing at you or turning around only to find a buddy lying there with a bullet through the head wasn't something one spoke about. The smell of the jungle, smoke, the acid scent of cannon fire, and the odor of death, all separate or mixed together, lingered on and on. We tried to shove that recollection into a box labeled Yesterday: Don't Open.

Talk often turns to "Who were the heroes?" Let me tell you who the heroes are. Anyone who puts on a military uniform and marches off to battle is a hero. Makes no difference if bullets whiz by your head or you never step on the battlefield. Putting on the uniform and making yourself available for service makes you a hero in my book.

After I left the military, I realized that traumatic experiences permeated civilian life as well. Things I learned in war became valuable tools for surviving peacetime. I began to realize that my own survival had come with help that I missed seeing the first time around. Unseen hands had pulled me in and out of scrapes while I never realized divine interventions had been at work all the time.

Perhaps my most important discovery came out of an extreme back injury that occurred while I was still in the army. I was in Indiana acting as an adviser with the Indiana National Guard, fulfilling my obligation for civilian duty that was required of an officer approaching twenty to thirty years of military service.

The dirt roads had a slick covering of oil. You don't mix oil and ice together or you almost have a skating rink. My sergeant was driving us down one of those back roads when the jeep slid out of control. When we tipped, I grabbed the roll bar, but my body went flying and flipping out. The unnatural twist and turning more than bent me out of shape.

I knew I had a serious problem, but I didn't want to go to a hospital, fearing that after working on me, the army might make me retire. Unfortunately, the pain had only begun. Eventually, I was swallowed by the agony and forced to face treatment for the damage. I ended up with a spinal fusion from the L1 to the S1 vertebrae in my spinal cord.

Intrusive surgery in that part of one's body is beyond terrible. I was left paralyzed from the waist down and couldn't even wiggle my toes. Before the doctors went any further, I had to regain the ability to move my big toe. Although it felt like an eternity before any sensation returned, eventually I got a wiggle. I knew I would walk again.

My Christmas of recovery turned into a Halloween of despair. My first operation required twenty-two units of blood. While I was recovering, I discovered that a second surgery would be necessary. I guess you wouldn't expect a disaster like that from an unscathed veteran of one of the worst conflicts of World War II.

———————

I really didn't like civilian life. I was army to the core. The hardest part of post-army life was recovering from what happened to my family.

Many years before my back operation, Joan and I had experienced a medical crisis that had ended unexpectedly in hope. The war had begun, and I was stationed at Fort Lewis, preparing to leave the country. Joan was pregnant and the "bulge" had begun to show. Then one morning there was no protrusion. Her stomach had become flat as the sidewalk. I immediately returned to Oklahoma.

We immediately went to see the medics at Fort Sill. In turn, they sent us on to Oklahoma City. Dr. Eskridge examined Joan carefully and then called us both in.

"The fetus is dead," the doctor said unceremoniously.

"Oh, no!" Joan cried.

"You're going back on the train?" the doctor asked.

We both nodded our heads.

"You'll probably miscarry on the way home, but if you don't, you'll need to take these records to the military hospital and let them care for you. Sorry, but that's the best I can do."

He shook my hand and walked out.

We were just kids and didn't know what to do except to take his advice seriously. With heavy hearts, we went home . . . but Joan didn't miscarry.

Because I had orders to leave for the front, we had no time: we needed to get Joan to the hospital and get this problem resolved. Unfortunately, I also had orders to be on a maneuver and couldn't even stay with her at the hospital. After all was settled, I could leave the country and Joan would return to her former home in Marlow, Oklahoma. We checked into the hospital with a staff of five ob-gyn doctors and prepared for the worst. Joan was checked and on her way to the procedure when the doctor stopped the gurney and made a final examination. He ran his hand over her belly and "Stop! The baby kicked!"

We were greatly relieved. The doctor couldn't explain how the baby was alive, and we didn't know what to think. Being as young as we were, we could only go home and be grateful.

The clock was running, and I had some final preparations as well as training that I had to complete before I shipped out. We kissed, and I told Joan I'd be back soon. We both knew that was a lie. She looked at me with those big gray eyes and tried not to cry. I didn't want to think about how long the separation might be before I saw her again. I waved and waved and was gone.

———————

Once I was back in the swing of preparation for battle, time moved faster, but the process took longer than I expected. Months passed before I was loaded on a navy ship heading for the Philippines. I knew the baby had to be developing fast, and that for a long time I would have no idea what my child looked like.

While the navy cruiser sailed across the Pacific Ocean, I

learned that the navy boys had a special ceremony for their men who had never crossed the equator. King Neptune of the Sea held a special court to initiate the sea dogs. The first-timers were called pollywogs while the veterans were shellbacks. The navy personnel harassed the boys with ridiculous exercises that ranged from blindfolding them to covering them with flour makeup to giving them a shampoo with mayonnaise. Being in the army exempted me from the initiations.

Suddenly, a voice boomed over the loudspeaker. "Major Arthur Shaw present yourself to King Neptune."

"What?" I turned to the soldier next to me. "I'm not a sailor. They got to be kidding."

He laughed. "Kidding is the right word. You better get over there."

I grudgingly walked between two sailors who escorted me to an elevated throne where King Neptune sat. The sailor held up his hand to speak like royalty announcing a military success.

"You are under severe penalty, Major Arthur Shaw, for the pain and suffering you have caused your wife." He gave me a hard, harsh stare, then broke into a smile. "Your wife just gave birth to your baby daughter."

The ship broke into applause.

———————

Our lives had been so heavily invested in the struggle to capture Okinawa that most of us felt like we had been there for a lifetime. And then it was all over.

The war simply stopped and we loaded up to get out of there. Of course, no one could fully express their gratitude for surviving the horrendous battles where so, so many had died. We would always have one foot planted forever in that island, though we would almost never talk about what we had seen.

After making our adjustment to being back in the States, I was sent to Fort Sill, which I knew like the back of my hand. My training in artillery had begun there and that's where I met my wife, Joan, in Lawton. The base was still humming and the big cannons firing in the practice fields. I was glad to be somewhere where a flying boxcar or a mortar could not fall out of the sky. Being home felt warm, friendly, and oh, so welcoming. In 1946, everything felt like a year of promise. I had barely settled in when I received orders that I was being assigned to the American Embassy in Turkey. Can you believe it? *Turkey!* Barely got home and was sent to another country I had never been to!

The airplane transport took off and I was on my way to Istanbul. I quickly learned that the influence of Mustafa Ataturk still swept through the country. After getting situated in the embassy, I discovered that my primary role was to help build a "West Point" in Turkey for training their military. We were to help them assemble an intelligent, informed, armed forces. All was going well until on June 25, 1945, North Korea invaded South Korea.

Our attention turned in a new direction. I became part of the process of organizing troops sent to Korea. We started putting together a Turkish Brigade to enter the conflict. One of the generals approached me about being his adjutant. Since I'd lived through the struggle in Okinawa and the Pacific, he knew I understood the war scene. Joan screamed when she heard about such a possibility and that was the end of that idea.

As the Korean conflict was winding down, I came back to the United States and picked up an assignment in assisting the

Indiana National Guard. Finally, in 1962, I retired as a Colonel in the United States Army. I had served my country, my family, and friends. I could always proudly salute the flag.

———————

The years slipped by. Joan and I settled into civilian life happy to watch our daughter grow and mature. I found my way doing various types of odd jobs. The army provided a good pension so I was at ease with those financial obligations. Making an adjustment from the rigid style of the military to an easygoing civilian life took some doing, but I continued to help with the Military Reserves and became involved with the Episcopal Church USA. I attended their conventions and worked in a local congregation. All the while, I kept trying to push my war experiences to the back of my mind, but they didn't stay down. Often, in the middle of the night, they'd come roaring back to life. Of course, I never talked to my wife or friends about the awful struggles I'd seen. I had a small storage box with a firm lid and a lock. I never opened it, but I knew the horrors of the past were buried in that antique box I left in a corner unopened.

During those years, Joan was a heavy smoker. Cigarette commercials were everywhere. No one thought anything about it. Somewhere along the way, rumors were heard that smoking wasn't good for you, but no one paid much attention. The warnings increased. Smoking continued. Everyone smoked.

Joan began coughing incessantly. A doctor warned that she appeared to have emphysema or something of that sort. The problem was that her lungs weren't working and processing her blood as they should. She struggled along but finally ended up spending most of her time in bed. During her last nine months, Joan lay in bed doing nothing but reading all the time. I did the cooking, cleaning, and everything I could do, but we were on a downhill slide and I couldn't stop the decline. Her breath shortened.

On December 6, 2002, at one in the morning, Joan slipped away. As overwhelmed as I was, I was relieved that her suffering was over. Her final journey had been hard and painful and now she was at rest. Our life together had been a great love affair and now I had to go on alone. *Alone* was the word that constantly lingered in my mind. Married on May 26, 1942, our marriage had lasted sixty years.

Death is natural. That old cliché that it's part of life is worn but true. During my World War II experiences, I had seen bodies in plastic bags stacked up like a cord of wood. Men blown to bits. People ripped apart. The horrors of death had been scattered around me, and somehow, I had walked through those tragedies, even though I still don't know how. I suppose that I never thought about the Specter coming to my house. The collapse of that which I held most dear was too great. How could I go on?

In war, death is all around you. One minute you're talking to a friend, you look away, and when you look back, he's lying there with a bullet through his helmet. You care about the guy. He's your buddy. And then in an instant he is gone. His face, his distant, unfocused eyes stare back at you empty. The image burns into your mind and doesn't go away. You end up never wanting to have a friendship with anybody in a uniform. They could all be gone in a flash. It's simply too much, way too much.

I didn't have much tolerance for so-called war-weary cases before I went to Leyte and Okinawa. After I crawled alongside cold bodies curled up around their rifles, their fingers already stiff, my bias changed. Any of us could have ended up in a psychiatric tent staring at the ceiling. Some men cracked like walnuts smashing against rocks. Others stopped talking; many became perpetually silent. Some of us sucked it up and went on. But the encounters, the experiences, the recollections never went away.

Some of the time, it seems the smell of death still hangs in the air. Horrible images keep returning. Dreams regurgitate what has been hidden at the bottom of your mind. Even decades later, those old memories will come flying back, screaming at you in the middle of the night. Humanity wasn't meant to witness best friends stacked up in a pile of lifeless soldiers awaiting their final journey to the grave.

But when death overwhelms your wife, your daughter, your granddaughter, the load is completely and totally unbearable, emotionally insufferable. You're afraid to go to sleep at night for what the dreams might say, and reluctant to get up in the morning because your body aches and there's a knot in your stomach. You feel tired all the time and forget things. You think your memory is going, and then you reflect and realize that the problem is depression. Behind the darkness is an anger that you can never quite get your hands around.

The formula is basic. Denial + anger + time = depression.

You can't laugh anymore. Sometimes you can't concentrate. You shuffle around like a zombie, but you know you must get over it. At the same time, you recognize that willpower isn't enough. Grieving is simply one hell of a mess.

In those moments of despair, I remembered lying flat on my

back in the hospital after my back surgery. For a while it had appeared that my legs wouldn't ever work again. Learning to walk again had seemed impossible. Then, in the midst of those dreaded log rolls, a voice had cut through the fog of my fears and I had moved without even a hint of pain. An unseen friend appeared out of nowhere, and though I couldn't see him, it, whatever, I could never forget that angelic voice. An angel had guided me through the maelstrom of struggle and I had survived. Surely, God had not abandoned me then and would not now.

I began to realize that I could do nothing about the past. What was done was settled. I needed to flip the light switch and let the yesterdays settle into the dim. And the future was no different. I didn't have a clue about what tomorrow would bring. All I could do was let it unfold when the sun came up once more. The only thing I could control was today.

No matter what had happened or might occur again, I could live for the hour at hand. All I really needed was one hour at a time. I decided that today could be faced with hope. Each morning, I would remember that this day had its own particular and important promise. I would pursue that dream.

Jesus once said, "Do not be anxious about your life, what you shall eat, or what you shall drink, nor about your body . . . do not be anxious about tomorrow, for tomorrow will be anxious for itself. Let the day's own trouble be sufficient for the day."

That would be good enough for me. All I have is today . . . and the possibilities that hope brings. Such will always be more than enough. I have chosen to live with that hope.

Acknowledgments

Special thanks to Susan Conway for her excellent oversight of the manuscript and many important observations. Her marine father participated in the battle for Okinawa, and Faye O'Dell is in this account. Memories of Digger O'Dell, as his buddies called him, add to the story of courage and honor.

We are indebted to Orlando R. Davidson, J. Carl Willems, and Joseph A. Kahl for their work *The Deadeyes: The Story of the 96th Infantry Division*, published by Infantry Journal, Inc., 1947.

The magnificent deeds of the Ninety-Sixth Infantry Division, the Deadeyes, remain as a constant reminder of the price paid for the American way of life. The division's cemetery on Okinawa will forever be a symbol of the valor and service that has preserved this nation.

Index

Aakerhaus, Kenneth, 185
A Company, 42, 110, 111, 112, 114,
    144–46, 149, 160, 170, 185, 242,
    245, 260, 279–80, 282, 297
Ada, Okla., 25–26, 27, 80
Addy, Leon, 274
aircraft, air strikes, 275–77, 283
    antiaircraft guns, 300
    Corsair, 203, 217
    Curtiss Helldiver, 96
    Japanese, 2, 4, 53, 203
Akio, 34–35
Alexander, Don, 106
Allyson, June, 315
Amamiya, General, 306
Amdahl, Aida, 254
America First, 157–58
Anderson, Beauford T. "Snuffy,"
    159–61, 162
Anderson, Woodrow, 242
Andrews, Leon, 211, 212
antiaircraft guns, 300
APA (troop attack transport), 10,
    12, 13
Aragachi, 302
Arends, John, 189–90
Arnold, "Swinging" Bill, 51–52, 56,
    66, 71, 78–80, 92, 93–95, 98,
    100–102, 136–39, 152–56, 159,
    172–73, 238–39, 250, 299–301,
    302, 304–306, 308–309, 311

God as viewed by, 137–38
mother and childhood trauma
    of, 94–95, 138, 172–73, 238, 239,
    308, 309
Arnsdorf, Garfield, 254
artillery, 14, 19, 27, 51, 54, 55, 65, 68,
    72, 85–87, 186, 243, 274, 289, 296,
    299, 300, 327
    Eleventh Marine Artillery, 169
    321st Field Artillery Battalion, 105
    361st Field Artillery Battalion, 3,
        14, 27, 51, 72, 77, 88, 92, 95, 136,
        169, 192, 242, 243, 251, 258, 299,
        306, 310, 315
    362nd Field Artillery Battalion, 105
    see also howitzers; mortars
Ashcraft, Clarence, 316
Ataturk, Mustafa, 327
atomic bomb, 310–11
atrocities, 15
Ault, George, 235

Baar, Bernard, 91
Baker, Merrill, 211
Bald Hill, 227–28
Ballard, Bill, 178–79, 236
BAR (Browning automatic rifle), 92,
    102, 134, 150, 228
Barron, James, 65
Bassett, Charles, 119–21
Bataan, 11

Battle of Midway, 36
Battle of the Bulge, 51
bazookas, 48
B Company, 29, 41–42, 78, 81, 83,
      110, 111, 113, 114, 141, 143–44,
      171, 232, 240, 242, 243, 252,
      260, 276, 297
Beery, Wallace, 315
Belman, Dave, 114
Bergman, Ingrid, 250
Best, Robert, 81
Big Apple Hill and Ridge, 293
Bland, Lee, 63–64
Blevins, Earl, 126–27, 131
Bolan, Robert, 142–43
Bolger, James, 62, 63
Bollinger, Captain, 212–13, 223–24
Boynton, Kenneth, 267, 268, 271
Bradford's Task Force, 197, 202
Bradley, James, 32–33, 86–87, 92,
      106, 163–64, 196–97, 247, 251,
      257–58, 261, 273, 283, 292, 300,
      303, 316
Bradley, John, 132–33, 136
Bridenbaugh, Neal, 254
Bronze Star, 136, 187
Brown, Tom, 155
Buckner, General, 249
Bulge, Battle of the, 51
bulldozers, 15, 19–20, 24, 33
burial caves, 31–32, 38, 72, 76, 181, 266
Bushboom, Arthur, 10
Butler, Clark, 254
Butler, Harold, 173
Byers, John, 211

Cactus Hill, 54, 65, 66–68, 72, 86,
      88–92, 93–98, 139
Cain, John, 67
Caldwell, Fred, 124–27
Camp Anza, 316
Campbell, Garland, 83

Carpenter, William, 4, 7
Carr, Jack, 83–85
caves, 68, 73, 75, 76, 120–21, 128–29,
      181, 183, 207–208, 218–19
   burial, 31–32, 38, 72, 76, 181, 266
   Command Center set up in,
      53–54, 105
   Japanese civilians hiding in,
      20–22, 24, 27, 38–41
   "lost platoon" in, 265–71
caves, Japanese forces in, 72, 84, 143,
      220, 222, 233, 235, 236, 246, 252
   at close of war, 304, 306
   flamethrowers used against,
      205–207, 225
   oil and gasoline used against, 222,
      225, 232
   smoke bomb used against,
      294–95
   tunnels connecting, 207, 208, 218,
      219, 220–22, 224–25, 232, 298
   white flags and, 252–53
C Company, 69, 81, 110, 112, 114,
      141–44, 174, 178, 235–36, 252, 260,
      263, 265, 274, 282–83, 293–94
Chambers, Earl, 84–85
Charlie Hill, 54, 244–45, 263, 265,
      274–76, 286
Chinen Peninsula, 244
Chittenden, Everett, 229–30
Cho, Isamu, 304–306
Christmas, 317
Clark, Prosser, 88–92, 97, 103
Clay Ridge, 67, 72, 73, 82
Cochran, James, 178, 179
Cochran, Keith, 267, 268, 271
Command, 72, 75, 77–78, 81, 82, 85,
      86, 95–98, 105, 110–11, 124, 147,
      148, 152, 155, 158, 168, 169, 199,
      202, 246, 262, 279, 283, 285, 296,
      298–99, 309
   cave headquarters of, 53–54, 105

Company A, 42, 110, 111, 112, 114,
 144–46, 149, 160, 170, 185, 242,
 245, 260, 279–80, 282, 297
Company B, 29, 41–42, 78, 81, 83,
 110, 111, 113, 114, 141, 143–44,
 171, 232, 240, 242, 243, 252, 260,
 276, 297
Company C, 69, 81, 110, 112, 114,
 141–44, 174, 178, 235–36, 252,
 260, 263, 265, 274, 282–83,
 293–94
Company E, 62–63, 95–97, 140, 162,
 204, 207–208, 253, 276, 279, 297
Company F, 65, 89–92, 97, 162, 171,
 209–10, 212–13, 222–24, 245–46,
 247, 259, 279
Company G, 73, 96, 125–26, 171,
 185, 191, 209–10, 218, 227, 246,
 262–63, 272, 277, 282, 286, 294,
 297–98
Company H, 103, 125, 127–28, 184
Company I, 83, 125, 127–28, 173–
 74, 181–82, 195, 205–206, 218,
 234, 298
Company K, 32, 57, 68, 173, 182,
 214–17
Company L, 124–29, 130–33, 136,
 179–80, 181, 193–94, 229,
 260, 282
Company M, 188, 262
Congressional Medal of Honor, 122,
 162, 187, 233, 288–89
Conical Hill, 242, 244–49, 251,
 262–65, 272, 277, 279
Coral Hill, 67, 72
coral reefs, 11, 15, 19, 29, 212
Corsair aircraft, 203, 217
cows, 27–28, 241
Coy, Robert, 263
Craft, Clarence, 286–89
Crags, the, 169, 183–86, 188
C rations, 186

Crowder, Jim, 210
Curtiss Helldiver airplanes, 96
Cutaway Hill, 286
crypts, 31–32, 38, 72, 76, 181, 266

Daily Oklahoman, 25
Deadeyes, *see* Ninety-Sixth Infantry
 Division
death, 80, 147, 176, 199, 226–27, 302,
 308, 309, 312, 329–30
 average American's view of, 44, 45
 depression and, 330–31
 fear of, 172–73
De Carlo, Yvonne, 315
de Havilland, Olivia, 314
depression, 330–31
Depression, Great, 2, 25, 156, 157
despair, 167–68
Dick Hill, 232, 235, 251, 284
 Dick Able, 240, 252
 Dick Baker, 240
 Dick Center, 240
 Dick Left, 240, 253–54, 259
 Dick Right, 240, 252
Dill, Macey, 232, 240, 253, 262, 298
Distinguished Service Cross, 30,
 136, 171, 187, 205, 230, 292
Dodd, Lloyd, 224
Doolittle, Jimmy, 78–79
Douthit, Maurice, 162–63
Dovel, David, 189
Doyle, Lieutenant, 145
D rations, 186
ducks (boats), 12
Duncan, Jim, 282
DuNiphin, Sergeant, 249

Easley, Claudius, 37, 56, 163, 196–98,
 202, 277, 300, 303–304
 death of, 304
 marksmanship of, 277
East China Sea, 11

Easy Hill, 244–45

E Company, 62–63, 95–97, 140, 162, 204, 207–208, 253, 276, 279, 297

Edmonson, Harmon, 244–45

Eighty-Eighth Chemical Mortar Battalion, 29, 113

Eleventh Marine Artillery, 169

Emiko, 34–35

Episcopal Church, 328

escarpment, Tanabaru, 54, 183–84, 195–97, 201

Farnsworth, John, 184

Fatigue Junction centers, 314

F Company, 65, 89–92, 97, 162, 171, 209–10, 212–13, 222–24, 245–46, 247, 259, 279

Fencil, Sanford, 174–75

Fierke, David, 105

First Battalion, 41, 56, 102, 103, 107, 136, 141, 149, 170, 174, 178, 185, 232, 240, 242, 251, 253, 258, 260, 274, 283, 292, 298

First Platoon, 132, 173, 241, 259

flamethrowers, 42, 81, 142–43, 204–205, 282

tanks with, 211–12, 246

used against caves, 205–207, 225

Flattop, 54

food, 186, 199, 301

Ford, Leo, 116, 118–21

Fort Sill, 17, 18, 327

Fox, John, 81

Fox Hill, 244–45

foxholes, 33–34, 212–13, 235, 282

spider holes, 15

French, Kenneth, 63–64

French, Orvil, 69

Frothinger, Richard, 249

Gaja (town), 245–47

Gaja Ridge, 246

Gard, Robert, 106–107

G Company, 73, 96, 125–26, 171, 185, 191, 209–10, 218, 227, 246, 262–63, 272, 277, 282, 286, 294, 297–98

General Langfitt, 317, 318

Gerrans, George, 171

Ginowan, 62, 73

Glassman, Robert, 179–80

Glenn, Robert, 105

Glover, George, 84–85

God and religion, 137–38, 139, 226–27, 230, 331

Episcopal Church, 328

Goins, Hans, 52, 66, 78–79, 100–101, 136–38, 172, 237–39, 250, 299, 302

graveyards and tombs, 31–32, 38, 72, 76, 181, 266

Great Depression, 2, 25, 156, 157

grenades, 84, 179, 234, 259, 282, 287

phosphorus, 233

Guam, 7

Hacksaw Ridge (Sawtooth Ridge; Maeda escarpment), 196, 197, 202–3, 211, 212, 214, 274

Hale, Fred, 41–43

Halloran, Colonel, 159, 197, 286, 293, 298

Halsey, William, Jr., 4, 7

hara-kiri, 14–15, 303, 305

Harp, William, 297

Hartline, Franklin, 190

Hartzer, Frank, 81

Hayes, John, 51, 155, 237, 238, 250, 251, 299

H Company, 103, 125, 127–28, 184

Hector Hill, 258, 286

Hen Hill, 258, 286

heroes, 322

Hiavac, Jaroslave, 105

Higa, Private, 39–41

Highway Five, 86
Hill, Elias, 210
Hill Nine, 195, 201
Hill 143, 202
Hill 167, 298
Hill Seven, 179–81, 185, 193
Hiroshima, 310
Hitler, Adolf, 157
Hodge, General, 247, 273
Hoffman, Marvin, 155, 156
howitzers, 3, 4–5, 38, 77, 169, 176,
      190, 232, 238, 259, 299, 300, 308
   105mm, 19, 20, 30, 51, 55, 56, 152
   155mm, 24, 48, 169
Hughes, Sam, 174
Hunter, Dick, 148–49
Hymer, Charles, 275–76

I Company, 83, 125, 127–28, 173–
      74, 181–82, 195, 205–206, 218,
      234, 298
Imperial Fleet, 12–13
Indiana National Guard, 323, 327
infiltrators, 82, 86, 88, 293–94
Iwa, 292
Iwo Jima, map of Allied invasion of,
      x–xi

Jackass Mail, 315
Jackson, Denton, 263
Jackson, Robert, 81
Japan:
   atomic bombing of, 310–11
   attack on mainland of, 307–11
   end of war with, 311–12
   occupation of, 313
   Tokyo, 7, 52, 78, 308, 313
Japanese civilians:
   hiding in caves, 20–22, 24, 27,
      38–41
   resistance movement among, 28,
      33–35

Shaw and, 21–23, 39–41
   suicides by, 31–32, 303
   women and children, 20–23,
      34–35, 73, 76, 78, 80, 90, 295,
      303, 308–309, 311–12
Japanese forces:
   aircraft of, 2, 4, 53, 203
   defenses of, 176
   expectations about Allied landing
      on Okinawa, 37, 54
   foxholes of, 15
   hara-kiri committed by, 14–15,
      303, 305
   infiltrators, 82, 86, 88, 293–94
   kamikazes and human torches, 11,
      17, 251
   Pearl Harbor attacked by, 2, 7, 36,
      158, 188
   pillboxes of, 42–43, 68, 75, 76, 89,
      170, 175–76, 181, 208, 210, 248,
      297–98
   prisoners seldom taken by, 15
   retreat of, 285
   suicides by, 14–15, 92, 303, 305–306
   surrender of, 311
   surrender invitations dropped
      onto, 304
   total casualties of, 306
Japanese forces in caves, 72, 84, 143,
      220, 222, 233, 235, 236, 246, 252
   at close of war, 304, 306
   flamethrowers used against,
      205–207, 225
   oil and gasoline used against, 222,
      225, 232
   smoke bomb used against, 294–95
   tunnels connecting, 207, 208, 218,
      219, 220–22, 224–25, 232, 298
   white flags and, 252–53
Japanese propaganda, 37
   Tokyo Rose, 5–6
Jesus, 331

Johnson, Charles, 56–57, 75, 76, 145,
 240–42, 258, 283
Jones, Frank, 252, 294
Jones, Horace, 59

Kakazu (village), 86, 185
Kakazu Ridge and Kakazu Gorge,
 86–87, 102–103, 106–11, 112–17,
 118–23, 124–29, 130–34, 135–36,
 139, 140, 169, 173–75, 192, 197
 casualties at, 134, 136–37
 lack of maps of, 106, 107
kamikazes and human torches, 11,
 17, 251
Kamiyama, 62
Kane, General, 11
Kaniku, 141, 169
Kansas City, 319–20
Kaye, Albert, 109–11
K Company, 32, 57, 68, 173, 182,
 214–17
Kent, Jim, 20–21, 30–32
King, Byron, 29, 260
King Hill, 244–46, 262, 263, 265
Korea, 313, 327
Korejwo, Walter, 32
K rations, 186, 301
Kufus, 11
Kyushu, 12

Lake, Veronica, 250
landings, 9–10
 on Okinawa, 9–16, 19, 29, 37, 44, 164
 on Okinawa, Japanese
 expectations about, 37, 54
L Company, 124–29, 130–33, 136,
 179–80, 181, 193–94, 229,
 260, 282
Lemons, Paul, 193–94
Lewis, J. R., 83
Lewis, Lee, 78–80, 100, 136–37,
 152–53, 155, 240, 299, 302

Leyte, 10, 12, 278, 317
 Battle of, 1–7, 65, 100
Lindbergh, Charles, 157–58
List, Ed, 260
lizards, 16
Long, Fred, 15, 16
Los Angeles Musicians' Association
 Orchestra, 319
"lost platoon," 265–71
Love Hill, 264–71, 277, 279
LST (landing ship, tank), 10, 12, 307
Lundman, PFC, 224
Luzon, 19

MacArthur, Douglas, 11, 19
machine gunners, 145
 Japanese, 235
MacKennis, John, Jr., 178, 179, 236
Maeda escarpment (Sawtooth Ridge;
 Hacksaw Ridge), 196, 197,
 202–203, 211, 212, 214, 274
Main, Marjorie, 315–16, 319
Makabe, 299
maps of Okinawa, x–xv
Marine Corps, US, 231–32, 299
 Eleventh Marine Artillery, 169
 Marine Raiders, 231
Martin, Lorne, 51, 301
Mashiki, 71, 103
Mason, James, 234, 235
Masters, Avery, 51, 54, 86, 87, 106, 310
May, Ed, 57, 69–70, 86, 247–49,
 275–76, 279, 291, 292
 death of, 292
McElheran, Bill, 119, 120
M Company, 188, 262
McQuiston, Art, 37–41, 45, 50, 53,
 66–69, 71–73, 78–81, 83, 85–86,
 92, 95, 98, 100–102, 105, 108,
 136–38, 152–55, 158, 159, 172,
 176, 183, 188, 190, 191, 202, 222,
 237–39, 243, 250–52, 256–59,

285, 290–91, 293–94, 296–97,
300–301, 302, 309
death of, 301, 302, 304, 308, 309
religious faith of, 137–38
Sally and, 101
Medal of Honor, 122, 162, 187, 233,
288–89
medals, 187
Bronze Star, 136, 187
Distinguished Service Cross, 30,
136, 171, 187, 205, 230, 292
Medal of Honor, 122, 162, 187, 233,
288–89
Silver Star, 69, 136, 187
Medeera, 302
Midway, Battle of, 36
Mikula, Joe, 63–64
Miles, Howard, 217–18
Military Reserves, 328
Mindoro, 307–8, 313–14
mines, 76
Mishabaru Hill, 67
Mitchell, Ed, 194
Mitchell, Willard "Hoss," 128–29,
130–31, 134, 135–36, 138, 193–94
Molly, Aunt, 27–28
Momobaru, 42
monsoon season and rain, 145,
148, 151, 256–61, 262–64, 272,
278–79, 291–92, 307
Moore, Lee, 204–205
Morris, George, 78–79, 100–101, 136,
137, 153–55, 240, 299, 302
mortars, 82, 83, 113–15
Anderson and, 161
Eighty-Eighth Chemical Mortar
Battalion, 29, 113
320mm "boxcar," 74–76, 103, 127,
141, 142, 144, 173, 300
Moskala, Edward, 122
movie stars, 250–51, 314–15
Muehrcke, Robert, 247–48

Nagasaki, 311
Naha, 12, 54
maps of, xiv, xv
Nakagusuku Castle, 247
Nauss, James, 276
Needle Rock, 202–203, 204, 212,
222–23
Neptune, King, 326–27
Newell, Philip, 252, 293
newspaper reporters, 175–76
New Year's Eve, 317
Ninety-Sixth Infantry Division
(Deadeyes), 14, 15, 26–27, 37–38,
55–56, 72, 162, 163, 168–69, 175,
176, 193, 231, 242, 296, 304, 306,
307, 313
cemetery on Okinawa, 312, 317
Deadeye Bowl, 316–17
Deadeye Dispatch, 314
Marjorie Main and, 315–16, 319
"Occupation Girl" for, 314–16
Ninety-Sixth Reconnaissance,
67, 68
Nishabaru Ridge, 72, 86–87, 106–107,
140, 152, 174–75, 185–86, 188,
191–92, 196, 197
Nolan, Daniel, 216–18, 221–22
North Korea, 327

Oboe Hill, 232, 235, 257–58, 260, 264,
265, 283
O'Dell, Ollie Faye "Digger," 231–32
O'Donnell, Joe, 97–98
O'Hara, Maureen, 250–51
Okinawa, 10
Big Apple Hill and Ridge, 293
Cactus Hill, 54, 65, 66–68, 72, 86,
88–92, 93–98, 139
caves on, *see* caves
Charlie Hill, 54, 244–45, 263, 265,
274–76, 286
Clay Ridge, 67, 72, 73, 82

Okinawa (*cont.*)
  Conical Hill, 242, 244–49, 251,
    262–65, 272, 277, 279
  coral reefs at, 11, 15, 19, 29, 212
  the Crags, 169, 183–86, 188
  Dick Hill, *see* Dick Hill
  end of battle for, 302–6, 307–
    308, 326
  Hill Nine, 195
  Hill Seven, 179–81, 185, 193
  Kakazu (village), 86, 185
  Kakazu Ridge, *see* Kakazu Ridge
    and Kakazu Gorge
  landing on, 9–16, 19, 29, 37, 44, 164
  landing on, Japanese expectations
    about, 37, 54
  Love Hill, 264–71, 277, 279
  maps of, x–xv
  Naha, 12, 54
  Naha, maps of, xiv, xv
  Ninety-Sixth Division Cemetery
    on, 312, 317
  Nishabaru Ridge, 72, 86–87, 106–
    107, 140, 152, 174–75, 185–86,
    188, 191–92, 196, 197
  Oboe Hill, 232, 235, 257–58, 260,
    264, 265, 283
  resistance movement among
    villagers of, 28, 33–35
  Ryukyuan language spoken on,
    10, 16, 21, 39–41
  Ryukyus Islands map, xiii
  Shuri, 212, 231, 232, 235, 242, 247,
    255, 257, 273–74, 279, 283, 289,
    190–91
  Shuri, maps of, xiv, xv
  snakes on, 15–16, 116–17
  soldiers sent back to the USA after,
    316–20
  Tanabaru escarpment, 54, 183–84,
    195–97, 201

  Tombstone Ridge, 72, 75, 77–
    81, 82, 87, 106, 140, 141, 148,
    152, 169, 170, 179, 181–82, 186,
    188, 191
  Yonabaru, 12, 54, 244, 274, 292
  Yonabaru, map of, xiv
Oklahoma:
  Ada, 25–26, 27, 80
  Oklahoma City, 25
  Oklahoma Times, 25
Olson, Albert, 51
Olson, Robert, 155
198th Battalion, 169
O'Neil, Owen, 210
O'Neil, Tony, 162
Operation Iceberg, maps of, x–xii
Orr, Clayton, 254
Ozato, 297, 303

Pacific Ocean, 11
Parrish, Delmar, 102
Pearl Harbor attack, 2, 7, 36, 158, 188
Philippines, 11, 18, 19, 325
Phillips, Ralph, 92
pillboxes, 42–43, 68, 75, 76, 89, 170,
    175–76, 181, 208, 210, 248,
    297–98
Pirates' Den, 68, 103, 106
Porter Hill, 72
Pritchard, James, 135
Purtlebaugh, Virgil, 97–98

Quarry Hill, 67

rain, 145, 148, 151, 256–61, 262–64,
    272, 278–79, 291–92, 307
Raleigh, Robert, 6
rations, 186, 301
Reagan, John, 226–27
Reber, Charles, 62, 63
reconnaissance, 107, 109

Ninety-Sixth Reconnaissance, 67, 68
    by Shaw, 83, 95–96, 169, 191, 297
Red Cross, 314, 317
Reed, Donna, 250
Reeder, PFC Bill, 204
Reeder, Sergeant, 274
Regimental Mine Platoon, 64
religion and God, 137–38, 139, 226–27, 230, 331
    Episcopal Church, 328
Renick, Charles C., 253–54
reporters, 175–76
Republicans, 157
resistance movement, 28, 33–35
Restuccia, John, 29–30
Reuter, Louis, 218–19, 220–22, 225
Rice, Jesse, 58–60
rifles:
    BAR automatic, 92, 102, 134, 150, 228
    Easley and, 277
Riley, Kyle, 67
Robertson, Alfred "Chief," 149–50
Roosevelt, Franklin Delano, 156, 157
    death of, 154–56, 157
Royster, Jack, 111, 112–14
Ruth, James, 210
Ryder, Lieutenant, 30
Ryukyuan language, 10, 16, 21, 39–41
Ryukyus Islands, map of, xiii

satchel charges, 174, 233, 252
Sawtooth Ridge (Hacksaw Ridge; Maeda escarpment), 196, 197, 202–203, 211, 212, 214, 274
Schiever, Donald, 282
Schneider, Michael, 254
Schweneger, Bill, 267, 268, 271
Second Battalion, 30, 62–63, 65, 73–75, 77–78, 103, 107, 140, 151, 171, 184, 201, 202, 209, 244, 247, 249, 258, 286, 288, 292
Second Platoon, 195, 249, 254, 263, 297
Seibert, Doc, 27–28, 200–201
763rd Battalion, 62, 69, 211–12, 244
Seventh Division, 33, 55–56, 163, 169, 197, 298
Seventy-Seventh Division, 231, 240, 303
Shaw, Arthur:
    adjustment to civilian life, 324, 327, 328
    Aunt Molly and, 27–28
    back injury and surgery of, 323–24, 327–28, 331
    boyhood paper route of, 25–26, 27
    cows milked by, 27–28
    as first man on Okinawa, 14
    in high school, 101
    as Indiana National Guard adviser, 323, 327
    memories of the war, 322, 330
    Okinawan civilians and, 21–23, 39–41
    reconnaissance by, 83, 95–96, 169, 191, 297
    retirement of, 328
    ruptured appendix of, 199–201
    Turkey assignment of, 327
Shaw, Beulah (mother), 200–201
Shaw, Joan (wife), 79, 80–81, 154, 319, 320–21, 327, 328
    Arthur's meeting of, 17–18, 327
    illness and death of, 328–29
    medical crisis of, 324–25
Shaw, Sharon (daughter), 320, 328
    birth of, 326
Shimabaku, 32
Shimuku, 37

Shuri, 212, 231, 232, 235, 242, 247, 255, 257, 273–74, 279, 283, 289, 290–91
  maps of, xiv, xv
Shuri Castle, 289, 290
Silver Star, 69, 136, 187
Sims, Jack, 79
Sisk, Gerald, 253–54
Sixth Army, 313
Smith, George, 280–81
Smith, Howard, 25–26, 27
Smith, Leo, 103
Smith, Lloyd, 90
Smith, Roger, 170–71
Smith, Stan, 173
smoke bombs, 293–95
Snafu Maru, 319
snakes, 15–16, 116–17
snipers, 14
Snyder, Bill, 62
Solch, Joseph, 133–34, 136
soldiers:
  sent back to US, 316–20
  training for, 18
soldiers, war's effects on, 44–45, 61–64, 80–81
  depression, 330–31
  despair, 167–68
  memories, 147, 322, 330
Sommers, Sergeant, 115–17
South Korea, 327
Spam, 186, 199, 301
spider holes, 15
Stare, Ed, 45, 68, 70, 71–72, 103–104
Starr, Charles, 227–29
Sterner, Cyril, 62, 64, 73, 140–41, 201
Stevens, John, 189–90
Stock, William, 259
Strand, Albert, 173, 214–17
Stretch, Harlan, 220–21
Stults, Hilton, 264–66

Sugar Hill, 54, 279, 286
suicides, 31–32, 92, 303, 305–306

Tanabaru (town), 202
Tanabaru escarpment, 54, 183–84, 195–97, 201
tanks, 43, 174, 184, 228–29, 235–36, 246
  flamethrowing, 211–12, 246
  763rd Battalion, 62, 69, 211–12, 244
Tenth Army, 231, 278
  maps of operations of, xii, xiv
Terry, Seymour, 233, 235, 240–42
Third Battalion, 57, 65, 68, 103, 127, 147–48, 201, 212, 283, 286
Third Platoon, 173, 185, 194, 298
Thorsen, Austin, 103
305th Infantry, 303
321st Field Artillery Battalion, 105
361st Engineer Battalion, 109
361st Field Artillery Battalion, 3, 14, 27, 51, 72, 77, 88, 92, 95, 136, 169, 192, 242, 243, 251, 258, 299, 306, 310, 315
361st Infantry, 315
362nd Field Artillery Battalion, 105, 242
381st Infantry Regiment, 27, 32, 56, 103, 176, 185, 193, 199, 209, 286, 293
382nd Infantry Regiment, 37, 56, 72, 140, 169, 170, 177, 185–86, 191, 193, 199, 201, 231, 232, 235, 253, 259, 264, 286, 298
383rd Infantry Regiment, 45–46, 56, 86, 103–104, 105, 122, 124, 150, 163–64, 191, 207, 226, 227, 242, 273, 274, 379, 283, 289, 292, 297
Tlougan, Ben, 245
Tokyo, 7, 52, 78, 308, 313
Tokyo Rose, 5–6

tombs and graveyards, 31–32, 38, 72, 76, 181, 266
Tombstone Ridge, 72, 75, 77–81, 82, 87, 106, 140, 141, 148, 152, 169, 170, 179, 181–82, 186, 188, 191
training, 18
Truman, Harry S., 155–56, 157, 162, 288–89
Tschoepe, Clifford, 263
Turkey, 327
Turner, R. D., 267–68, 271
Turner, Richmond K., 168
Tway, Howard, 64
Twenty-Seventh Division, 169, 197

Uchitomari, 67
Ushijima, Mitsuru, 290–91, 304–305
  suicide of, 305–306

Vanderlinden, Captain, 103
Van Vulpen, John, 114–17, 276

war correspondents, 175–76
Weasel cargo carrier, 278
Weiner, George, 195, 205–207
Weingartner, Harold, 281–82
Wheeler, Gordon, 46–49
White, Tom, 150
white flags, 252–53

Williams, Donald, 268–71
Williams, John, 286
Wilson, Al, 260
women and children, 20–23, 34–35, 73, 76, 78, 80, 90, 295, 303, 308–309, 311–12
World War I, 51, 56
World War II:
  American opposition to involvement in, 157–58
  atomic bombing of Japan, 310–11
  Battle of Midway, 36
  Battle of Leyte, 1–7, 65, 100
  Battle of the Bulge, 51
  end of war with Japan, 311–12
  Pearl Harbor attack, 2, 7, 36, 158, 188
WPA, 157

Yap, 1–2
Yokohama, 11
Yonabaru, 12, 54, 244, 274, 292
  map of, xiv
Yonabaru Bay, 244
Young, Hugh, 260
Young, James, 180–82
Yuza Ridge, 297–98, 303

Zebra Hill, 235, 283
Zeros, 53